# The ARRL's Amateur Extra Q&A

## Upgrade to an Amateur Extra Class Ham License

**By: Stephen Horan, AC5RI**
**Edited by Chuck Hutchinson, K8CH**

**Production Staff:**
David Pingree, N1NAS, Senior Technical Illustrator: Technical Illustrations
Kathy Ford, Proofreader
Paul Lappen, Production Assistant: Layout
Sue Fagan, Graphic Design Supervisor: Cover Design
Michelle Bloom, WB1ENT, Production Supervisor: Layout

**Published By:**
ARRL—The national association for Amateur Radio
Newington, CT 06111-1494

Printed in USA



ISBN: 0-87259-888-8

First Edition
Second Printing, 2005

This book may be used for Amateur Extra class license exams until the Volunteer Examiner Coordinator's Question Pool Committee issues a new revision of the Extra class question pool. Originally scheduled to be used for exams given through June 30, 2006, the Question Pool Committee later suspended that revision date. *QST* and *ARRLWeb* (**www.arrl.org**) will have news about a revised Extra class question pool and any FCC Rules changes that may affect the current question pool.

We strive to produce books without errors. Sometimes mistakes do occur, however. When we become aware of problems in our books (other than obvious typographical errors that should not cause our readers any problems) we post an Adobe Portable Document Format (PDF) file on *ARRLWeb*. If you think you have found an error, please check **www.arrl.org/notes** for corrections. If you don't find a correction there, please let us know, either using the Feedback Form in the back of this book or by sending an e-mail to **pubsfdbk@arrl.org**.

# Contents

# Foreword

When you decided to go for an Amateur Extra license, you took the first step toward full access to every bit of Amateur Radio frequency spectrum. Once you've earned that Amateur Extra, you will be permitted to operate with all of the privileges that the Federal Communications Commission grants to Amateur Radio Operators.

This first edition of *ARRL's Amateur Extra Q & A* continues ARRL's proud tradition of providing the most complete license preparation and study materials available. With more than 800 questions in the Element 4 question pool, there is a lot of material for you to master. This volume contains every one of those questions, and with each you'll find a brief explanation of the right answer.

Stephen Horan, AC5RI, is the author of this fine book. Stephen has been a licensed amateur since 1996 and he helped to start the Amateur Radio license classes for the Mesilla Valley Radio Club. He has developed instructional materials for the three theory classes that the club teaches. He mostly uses PSK 31 and packet modes from his home shack.

Professionally, he is a faculty member of the Klipsch School of Electrical and Computer Engineering at New Mexico State University. He is the faculty advisor for the NMSU Amateur Radio Club, W5GB. He also teaches in the communications area and performs research for NASA and the Air Force, including building nanosatellites. We are very pleased that he has shared his experience and expertise with all of us.

This first edition of *ARRL's Amateur Extra Q & A* represents the work and expertise of the author and the many ARRL staff members who have helped bring this book into being. You too can help us make this the best possible book that it can be. Your part is to provide suggestions or any corrections you think need to be made. Use the handy Feedback Form at the back of this book, and send the form to us. Alternatively, you can e-mail your comments to: **pubsfdbk@arrl.org**. Your comments and suggestions are important to us. Thanks, and good luck!

David Sumner, K1ZZ
Executive Vice President, ARRL
Newington, Connecticut
March 2003

# How to Use This Book

To earn an Amateur Extra class Amateur Radio license, you must pass (or receive credit for) exam Elements 1, 2, 3 and 4. This book is designed to help you prepare for and pass the Element 4 Amateur Extra class written exam. If you do not already have a General Amateur Radio license and valid credit for passing the Morse code exam you will need some additional study materials. In that case, see The ARRL Study Materials section on the next page and additional infomation in the Introduction chapter of this book.

The Amateur Extra class written exam requires that you know some electronics theory and Amateur Radio operating practices and procedures. You will learn more about the rules and regulations governing the Amateur Service, as contained in Part 97 of Title 47 of the Code of Federal Regulations–the Federal Communications Commission (FCC) Rules.

The Element 4 exam consists of 50 questions taken from the question pool in this book. A passing score is 74%, so you must answer 37 of the 50 questions correctly to pass. (Another way to look at this is that you can get as many as 13 questions wrong, and still pass the test.)

The questions and multiple-choice answers in this book are printed exactly as they were written by the Volunteer Examiner Coordinator's Question Pool Committee, and exactly as they will appear on your exam. (Be careful, though. The letter positions of the answers may be scrambled, so you can't simply memorize an answer letter for each question.) In this book, the letter of the correct answer is printed in **boldface type** just before the explanation. If you want to study without knowing the correct answer right away, simply cover the answer letters with your hand or a slip of paper as you read down the page.

# ARRL Study Materials

ARRL offers a variety of study materials to help ensure your success on exam day. For the Element 2 Technician written exam, ARRL's *Now You're Talking!* includes friendly, easy-to-understand theory and rules explanations. This book will also help you set up and operate your first Amateur Radio station. The entire Technician question pool is included. The *ARRL Technician Class Video Course* creates a classroom on your TV screen, with your own personal instructors to make sure you understand each topic. The Course Notes book includes the complete question pool. *ARRL's Tech Q & A* has brief explanations to go along with every question in the question pool, printed directly after each question. Perfect for a quick review before the exam or as a brief refresher for anyone already familiar with the material.

*The ARRL General Class License Manual* has detailed explanations of all the material covered by the Element 3 General class written exam. The complete General class question pool is included. *ARRL's General Q & A* has brief explanations after each question to refresh your memory or review the material just before your exam.

*ARRL's Your Introduction to Morse Code* is offered as a set of two audio cassette tapes or two audio CDs. You will learn all the characters required for the Element 1, 5 word-per-minute Morse code exam. You are introduced to each character and then you are given practice with that character. Each character is used in words or text before you move on to the next one. There is plenty of practice at 5 wpm to prepare you for your exam.

When you are ready to upgrade to the Amateur Extra license, *The ARRL Extra Class License Manual* will help you prepare. The book provides detailed explanations and examples of all types of calculations used on the exam. The complete Element 4 Extra class question pool is included. *ARRL's Amateur Extra Q & A* has brief explanations after each question to refresh your memory or review the material just before your exam.

# Introduction

## The Amateur Extra License

Every Amateur Radio operator thinks about trying to earn his or her Amateur Extra class license at one time or another. It certainly is a worthy goal to work toward! Maybe you hesitate to actually take the exam, however, because you think the theory is much too hard for you to understand. Perhaps you have little or no math or electronics background. Once you make the commitment to study and learn what it takes to pass the exam, however, you will be able to do it. This *ARRL Extra Class Q&A* will teach you the answer to every question you need to know to go from a General class license to a proud Amateur Extra! The key is that you must make the commitment, and be willing to study. With full Amateur privileges, you will be able to experience all the excitement of Amateur Radio!

It may take more than one attempt to pass the exam, but many amateurs do succeed the first time. There is no limit to how many times you can take the test. Many Volunteer Examiner Teams have several exam versions available, so you may even be able to try the exam again at the same exam session, if necessary. Time and available exam versions may limit the number of times you can try the exam at a single exam session. If you don't pass after a couple of tries, you certainly will benefit from more study of the question pool before you try again.

Segments of the 80, 40, 20 and 15-meter bands are reserved for the exclusive use of Amateur Extra class operators. These frequencies are where some of the juiciest DX stations hang out, and you also will find many contest stations in these band segments. So if you want to be sure you aren't missing out on those rare DX QSL cards and extra contest points, you'll want to earn your Amateur Extra class license! Of course, there are many other reasons for wanting the highest class license.

If you don't already hold a General class license, you also will have to pass the Element 3 written exam. If you don't have a Technician license, you will have to pass the Element 2 written exam, as well. To reach any rung on the Amateur Radio license ladder, you must pass all the lower exam elements.

If you have not yet passed the 5-wpm (Element 1) Morse code exam, you also will have to pass that to earn your Extra class license. There are many good Morse code training techniques, including ARRL's *Your Introduction to Morse Code* and W1AW code practice. There are some good computer programs, as well. *Ham University* is a Morse code training program available from ARRL. In addition to teaching you Morse code, *Ham University* will drill you on questions from any of the exam question pools. Remember, the most enjoyable way to practice your Morse code skills and increase your code speed is with on-the-air operating! Many students are ready to pass the code exam after only a few weeks of study. Most people can pass that exam by the time they have learned all the required characters.

Chapter 1 of this book, Commission's Rules, covers those questions on FCC Part 97 Rules that you will be tested on for your Amateur Extra class license. We recommend that you also obtain a copy of *The ARRL's FCC Rule Book*. That book includes a complete copy of Part 97, along with detailed explanations for all the rules governing Amateur Radio.

The other chapters cover the remaining eight subelements for the Amateur Extra class license exam. All of the questions in the Extra class question pool are covered in this book.

Whether you now hold a Novice, Technician, Technician Plus (Technician with Morse code credit), General or Advanced license, or even if you don't have any license yet, you will find the exclusive operating privileges available to an Amateur Extra class licensee to be worth the time spent learning about your hobby. After passing the FCC Element 4 written exam, you will be allowed to operate on any frequency assigned to the Amateur Radio Service.

## An Overview of Amateur Radio

Earning an Amateur Radio license, at whatever level, is a special achievement. The 600,000 or so people in the US who call themselves Amateur Radio operators, or hams, are part of a global fraternity. Radio amateurs provide a voluntary, noncommercial, communication service. This is especially true during natural disasters or other emergencies. Hams have made many important contributions to the field of electronics and communications, and this tradition continues today. Amateur Radio experimentation is yet another reason many people become part of this self-disciplined group of trained operators, technicians and electronics experts — an asset to any country. Hams pursue their hobby purely for personal enrichment in technical and operating skills, without any type of payment except the personal satisfaction they feel from a job well done!

Radio signals do not know territorial boundaries, so hams have a unique ability to enhance international goodwill. Hams become ambassadors of their country every time they put their stations on the air.

**Many active Amateur Radio operators enjoy collecting colorful QSL cards, many of them from countries around the world.**

Amateur Radio has been around since the early 1900s. Hams have always been at the forefront of technology. Today, hams relay signals through their own satellites, bounce signals off the moon, relay messages automatically through computerized radio networks and use any number of other "exotic" communications techniques. Amateurs talk from hand-held transceivers through mountaintop repeater stations that can relay their signals to other hams' cars or homes. Hams send their own pictures by television, talk with other hams around the world by voice or, keeping alive a distinctive traditional skill, tap out messages in Morse code. When emergencies arise, radio amateurs are on the spot to relay information to and from disaster-stricken areas that have lost normal lines of communication.

The US government, through the Federal Communications Commission (FCC), grants all US Amateur Radio licenses. This licensing procedure ensures operating skill and electronics know-how. Without this skill, radio operators, because of improperly adjusted equipment or neglected regulations, might unknowingly cause interference to other services using the radio spectrum.

## Who Can Be a Ham?

The FCC doesn't care how old you are or whether you're a US citizen. If you pass the examination, the Commission will issue you an amateur license. Any person (except the agent of a foreign government) may take the exam and, if successful, receive an amateur license. It's important to understand that if a citizen of a foreign country receives an amateur license in this manner, he or she is a US Amateur Radio operator. (This should not be confused with a reciprocal permit for alien amateur licensee, which allows visitors from certain countries who hold valid amateur licenses in their homelands to operate their own stations in the US without having to take an FCC exam.)

### License Structure

Anyone earning a new Amateur Radio license can earn one of three license classes — Technician, General and Amateur Extra. These vary in degree of knowledge required and frequency privileges granted. Higher class licenses have more comprehensive examinations. In return for passing a more difficult exam you earn more frequency privileges (frequency space in the radio spectrum). The vast majority of beginners start with the most basic license, the Technician, although it's possible to start with any class of license.

Technician licensees who learn the international Morse code and pass an exam to demonstrate their knowledge of code at 5 words per minute gain some frequency privileges on four of the amateur high-frequency (HF) bands. This license was previously called the Technician Plus license, and many amateurs will refer to it by that name. **Table 1** lists the amateur license classes you can earn, along with a brief description of their exam requirements and operating privileges.

If you now hold a General license, you may already be an HF operator, having experienced the thrill of *working* (contacting) other Amateur Radio operators in just about any country in the world. An Amateur Extra license allows you full access to all frequencies and privileges permitted to radio amateurs. See **Table 2**.

Although there are also other amateur license classes, the FCC is no longer issuing new licenses for these classes. The Novice license was long considered the beginner's license. Exams for this license were discontinued as of April 15, 2000. The FCC also stopped issuing new Advanced class licenses on that date. They will continue to renew previously issued licenses, however, so you will probably meet some Novice and Advanced class licensees on the air.

## Learning Morse Code

Learning Morse code is a matter of practice. Instructions on learning the code, how to handle a telegraph key, and so on, can be found in *The ARRL General Class License Manual*, published by the ARRL. In addition, *Your Introduction to Morse Code*, ARRL's package to teach Morse code, is available with two cassette tapes or two audio CDs. *Your Introduction to Morse Code* was designed for beginners, and will help you learn Morse code. You will be ready to pass your 5 word-per-minute code exam when you finish the lessons on *Your Introduction to Morse Code*. You can purchase any of these products from your local Amateur Radio equipment dealer or directly from the ARRL, 225 Main St,

Table 1

Amateur Operator Licenses†

| *Class* | *Code Test* | *Written Examination* | *Privileges* |
|---|---|---|---|
| Technician | | Basic theory and regulations. (Element 2)* | All amateur privileges above 50.0 MHz. |
| Technician with Morse code credit | 5 wpm (Element 1) | Basic theory and regulations. (Element 2)* | All "Novice" HF privileges in addition to all Technician privileges. |
| General | 5 wpm (Element 1) | Basic theory and regulations; General theory and regulations. (Elements 2 and 3) | All amateur privileges except those reserved for Advanced and Amateur Extra class. |
| Amateur Extra privileges. | 5 wpm (Element 1) | All lower exam elements, plus Extra-class theory (Elements 2, 3 and 4) | All amateur |

†A licensed radio amateur will be required to pass only those elements that are not included in the examination for the amateur license currently held.

*If you have a Technician-class license issued before March 21, 1987, you also have credit for Elements 1 and 3. You must be able to prove your Technician license was issued before March 21, 1987 to claim this credit.

Newington, CT 06111. To place an order, call, toll-free, **888-277-5289**. You can also send e-mail to: **pubsales@arrl.org** or check out our World Wide Web site: **www.arrl.org/** Prospective new amateurs can call: **800-32-NEW HAM (800-326-3942)** for additional information.

Besides listening to code tapes or CDs, some on-the-air operating experience will be a great help in building your code speed. When you are in the middle of

Table 2
Amateur Operating Privileges

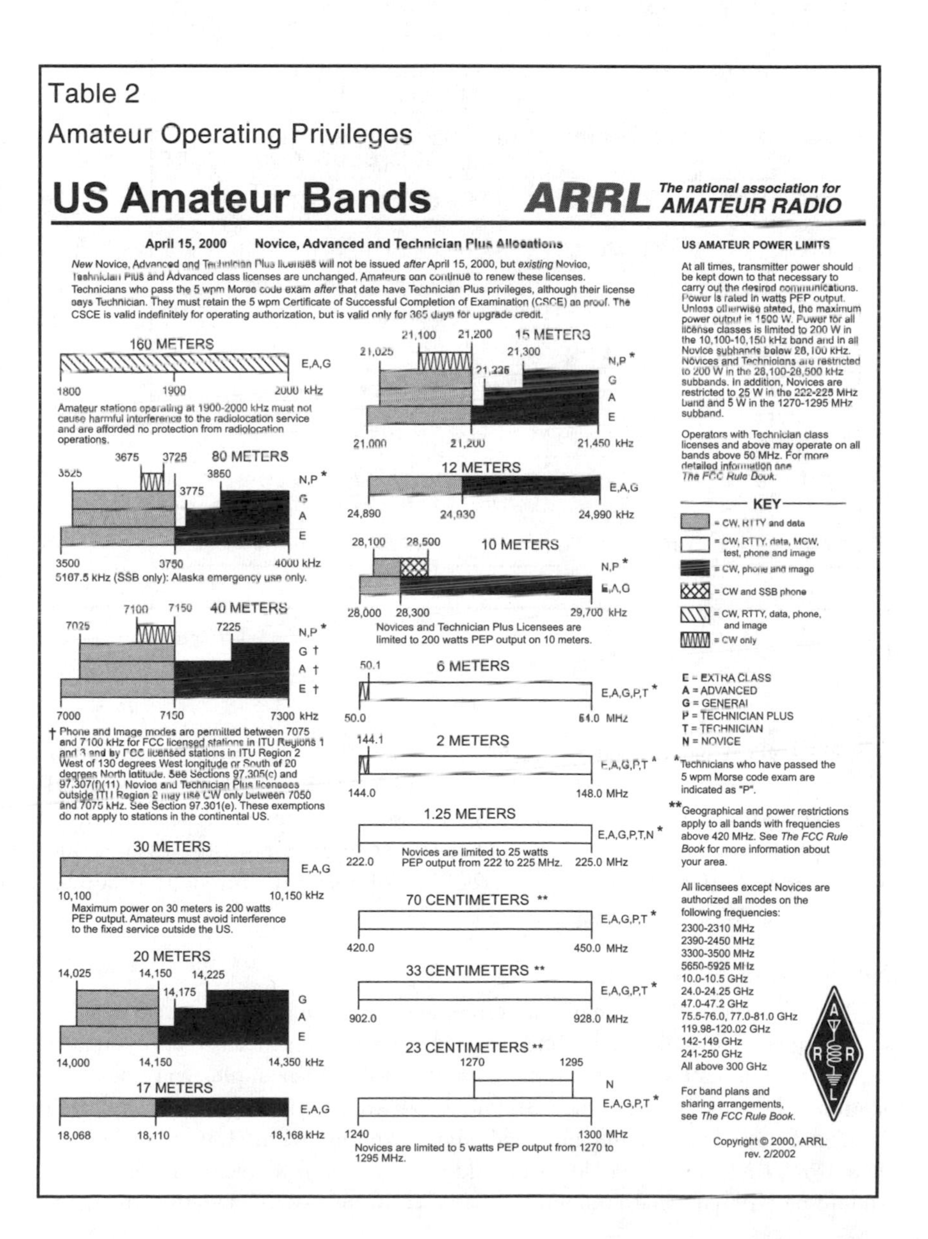

Table 3
W1AW Schedule

| W1AW Schedule | | | | | | | | |
|---|---|---|---|---|---|---|---|---|
| PACIFIC | MTN | CENT | EAST | MON | TUE | WED | THU | FRI |
| 6 AM | 7 AM | 8 AM | 9 AM | | FAST CODE | SLOW CODE | FAST CODE | SLOW CODE |
| 7 AM-1 PM | 8 AM-2 PM | 9 AM-3 PM | 10 AM-4 PM | VISITING OPERATOR TIME (12 PM-1 PM CLOSED FOR LUNCH) | | | | |
| 1 PM | 2 PM | 3 PM | 4 PM | FAST CODE | SLOW CODE | FAST CODE | SLOW CODE | FAST CODE |
| 2 PM | 3 PM | 4 PM | 5 PM | CODE BULLETIN | | | | |
| 3 PM | 4 PM | 5 PM | 6 PM | TELEPRINTER BULLETIN | | | | |
| 4 PM | 5 PM | 6 PM | 7 PM | SLOW CODE | FAST CODE | SLOW CODE | FAST CODE | SLOW CODE |
| 5 PM | 6 PM | 7 PM | 8 PM | CODE BULLETIN | | | | |
| 6 PM | 7 PM | 8 PM | 9 PM | TELEPRINTER BULLETIN | | | | |
| 6$^{45}$ PM | 7$^{45}$ PM | 8$^{45}$ PM | 9$^{45}$ PM | VOICE BULLETIN | | | | |
| 7 PM | 8 PM | 9 PM | 10 PM | FAST CODE | SLOW CODE | FAST CODE | SLOW CODE | FAST CODE |
| 8 PM | 9 PM | 10PM | 11 PM | CODE BULLETIN | | | | |

a contact via Amateur Radio, and have to copy the code the other station is sending to continue the conversation, your copying ability will improve quickly!

ARRL's Maxim Memorial Station, W1AW, transmits code practice and information bulletins of interest to all amateurs. These code-practice sessions and Morse code bulletins provide an excellent opportunity for code practice. **Table 3** is a W1AW operating schedule.

## Station Call Signs

Many years ago, by international agreement, the nations of the world decided to allocate certain call-sign prefixes to each country. This means that if you hear a radio station call sign beginning with W or K, for example, you know the station is licensed by the United States. A call sign beginning with the letter G is licensed by Great Britain, and a call sign beginning with VE is from Canada. *The ARRL DXCC List* is an operating aid no ham who is active on the HF bands should be without. That booklet, available from the ARRL, includes the com-

W1AW's schedule is at the same local time throughout the year. The schedule according to your local time will change if your local time does not have seasonal adjustments that are made at the same time as North American time changes between standard time and daylight time. From the first Sunday in April to the last Sunday in October, UTC = Eastern Time + 4 hours. For the rest of the year, UTC = Eastern Time + 5 hours.

♦ **Morse code transmissions:**

Frequencies are 1.818, 3.5815, 7.0475, 14.0475, 18.0975, 21.0675, 28.0675 and 147.555 MHz.

Slow Code = practice sent at 5, 7½, 10, 13 and 15 wpm.

Fast Code = practice sent at 35, 30, 25, 20, 15, 13 and 10 wpm.

Code practice text is from the pages of *QST*. The source is given at the beginning of each practice session and alternate speeds within each session. For example, "Text is from July 2001 *QST*, pages 9 and 81," indicates that the plain text is from the article on page 9 and mixed number/letter groups are from page 81. Code bulletins are sent at 18 wpm.

W1AW qualifying runs are sent on the same frequencies as the Morse code transmissions. West Coast qualifying runs are transmitted on approximately 3.590 MHz by K6YR. See "Contest Corral" in this issue. At the beginning of each code practice session, the schedule for the next qualifying run is presented. Underline one minute of the highest speed you copied, certify that your copy was made without aid, and send it to ARRL for grading. Please include your name, call sign (if any) and complete mailing address. The fee structure is $10 for a certificate, and $7.50 for endorsements.

♦ **Teleprinter transmissions:**

Frequencies are 3.625, 7.095, 14.095, 18.1025, 21.095, 28.095 and 147.555 MHz.

Bulletins are sent at 45.45-baud Baudot and 100-baud AMTOR, FEC Mode B. 110-baud ASCII will be sent only as time allows.

On Tuesdays and Fridays at 6:30 PM Eastern Time, Keplerian elements for many amateur satellites are sent on the regular teleprinter frequencies.

♦ **Voice transmissions:**

Frequencies are 1.855, 3.99, 7.29, 14.29, 18.16, 21.39, 28.59 and 147.555 MHz.

♦ **Miscellanea:**

On Fridays, UTC, a DX bulletin replaces the regular bulletins.

W1AW is open to visitors from 10 AM until noon and from 1 PM until 3:45 PM on Monday through Friday. FCC licensed amateurs may operate the station during that time. Be sure to bring your current FCC amateur license or a photocopy.

In a communication emergency, monitor W1AW for special bulletins as follows: voice on the hour, teleprinter at 15 minutes past the hour, and CW on the half hour.

Headquarters and W1AW are closed on New Year's Day, President's Day, Good Friday, Memorial Day, Independence Day, Labor Day, Thanksgiving and the following Friday, and Christmas Day and the following day.

mon call-sign prefixes used by amateurs in virtually every location in the world. It also includes a check-off list to help you keep track of the countries you contact as you work toward collecting QSL cards from 100 or more countries to earn the prestigious DX Century Club award. (DX is ham lingo for distance, generally taken on the HF bands to mean any country outside the one from which you are operating.)

The International Telecommunication Union (ITU) radio regulations outline the basic principles used in forming amateur call signs. According to these regulations, an amateur call sign must be made up of one or two characters (the first one may be a numeral) as a prefix, followed by a numeral, and then a suffix of not more than three letters. The prefixes W, K, N and A are used in the United States. When the letter A is used in a US amateur call sign, it will always be with a two-letter prefix, AA to AL. The continental US is divided into 10 Amateur Radio call districts (sometimes called areas), numbered 0 through 9. **Figure 1** is a map showing the US call districts.

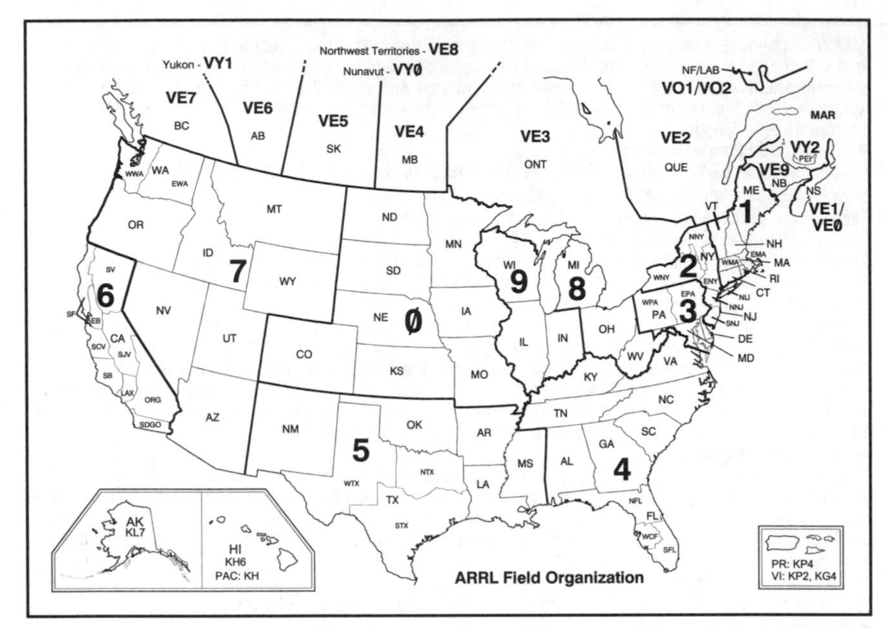


**Figure 1—There are 10 US call areas. Hawaii is part of the sixth call area, and Alaska is part of the seventh.**

For information on the FCC's call-sign assignment system, and a table listing the blocks of call signs for each license class, see *ARRL's FCC Rule Book*. You may keep the same call sign when you change license class, if you wish. You must indicate that you want to receive a new call sign when you fill out an FCC Form 605 to apply for the exam or change your address.

The FCC also has a vanity call sign system. Under this system the FCC will issue a call sign selected from a list of preferred available call signs. While there is no fee for an Amateur Radio license, there is a fee for the selection of a vanity call sign. The current fee is $14.50 for a 10-year Amateur Radio license, paid upon application for a vanity call sign and at license renewal after that. (That fee may change as costs of administering the program change.) The latest details about the vanity call sign system are available from ARRL Regulatory Information, 225 Main Street, Newington, CT 06111-1494 and on *ARRLWeb* at **www.arrl.org/**

# Earning a License

## Forms and Procedures

To renew or modify a license, you can file a copy of FCC Form 605. In addition, hams who have held a valid license that has expired within the past two years may apply for reinstatement with an FCC Form 605.

**Josh Abramowicz, KB3GWY, logs as his sister Amy runs stations during the Pennsylvania QSO Party held the second weekend of October each year. Operating from a cabin at Blue Mountain Scout Reservation in Schuylkill County Pennsylvania, Josh and Amy, along with their father Mark, NT3V, enjoyed a pleasant fall weekend of camping and ham radio.**

Licenses are normally good for ten years. Your application for a license renewal must be submitted to the FCC no more than 90 days before the license expires. (We recommend you submit the application for renewal between 90 and 60 days before your license expires.) If the FCC receives your renewal application before the license expires, you may continue to operate until your new license arrives, even if it is past the expiration date. If you forget to apply before your license expires, you may still be able to renew your license without taking another exam. There is a two-year grace period, during which you may apply for renewal of your expired license. Use an FCC Form 605 to apply for reinstatement (and your old call sign). If you apply for reinstatement of your expired license under this two-year grace period, you may not operate your station until your new license is issued. If you move or change addresses you should use an FCC Form 605 to notify the FCC of the change. If your license is lost or destroyed, however, just write a letter to the FCC explaining why you are requesting a new copy of your license.

You can ask one of the Volunteer Examiner Coordinators' offices to file your renewal application electronically if you don't want to mail the form to the FCC. You must still mail the form to the VEC, however. The ARRL/VEC Office will electronically file application forms. This service is free for any ARRL member.

## Electronic Filing

You can also file your license renewal or address modification using the Universal Licensing System (ULS) on the World Wide Web. To use ULS, you must have an FCC Registration Number, or FRN. Obtain your FRN by registering with the Commission Registration System, known as CORES.

Described as an agency-wide registration system for anyone filing applications with or making payments to the FCC, CORES will assign a unique 10-digit FCC Registration Number, or FRN to all registrants. All Commission systems that handle financial, authorization of service, and enforcement activities will use the FRN. The FCC says use of the FRN will allow it to more rapidly verify fee payment. Amateurs mailing payments to the FCC — for example as part of a vanity call sign application — would include their FRN on FCC Form 159.

The on-line filing system and further information about CORES is available by visiting the FCC Web site, **www.fcc.gov** and clicking on the Commission Registration System link. Follow the directions on the Web site. It is also possible to register on CORES using a paper Form 160.

When you register with CORES you must supply a Taxpayer Identification Number, or TIN. For individuals, this is usually a Social Security Number. Club stations must obtain an Assigned Taxpayer Identification Number (ATIN) before registering on CORES.

Anyone can register on CORES and obtain an FRN. CORES/FRN is "entity registration." You don't need a license to be registered.

Once you have registered on CORES and obtained your FRN, you can proceed to renew or modify your license using the Universal Licensing System (ULS), also on the World Wide Web. Go to **www.fcc.gov/uls** and click on the "Online Filing" button. Follow the directions provided on the Web page to connect to the FCC's ULS database.

## Paper Filing

The FCC has a set of detailed instructions for the Form 605, which are included with the form. To obtain a new Form 605, call the FCC Forms Distribution Center at 800-418-3676. You can also write to: Federal Communications Commission, Forms Distribution Center, 9300 E. Hampton Drive Capital Heights, MD 20743 (specify "Form 605" on the envelope). The Form 605 also is available from the FCC's fax on demand service. Call 202-418-0177 and ask for form number 000605. Form 605 also is available via the Internet. The World Wide Web location is: **www.fcc.gov/formpage.html** or you can receive the form via ftp to: **ftp.fcc.gov/pub/Forms/Form605**.

The ARRL/VEC has created a package that includes the portions of Form 605 that are needed for amateur applications, as well as a condensed set of instructions for completing the form. Write to: ARRL/VEC, Form 605, 225 Main Street, Newington, CT 06111-1494. (Please include a large business-sized stamped self-addressed envelope with your request.) **Figure 2** is a sample of those portions of an FCC Form 605 that you would complete to submit a change of address to the FCC.

Most of the form is simple to fill out. You will need to know that the Radio Service Code for box 1 is HA for Amateur Radio. (Just remember HAm radio.) You will have to include a "Taxpayer Identification Number" on the Form. This is normally your Social Security Number. If you don't want to write your Social Security Number on this form, then you can register with CORES as described above. When you receive your FRN from the FCC, you can use that number instead of your Social Security Number on the Form. Of course, you will have to supply your Social Security Number to register with the CORES.

The telephone number, fax number and e-mail address information is optional. The FCC will use that information to contact you in case there is a problem with your application.

Page two of the Form includes six General Certification Statements. Statement five may seem confusing. Basically, this statement means that you do not plan to install an antenna over 200 feet high, and that your permanent station location will not be in a designated wilderness area, wildlife preserve or nationally recognized scenic and recreational area. The sixth statement indicates that you are familiar with the FCC RF Safety Rules, and that you will obey them.

## Volunteer Examiner Program

Before you can take an FCC exam, you'll have to fill out a copy of the National Conference of Volunteer Examiner Coordinators' (NCVEC) Quick Form 605. This form is used as an application for a new license or an upgraded license. The NCVEC Quick Form 605 is only used at license exam sessions. This form includes some information that the Volunteer Examiner Coordinator's office will need to process your application with the FCC. See **Figure 3**. You should not use an NCVEC Quick Form 605 to apply for a license renewal or modification with the FCC. *Never* mail these forms to the FCC, because that will result in a rejection of the application. Likewise, an FCC Form 605 can't be used for an exam application.

All US amateur exams are administered by Volunteer Examiners who are certified by a Volunteer-Examiner Coordinator (VEC). *The ARRL's FCC Rule Book* contains more details about the Volunteer-Examiner program.

## Finding an Exam Opportunity

To determine where and when exams will be given in your area, contact the ARRL/VEC office, or watch for announcements in the Hamfest Calendar and Coming Conventions columns in *QST*. Many local clubs sponsor exams, so they are another good source of information on exam opportunities. Upcoming exams are listed on *ARRLWeb* at: **www.arrl.org/arrlvec/examsearch.phtml**. Registration deadlines, and the time and location of the exams, are mentioned prominently in publicity releases about upcoming sessions.

## Taking the Exam

By the time examination day rolls around, you should have already prepared yourself. This means getting your schedule, supplies and mental attitude ready. Plan your schedule so you'll get to the examination site with plenty of time to spare. There's no harm in being early. In fact, you might have time to discuss hamming with another applicant, which is a great way to calm pretest nerves. Try not to discuss the material that will be on the examination, as this may make you even more nervous. By this time, it's too late to study anyway!

**FCC 605**
**Main Form**

**Quick-Form Application for Authorization in the Ship, Aircraft, Amateur, Restricted and Commercial Operator, and General Mobile Radio Services**

Approved by OMB 3060 - 0850
See instructions for public burden estimate

1) Radio Service Code: HA

**Application Purpose** (Select only one) (MD)

| 2) | **NE** – New<br>**MD** – Modification<br>**AM** – Amendment | **RO** – Renewal Only<br>**RM** – Renewal / Modification<br>**CA** – Cancellation of License | **WD** – Withdrawal of Application<br>**DU** – Duplicate License<br>**AU** – Administrative Update |
|---|---|---|---|

| | |
|---|---|
| 3) If this request if for Developmental License or STA (Special Temporary Authorization) enter the appropriate code and attach the required exhibit as described in the instructions. Otherwise enter N (Not Applicable). | ( N ) D S N/A |
| 4) If this request is for an Amendment or Withdrawal of Application, enter the file number of the pending application currently on file with the FCC. | File Number |
| 5) If this request is for a Modification, Renewal Only, Renewal / Modification, Cancellation of License, Duplicate License, or Administrative Update, enter the call sign (serial number for Commercial Operator) of the existing FCC license. If this is a request for consolidation of DO & DM Operator Licenses, enter serial number of DO. | Call Sign/Serial #<br>WR1B |
| 6) If this request is for a New, Amendment, Renewal Only, or Renewal Modification, enter the requested expiration date of the authorization (this item is optional). | MM DD |
| 7) Does this filing request a Waiver of the Commission's rules? If 'Y', attach the required showing as described in the instructions. | ( ) Yes No |
| 8) Are attachments (other than associated schedules) being filed with this application? | ( ) Yes No |

**Applicant Information**

9) FCC Registration Number (FRN): 0003-3573-99

10) Applicant /Licensee is a(n): ( I ) Individual Unicorporated Association Trust Government Entity Joint Venture Corporation Limited Liability Corporation Partnership Consortium

| 11) First Name (if individual): Larry | MI: D | Last Name: Wolfgang | Suffix: |
|---|---|---|---|

11a) Date of Birth (required for Amateur Radio or Commercial Operators (including Restricted Radiotelephone)): 07 (mm)/09 (dd)/52 (yy)

12) Entity Name (if other than individual):

13) Attention To:

| 14) P.O. Box: | And/Or | 15) Street Address: 225 Main Street | |
|---|---|---|---|
| 16) City: Newington | 17) State: CT | 18) Zip: 06111 | 19) Country: USA |
| 20) Telephone Number: 860-594-0200 | | 21) FAX: | |

22) E-Mail Address: wr1b@arrl.net

FCC 605 – Main Form
November 2001 - Page 1

**Figure 2—This sample FCC Form 605 shows the sections you should complete to notify the FCC of a change in your address.**

**Fee Status**

| | |
|---|---|
| 23) Is the applicant exempt from FCC application Fees? | ( N ) Yes No |
| 24) Is the applicant exempt from FCC regulatory Fees? | ( N ) Yes No |

**General Certification Statements**

| | |
|---|---|
| 1) | The Applicant waives any claim to the use of any particular frequency or of the electromagnetic spectrum as against the regulatory power of the United States because of the previous use of the same, whether by license or otherwise, and requests an authorization in accordance with this application. |
| 2) | The applicant certifies that all statements made in this application and in the exhibits, attachments, or documents incorporated by reference are material, are part of this application, and are true, complete, correct, and made in good faith. |
| 3) | Neither the Applicant nor any member thereof is a foreign government or a representative thereof. |
| 4) | The applicant certifies that neither the applicant nor any other party to the application is subject to a denial of Federal benefits pursuant to Section 5301 of the Anti-Drug Abuse Act of 1988, 21 U.S.C. § 862, because of a conviction for possession or distribution of a controlled substance. **This certification does not apply to applications filed in services exempted under Section 1.2002(c) of the rules, 47 CFR § 1.2002(c).** See Section 1.2002(b) of the rules, 47 CFR § 1.2002(b), for the definition of "party to the application" as used in this certification. |
| 5) | Amateur or GMRS Applicant certifies that the construction of the station would NOT be an action which is likely to have a significant environmental effect (see the Commission's Rules 47 CFR Sections 1.1301-1.1319 and Section 97.13(a) Rules (available at web site http://www.fcc.gov/wtb/rules.html). |
| 6) | Amateur Applicant certifies that they have READ and WILL COMPLY WITH Section 97.13(c) of the Commission's Rules (available at web site http://www.fcc.gov/wtb/rules.html) regarding RADIOFREQUENCY (RF) RADIATION SAFETY and the amateur service section of OST/OET Bulletin Number 65 (available at web site http://www.fcc.gov/oet/info/documents/bulletins/). |

**Certification Statements For GMRS Applicants**

| | |
|---|---|
| 1) | Applicant certifies that he or she is claiming eligibility under Rule Section 95.5 of the Commission's Rules. |
| 2) | Applicant certifies that he or she is at least 18 years of age. |
| 3) | Applicant certifies that he or she will comply with the requirement that use of frequencies 462.650, 467.650, 462.700 and 467.700 MHz is not permitted near the Canadian border North of Line A and East of Line C. These frequencies are used throughout Canada and harmful interference is anticipated. |
| 4) | Non-Individual applicants certify that they have NOT changed frequency or channel pairs, type of emission, antenna height, location of fixed transmitters, number of mobile units, area of mobile operation, or increase in power. |

**Signature**

25) Typed or Printed Name of Party Authorized to Sign

| First Name: Larry | MI. D | Last Name: Wolfgang | Suffix: |
|---|---|---|---|
| 26) Title: | | | |
| Signature: Larry D. Wolfgang | | | 27) Date: 1/2/2002 |

| |
|---|
| Failure to Sign This Application May Result in Dismissal Of The Application And Forfeiture Of Any Fees Paid |

| |
|---|
| WILLFUL FALSE STATEMENTS MADON THIS FOR OR ANY ATTACHMENTS ARE PUNISHRABLE BY FINE AND/OR IMPRISONMENT (U.S. Code, Title 18, Section 1001) AND / OR REVOCATION OF ANY STATION LICENSE OR CONSTRUCTION PERMIT (U.S. Code, Title 47, Section 312(a)(1)), AND / OR FORFEITURE (U.S. Code, Title 47, Section 503). |

**FCC 605 – Main Form**
**November 2001 - Page 2**

## NCVEC QUICK-FORM 605 APPLICATION FOR AMATEUR OPERATOR/PRIMARY STATION LICENSE

**SECTION 1 - TO BE COMPLETED BY APPLICANT**

| PRINT LAST NAME | SUFFIX | FIRST NAME | INITIAL | STATION CALL SIGN (IF ANY) |
|---|---|---|---|---|
| REED | | DANA | G | KD1CW |

| MAILING ADDRESS (Number and Street or P.O. Box) | SOCIAL SECURITY NUMBER / TIN (OR FCC LICENSEE ID #) |
|---|---|
| 70 BROOKS POND ROAD | 000-00-0000 |

| CITY | STATE CODE | ZIP CODE (5 or 9 Numbers) | E-MAIL ADDRESS (OPTIONAL) |
|---|---|---|---|
| SPENCER | MA | 01562-1006 | starline@fis.net |

| DAYTIME TELEPHONE NUMBER (Include Area Code) OPTIONAL | FAX NUMBER (Include Area Code) OPTIONAL | ENTITY NAME (IF CLUB, MILITARY RECREATION, RACES) |
|---|---|---|
| (555)555-8853 | | |

Type of Applicant: ☒ Individual ☐ Amateur Club ☐ Military Recreation ☐ RACES (Modify Only)

TRUSTEE OR CUSTODIAN CALL SIGN

SIGNATURE OF RESPONSIBLE CLUB OFFICIAL

**I HEREBY APPLY FOR** (Make an X in the appropriate box(es))

☐ **EXAMINATION** for a **new** license grant

☒ **EXAMINATION** for **upgrade** of my license class

☐ **CHANGE** my **name** on my license to my new name

Former Name: ______________ (Last name) (Suffix) (First name) (MI)

☐ **CHANGE** my mailing address to **above** address

☐ **CHANGE** my station **call sign** systematically

Applicant's Initials: ______________

☐ **RENEWAL** of my license grant.

| Do you have another license application on file with the FCC which has not been acted upon? | PURPOSE OF OTHER APPLICATION | PENDING FILE NUMBER (FOR VEC USE ONLY) |
|---|---|---|
| | | |

**I certify that:**

- I waive any claim to the use of any particular frequency regardless of prior use by license or otherwise;
- All statements and attachments are true, complete and correct to the best of my knowledge and belief and are made in good faith;
- I am not a representative of a foreign government;
- I am not subject to a denial of Federal benefits pursuant to Section 5301of the Anti-Drug Abuse Act of 1988, 21 U.S.C. § 862;
- The construction of my station will NOT be an action which is likely to have a significant environmental effect (See 47 CFR Sections 1.301-1.319 and Section 97.13(a));
- I have read and WILL COMPLY with Section 97.13(c) of the Commission's Rules regarding RADIOFREQUENCY (RF) RADIATION SAFETY and the amateur service section of OST/OET Bulletin Number 65.

**Signature of applicant** (Do not print, type, or stamp. Must match applicant's name above.)

X Dana G. Reed    Date Signed: January 14, 2002

**SECTION 2 - TO BE COMPLETED BY ALL ADMINISTERING VEs**

Applicant is qualified for operator license class:

☐ **NO NEW LICENSE OR UPGRADE WAS EARNED**

☐ **TECHNICIAN** Element 2

☐ **GENERAL** Elements 1, 2 and 3

☑ **AMATEUR EXTRA** Elements 1, 2, 3 and 4

| DATE OF EXAMINATION SESSION | 1-14-02 |
|---|---|
| EXAMINATION SESSION LOCATION | Northfield MA |
| VEC ORGANIZATION | ARRL DØ1 |
| VEC RECEIPT DATE | |

**I CERTIFY THAT I HAVE COMPLIED WITH THE ADMINISTERING VE REQUIREMENTS IN PART 97 OF THE COMMISSION'S RULES AND WITH THE INSTRUCTIONS PROVIDED BY THE COORDINATING VEC AND THE FCC.**

| VEs NAME (Print First, MI, Last, Suffix) | VEs STATION CALL SIGN | VEs SIGNATURE (Must match name) | DATE SIGNED |
|---|---|---|---|
| 1st: Richard W. Stycharz Jr | KD1XP | [signature] | 1-14-02 |
| 2nd: Richard G. Peters | AA1XU | [signature] | 1-14-02 |
| 3rd: Robert Weissman | W1CKT | [signature] | 1-14-02 |

NCVEC FORM 605 - APRIL 2000
FOR VE/VEC USE ONLY - Page 1

**Figure 3—This sample NCVEC Quick Form 605 shows how your form will look after you have completed your upgrade to Amateur Extra.**

## INSTRUCTIONS FOR COMPLETING APPLICATION FORM NCVEC FORM 605

**ARE WRITTEN TESTS AN FCC-LICENSE REQUIREMENT? ARE THERE EXEMPTIONS?**

Beginning April 15, 2000, you may be examined on only three classes of operator licenses, each authorizing varying levels of privileges. The class for which each examinee is qualified is determined by the degree of skill and knowledge in operating a station that the examinee demonstrates to volunteer examiners (VEs) in his or her community. The demonstration of this know-ledge is required in order to obtain an Amateur Operator/Primary Station License. There is no exemption from the written exam requirements for persons with difficulty in reading, writing, or because of a handicap or disability. There are exam accommo-dations that can be afforded examinees (see ACCOMMODATING A HANDICAPPED PERSON below). Most new amateur operators start at the Technician class and then advance one class at a time. The VEs give examination credit for the license class currently (and in some cases, previously) held so that examinations required for that license need not be repeated. The written examinations are constructed from question pools that have been made public (see: <http//www.arrl.org/arrlvec/pools.html>.) Helpful study guides and training courses are also widely avail-able. To locate examination opportunities in your area, contact your local club, VE group, one of the 14 VECs or see the online listings at: <http://www.w5yi.org/vol-exam.htm> or <http//www.arrl.org/arrlvec/examsearch.phtml>.

**IS KNOWLEDGE OF MORSE CODE AN FCC-LICENSE REQUIREMENT? ARE THERE EXEMPTIONS?**

Some persons have difficulty in taking Morse code tests because of a handicap or disability. There is available to all otherwise qualified persons, handicapped or not, the Technician Class operator license that does not require passing a Morse code examination. Because of international regulations, how-ever, any US FCC licensee seeking access to the HF bands (frequencies below 30 MHz) must have demonstrated proficiency in Morse code. If a US FCC licensee wishes to gain access to the HF bands, there is no exemption available from this Morse code proficiency requirement. If licensed as a Tech-nician class, upon passing a Morse code examination operation on certain HF bands is permitted.

**THE REASON FOR THE MORSE CODE EXAMINATION**

Telegraphy is a method of electrical communication that the Amateur Radio Service community strongly desires to preserve. The FCC supports this objective by authorizing additional operating privileges to amateur operators who pass a Morse Code examination. Normally, to attain this skill, intense practice is required. Annually, thousands of amateur operators prove, by passing examinations, that they have acquired the skill. These examinations are prepared and administered by amateur ope-rators in the local community who volunteer their time and effort.

**THE EXAMINATION PROCEDURE**

The volunteer examiners (VEs) send a short message in the Morse code. The examinee must decipher a series of audible dots and dashes into 43 different alphabetic, numeric, and punctuation characters used in the message. Usually a 10-question quiz is then administered asking questions about items contained in the message.

**ACCOMMODATING A HANDICAPPED PERSON**

Many handicapped persons accept and benefit from the personal challenge of passing the examination in spite of their hardships. For handicapped persons who have difficulty in proving that they can decipher messages sent in the Morse code, the VEs make exceptionally accommodative arrangements. To assist such persons, the VEs will:

- adjust the tone in frequency and volume to suit the examinee.
- administer the examination at a place convenient and com-fortable to the examinee, even at bedside.
- for a deaf person, they will send the dots and dashes to a vibrating surface or flashing light.
- write the examinee's dictation.
- where warranted, they will pause in sending the message after each sentence, each phrase, each word, or in extreme cases they will pause the exam message character-by-character to allow the examinee additional time to absorb, to interpret or even to speak out what was sent.
- or they will even allow the examinee to send the message, rather than receive it.

Should you have any questions, please contact your local volunteer examiner team, or contact one of the 14 volunteer examiner coordinator (VEC) organizations. For contact information for VECs, or to contact the FCC, call 888-225-5322 (weekdays), or write to FCC, 1270 Fairfield Road, Gettysburg PA 17325-7245. Fax 717-338-2696. Also see the FCC web at: <http//www.fcc.gov/wtb/amateur/>.

## RENEWING, MODIFYING OR REINSTATING YOUR AMATEUR RADIO OPERATOR/PRIMARY STATION LICENSE

**RENEWING YOUR AMATEUR LICENSE**

The NCVEC Form 605 may also be used to renew or modify your Amateur Radio Operator/Primary Station license. License renewal may only be completed during the final 90 days prior to license expiration, or up to two years after expiration. Changes to your mailing address, name and requests for a sequential change of your station call sign appropriate for your license class may be requested at any time. This form may not be used to apply for a specific ("Vanity") station call sign.

**REINSTATING YOUR AMATEUR LICENSE**

This form may also be used to reinstate your Amateur Radio Operator/Station license if it has been expired less than the two year grace period for renewal. After the two year grace period you must retake the amateur license examinations to become relicensed. You will be issued a new systematic call sign.

**RENEWING OR MODIFYING YOUR LICENSE**

On-line renewal: You can submit your renewal or license modifications to FCC on-line via the internet/WWW at: <http://www.fcc.gov/wtb/uls>. To do so, you must first register in ULS by following the "TIN/Call Sign Registration" tab procedures, then choose the "Connecting to ULS" tab procedures and use their special dial-in to an FCC 800# modem-only access system.

Renewal by mail: If you choose to renew by mail, you can mail the "FCC Form 605" to FCC. You can obtain FCC Form 605 via the internet at <http://www.fcc.gov/formpage.html> or <ftp://ftp.fcc.gov/pub/Forms/Form605/>. It's available by fax at 202-418-0177 (request Form 000605). The FCC Forms Distribution Center will accept form orders by calling 800-418-3676. FCC Form 605 has a main form, plus a Schedule D. The main form is all that is needed for renewals. Mail FCC Form 605 to: FCC, 1270 Fairfield Rd, Gettysburg PA 17325-7245. This is a free FCC service.

The NCVEC Form 605 application can be used for a license renewal, modification or reinstatement. NCVEC Form 605 can be processed by VECs, but not all VECs provide this as a routine service. ARRL Members can submit NCVEC Form 605 to the ARRL/VEC for process-ing. ARRL Members or others can choose to submit their NCVEC Form 605 to a local VEC (check with the VEC office before forwarding), or it can be returned with a $6.00 application fee to: The W5YI Group, Inc., P.O. Box 565101, Dallas, Texas 75356 (a portion of this fee goes to the National Conference of VECs to help defray their expenses). The NCVEC Form 605 may not be returned to the FCC since it is an internal VEC form. Once again, the service provided by FCC is free.

**THE FCC APPLICATION FORM 605**

The FCC version of the Form 605 may not be used for applications submitted to a VE team or a VEC since it does not request information needed by the administering VEs. The FCC Form 605 may, however, be used to routinely renew or modify your license without charge. It should be sent to the FCC, 1270 Fairfield Rd., Gettysburg PA 17325-7245.

**CLUB AND MILITARY RECREATION CALL SIGN ADMINISTRATORS**

The NCVEC Form 605 may also be used for the processing of applications for Amateur Service club and military recreation station call signs and for the modification of RACES stations. No fee may be charged by an administrator for this service. As of March 9, 2000, FCC had not yet implemented the Call Sign Administrator System.

**NCVEC FORM 605 - APRIL 2000**
**FOR VE/VEC USE ONLY - Page 2**

What supplies will you need? First, be sure you bring your current original Amateur Radio license, if you have one. Bring a photocopy of your license, too, as well as the original and a photocopy of any Certificates of Successful Completion of Examination (CSCE) that you plan to use for exam credit. Bring along several sharpened number 2 pencils and two pens (blue or black ink). Be sure to have a good eraser. A pocket calculator may also come in handy. You may use a programmable calculator if that is the kind you have, but take it into your exam "empty" (cleared of all programs and constants in memory). Don't program equations ahead of time, because you may be asked to demonstrate that there is nothing in the calculator memory. The examining team has the right to refuse a candidate the use of any calculator that they feel may contain information for the test or could otherwise be used to cheat on the exam.

The Volunteer Examiner Team is required to check two forms of identification before you enter the test room. This includes your *original* Amateur Radio license, if you have one—not a photocopy. A photo ID of some type is best for the second form of ID, but is not required by the FCC. Other acceptable forms of identification include a driver's license, a piece of mail addressed to you or a birth certificate.

The following description of the testing procedure applies to exams coordinated by the ARRL/VEC, although many other VECs use a similar procedure.

## Code Test

The code test is usually given before the written exams. If you don't plan to take the code exam, just sit quietly while the other candidates give it a try.

Before you take the code test, you'll be handed a piece of paper to copy the code as it is sent. The test will begin with about a minute of practice copy. Then comes the actual test: at least five minutes of Morse code. You are responsible for knowing the 26 letters of the alphabet, the numerals 0 through 9, the period, comma, question mark, and the procedural signals $\overline{AR}$ ( + ), $\overline{SK}$, $\overline{BT}$ ( = or double dash) and $\overline{DN}$ (/ or fraction bar, sometimes called the "slant bar").

You may copy the entire text word for word, or just take notes on the content. At the end of the transmission, the examiner will hand you 10 questions about the text. Fill in the blanks with your answers. (You must spell each answer exactly as it was sent.) If you get at least 7 correct, you pass! Alternatively, the exam team has the option to look at your copy sheet if you fail the 10-question exam. If you have one minute of solid copy (25 characters), the examiners can certify that you passed the test on that basis. The format of the test transmission is generally similar to one side of a normal on-the-air amateur conversation.

A sending test may not be required. The Commission has decided that if applicants can demonstrate receiving ability, they most likely can also send at that speed. But be prepared for a sending test, just in case! Subpart 97.503(a) of the FCC Rules says, "A telegraphy examination must be sufficient to prove that the examinee has the ability to send correctly by hand and to receive correctly by ear texts in the international Morse code at not less than the prescribed speed..."

## Written Tests

After the code tests are administered, you'll take the written examination. The examiner will give each applicant a test booklet, an answer sheet and scratch paper. After that, you're on your own. The first thing to do is read the instructions. Be sure to sign your name every place it's called for. Do all of this at the beginning to get it out of the way.

Next, check the examination to see that all pages and questions are there. If not, report this to the examiner immediately. When filling in your answer sheet make sure your answers are marked next to the numbers that correspond to each question.

Go through the entire exam, and answer the easy questions first. Next, go back to the beginning and try the harder questions. Leave the really tough questions for last. Guessing can only help, as there is no additional penalty for answering incorrectly.

If you have to guess, do it intelligently: At first glance, you may find that you can eliminate one or more "distracters." Of the remaining responses, more than one may seem correct; only one is the best answer, however. To the applicant who is fully prepared, incorrect distracters to each question are obvious. Nothing beats preparation!

After you've finished, check the examination thoroughly. You may have read a question wrong or goofed in your arithmetic. Don't be overconfident. There's no rush, so take your time. Think, and check your answer sheet. When you feel you've done your best and can do no more, return the test booklet, answer sheet and scratch pad to the examiner.

The Volunteer-Examiner Team will grade the exam while you wait. The passing mark is 74%. (That means 37 out of 50 questions correct — or no more than 13 incorrect answers on the Element 4 exam.) You will receive a Certificate of Successful Completion of Examination (CSCE) showing all exam elements that you pass at that exam session. If you are already licensed, and you pass the exam elements required to earn a higher license class, the CSCE authorizes you to operate with your new privileges immediately. When you use these new privileges, you must sign your call sign followed by the slant mark ("/"; on voice, say "stroke" or "slant") and the letters "KT," if you are upgrading from a Novice to a Technician with code license. You only have to follow this special identification procedure until your new license is granted by the FCC, however.

If you pass only some of the exam elements required for a license, you will still receive a CSCE. That certificate shows what exam elements you passed, and is valid for 365 days. Use it as proof that you passed those exam elements so you won't have to take them over again next time you try for the license.

# And Now, Let's Begin

The complete Amateur Extra question pool (Element 4) is printed in this book. Each chapter lists all the questions for a particular subelement. A brief explanation about the correct answer is given after each question.

**Table 4** shows the study guide or syllabus for the Element 4 exam as released by the Volunteer-Examiner Coordinators' Question Pool Committee in July 2002. The syllabus lists the topics to be covered by the Amateur Extra exam, and so forms the basic outline for the remainder of this book. Use the syllabus to guide your study.

The question numbers used in the question pool refer to this syllabus. Each question number begins with a syllabus-point number (for example, E1C or E7E). The question numbers end with a two-digit number. For example, question E3B09 is the ninth question about the E3B syllabus point.

The Question Pool Committee designed the syllabus and question pool so there are the same number of points in each subelement as there are exam questions from that subelement. For example, three exam questions on the Amateur Extra exam must be from the "Radio-Wave Propagation" subelement, so there are three groups for that point. These are numbered E3A, E3B and E3C. While not a requirement of the FCC Rules, the Question Pool Committee recommends that one question be taken from each group to make the best possible license exams.

Good luck with your studies!

---

**Table 4**

**Amateur Extra Class (Element 4) Syllabus**

**Required for Amateur Extra Licenses**

***SUBELEMENT E1 — COMMISSION'S RULES***

***[7 Exam Questions — 7 Groups]***

E1A Operating standards: frequency privileges for Extra class amateurs; emission standards; message forwarding; frequency sharing between ITU Regions; FCC modification of station license; 30-meter band sharing; stations aboard ships or aircraft; telemetry; telecommand of an amateur station; authorized telecommand transmissions

E1B Station restrictions: restrictions on station locations; restricted operation; teacher as control operator; station antenna structures; definition and operation of remote control and automatic control; control link

E1C Reciprocal operating: reciprocal operating authority; purpose of reciprocal agreement rules; alien control operator privileges; identification (Note: This includes CEPT and IARP)

E1D Radio Amateur Civil Emergency Service (RACES): definition; purpose; station registration; station license required; control operator requirements; control operator privileges; frequencies available; limitations on use of

RACES frequencies; points of communication for RACES operation; permissible communications

E1E Amateur Satellite Service: definition; purpose; station license required for space station; frequencies available; telecommand operation: definition; eligibility; telecommand station (definition); space telecommand station; special provisions; telemetry: definition; special provisions; space station: definition; eligibility; special provisions; authorized frequencies (space station); notification requirements; earth operation: definition; eligibility; authorized frequencies (Earth station)

E1F Volunteer Examiner Coordinators (VECs): definition; VEC qualifications; VEC agreement; scheduling examinations; coordinating VEs; reimbursement for expenses; accrediting VEs; question pools; Volunteer Examiners (VEs): definition; requirements; accreditation; reimbursement for expenses; VE conduct; preparing an examination; examination elements; definition of code and written elements; preparation responsibility; examination requirements; examination credit; examination procedure; examination administration; temporary operating authority

E1G Certification of external RF power amplifiers and external RF power amplifier kits; Line A; National Radio Quiet Zone; business communications; definition and operation of spread spectrum; auxiliary station operation

***SUBELEMENT E2 — OPERATING PROCEDURES***

***[5 Exam Questions -- 5 Groups]***

E2A Amateur Satellites: orbital mechanics; frequencies available for satellite operation; satellite hardware; satellite operations

E2B Television: fast scan television (FSTV) standards; slow scan television (SSTV) standards; facsimile (fax) communications

E2C Contest and DX operating; spread-spectrum transmissions; automatic HF forwarding; selecting your operating frequency

E2D Operating VHF / UHF digital modes: packet clusters; digital bulletin boards; Automatic Position Reporting System (APRS)

E2E Operating HF digital modes

***SUBELEMENT E3 — RADIO-WAVE PROPAGATION***

***[3 Exam Questions -- 3 Groups]***

E3A Earth-Moon-Earth (EME or moonbounce) communications; meteor scatter

E3B Transequatorial; long path; gray line

E3C Auroral propagation; selective fading; radio-path horizon; take-off angle over flat or sloping terrain; earth effects on propagation

***SUBELEMENT E4 — AMATEUR RADIO PRACTICES***

***[5 Exam Questions — 5 Groups]***

E4A Test equipment: spectrum analyzers (interpreting spectrum analyzer displays; transmitter output spectrum), logic probes (indications of high and low states in digital circuits; indications of pulse conditions in digital circuits)

E4B Frequency measurement devices (i.e., frequency counter, oscilloscope Lissajous figures, dip meter); meter performance limitations; oscilloscope performance limitations; frequency counter performance limitations

E4C Receiver performance characteristics (i.e., phase noise, desensitization, capture effect, intercept point, noise floor, dynamic range {blocking and

IMD}, image rejection, MDS, signal-to-noise-ratio); intermodulation and cross-modulation interference

E4D Noise suppression: vehicular system noise; electronic motor noise; static; line noise

E4E Component mounting techniques (i.e., surface, dead bug (raised), circuit board; direction finding: techniques and equipment; fox hunting

## *SUBELEMENT E5 — ELECTRICAL PRINCIPLES*

### *[9 Exam Questions — 9 Groups]*

E5A Characteristics of resonant circuits: Series resonance (capacitor and inductor to resonate at a specific frequency); Parallel resonance (capacitor and inductor to resonate at a specific frequency); half-power bandwidth

E5B Exponential charge/discharge curves (time constants): definition; time constants in RL and RC circuits

E5C Impedance diagrams: Basic principles of Smith charts; impedance of RLC networks at specified frequencies; PC based impedance analysis (including Smith Charts)

E5D Phase angle between voltage and current; impedances and phase angles of series and parallel circuits

E5E Algebraic operations using complex numbers: rectangular coordinates (real and imaginary parts); polar coordinates (magnitude and angle)

E5F Skin effect; electrostatic and electromagnetic fields

E5G Circuit Q; reactive power; power factor

E5H Effective radiated power; system gains and losses

E5I Photoconductive principles and effects

## *SUBELEMENT E6 — CIRCUIT COMPONENTS*

### *[5 Exam Questions — 5 Groups]*

E6A Semiconductor material: Germanium, Silicon, P-type, N-type; Transistor types: NPN, PNP, junction, power; field-effect transistors (FETs): enhancement mode; depletion mode; MOS; CMOS; N-channel; P-channel

E6B Diodes: Zener, tunnel, varactor, hot-carrier, junction, point contact, PIN and light emitting; operational amplifiers (inverting amplifiers, noninverting amplifiers, voltage gain, frequency response, FET amplifier circuits, single-stage amplifier applications); phase-locked loops

E6C TTL digital integrated circuits; CMOS digital integrated circuits; gates

E6D Vidicon and cathode-ray tube devices; charge-coupled devices (CCDs); liquid crystal displays (LCDs); toroids: permeability, core material, selecting, winding

E6E Quartz crystal (frequency determining properties as used in oscillators and filters); monolithic amplifiers (MMICs)

## *SUBELEMENT E7 — PRACTICAL CIRCUITS*

### *[7 Exam Questions — 7 Groups]*

E7A Digital logic circuits: Flip flops; Astable and monostable multivibrators; Gates (AND, NAND, OR, NOR); Positive and negative logic

E7B Amplifier circuits: Class A, Class AB, Class B, Class C, amplifier operating efficiency (i.e., DC input versus PEP), transmitter final amplifiers; amplifier circuits: tube, bipolar transistor, FET

E7C Impedance-matching networks: Pi, L, Pi-L; filter circuits: constant K, M-derived, band-stop, notch, crystal lattice, pi-section, T-section, L-section, Butterworth, Chebyshev, elliptical; filter applications (audio, IF, digital signal processing {DSP})

E7D Oscillators: types, applications, stability; voltage-regulator circuits: discrete, integrated and switched mode

E7E Modulators: reactance, phase, balanced; detectors; mixer stages; frequency synthesizers

E7F Digital frequency divider circuits; frequency marker generators; frequency counters

E7G Active audio filters: characteristics; basic circuit design; preselector applications

***SUBELEMENT E8 -- SIGNALS AND EMISSIONS***

***[4 Exam Questions — 4 Groups]***

E8A AC waveforms: sine wave, square wave, sawtooth wave; AC measurements: peak, peak-to-peak and root-mean-square (RMS) value, peak-envelope-power (PEP) relative to average

E8B FCC emission designators versus emission types; modulation symbols and transmission characteristics; modulation methods; modulation index; deviation ratio; pulse modulation: width; position

E8C Digital signals: including CW; digital signal information rate vs bandwidth; spread-spectrum communications

E8D Peak amplitude (positive and negative); peak-to-peak values: measurements; Electromagnetic radiation; wave polarization; signal-to-noise (S/N) ratio

***SUBELEMENT E9 — ANTENNAS***

***[5 Exam Questions — 5 Groups]***

E9A Isotropic radiators: definition; used as a standard for comparison; radiation pattern; basic antenna parameters: radiation resistance and reactance (including wire dipole, folded dipole), gain, beamwidth, efficiency

E9B Free-space antenna patterns: E and H plane patterns (i.e., azimuth and elevation in free-space); gain as a function of pattern; antenna design (computer modeling of antennas)

E9C Phased vertical antennas; radiation patterns; beverage antennas; rhombic antennas: resonant; terminated; radiation pattern; antenna patterns: elevation above real ground, ground effects as related to polarization, take-off angles as a function of height above ground

E9D Space and satellite communications antennas: gain; beamwidth; tracking; losses in real antennas and matching: resistivity losses, losses in resonating elements (loading coils, matching networks, etc. {i.e., mobile, trap}); SWR bandwidth; efficiency

E9E Matching antennas to feed lines; characteristics of open and shorted feed lines: ⅛ wavelength; ¼ wavelength; ½ wavelength; feed lines: coax versus open-wire; velocity factor; electrical length; transformation characteristics of line terminated in impedance not equal to characteristic impedance; use of antenna analyzers

# Subelement E1

## Subelement E1
## Commission's Rules

The Extra Class (Element 4) written examination consists of 50 questions taken from the Extra Class examination pool. This pool is prepared by the Volunteer Examiner Coordinators' Question Pool Committee. A certain number of questions are taken from each of the 9 subelements.

There will be seven examination questions over the seven groups of questions covering the Commission's Rules. The question groups are labeled E1A through E1G. The correct answer (A, B, C, or D) is given in bold following the question and the possible responses at the beginning of an explanation section. After many of the explanations in this subelement, you will see a reference to Part 97 of the FCC rules set inside square brackets, like [97.301(b)]. This tells you where to look for the exact wording in the Rules as they relate to that question. For a complete copy of Part 97, along with simple explanations of the Rules governing Amateur Radio, see *The FCC Rule Book* published by ARRL.

You'll also find FCC rules online at **http://www.arrl.org/FandES/field/regulations/rules-regs.html**. In addition to Part 97, you'll find other parts of the FCC rules. These include Part 1 and Part 17.

### E1A Operating standards: frequency privileges for Extra class amateurs; emission standards; message forwarding; frequency sharing between ITU Regions; FCC modification of station license; 30-meter band sharing; stations aboard ships or aircraft; telemetry; telecommand of an amateur station; authorized telecommand transmissions

**E1A01 What exclusive frequency privileges in the 80-meter band are authorized to Amateur Extra Class control operators?**

A. 3525-3775 kHz
B. 3500-3525 kHz
C. 3700-3750 kHz
D. 3500-3550 kHz

**B** In the 80-meter band, only Amateur Extra Class licensees have transmitting privileges from 3500 to 3525 kHz. [97.301]

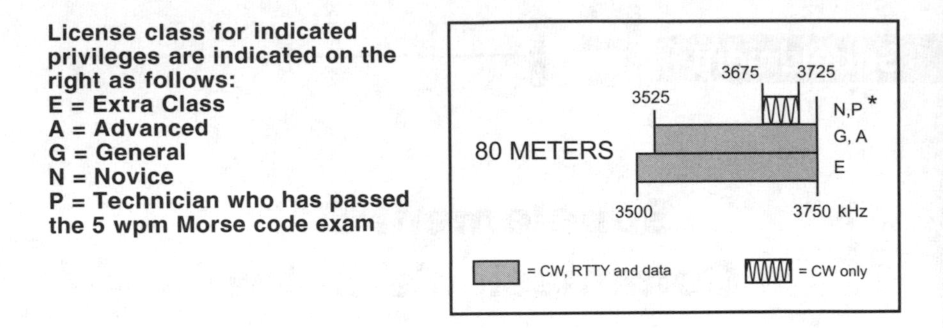


**E1A02** **What exclusive frequency privileges in the 75-meter band are authorized to Amateur Extra class control operators?**

A. 3775-3800 kHz
B. 3800-3850 kHz
C. 3750-3775 kHz
D. 3800-3825 kHz

**C** Amateur Extra Class licensees have exclusive transmitting privileges in the 75-meter band from 3750 to 3775 kHz. [97.301]

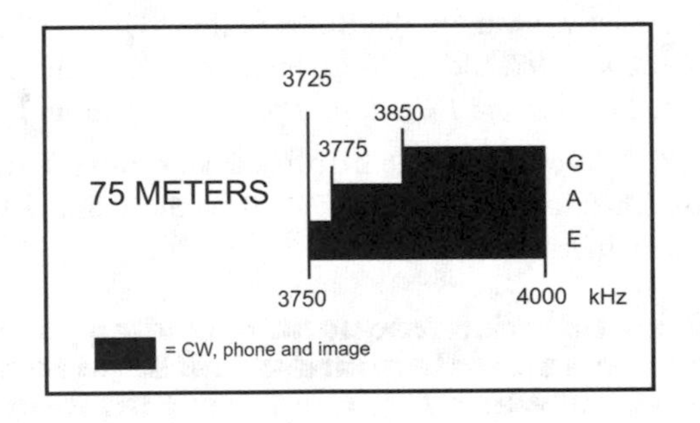


**E1A03** **What exclusive frequency privileges in the 40-meter band are authorized to Amateur Extra class control operators?**

A. 7000-7025 kHz
B. 7000-7050 kHz
C. 7025-7050 kHz
D. 7100-7150 kHz

**A** This is another question on which license class has use of a given band segment. Amateur Extra Class licensees have exclusive transmitting privileges from 7000 to 7025 kHz. [97.301]

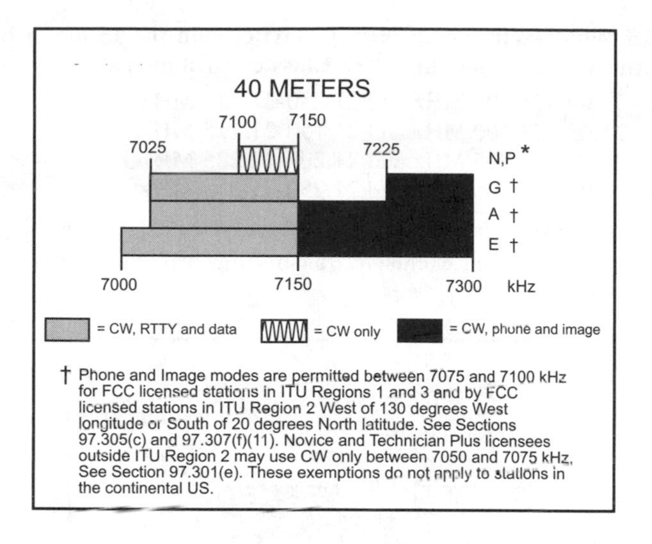


**E1A04 What exclusive frequency privileges in the 20-meter band are authorized to Amateur Extra Class control operators?**

A. 14.100-14.175 MHz and 14.150-14.175 MHz
B. 14.000-14.125 MHz and 14.250-14.300 MHz
C. 14.025-14.050 MHz and 14.100-14.150 MHz
D. 14.000-14.025 MHz and 14.150-14.175 MHz

**D** Amateur Extra Class licensees have exclusive frequency privileges from 14.000 to 14.025 MHz and exclusive transmitting privileges from 14.150 to 14.175 MHz. [97.301]

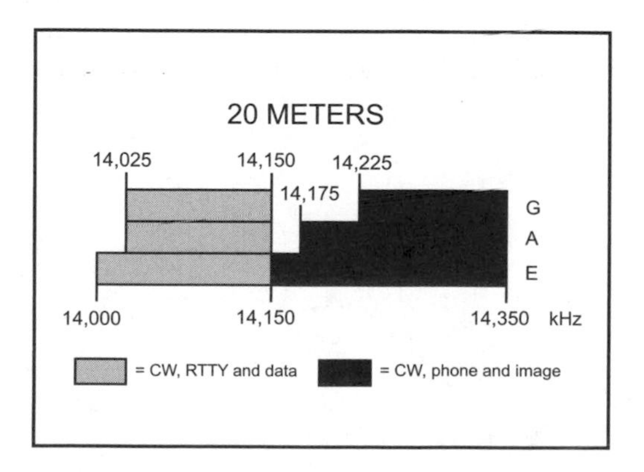

**E1A05 What exclusive frequency privileges in the 15-meter band are authorized to Amateur Extra Class control operators?**

A. 21.000-21.200 MHz and 21.250-21.270 MHz
B. 21.050-21.100 MHz and 21.150-21.175 MHz
C. 21.000-21.025 MHz and 21.200-21.225 MHz
D. 21.000-21.025 MHz and 21.250-21.275 MHz

**C** Amateur Extra Class licensees have exclusive operating privileges from 21.000 to 21.025 MHz and exclusive transmitting privileges from 21.200 to 21.225 MHz. [97.301]

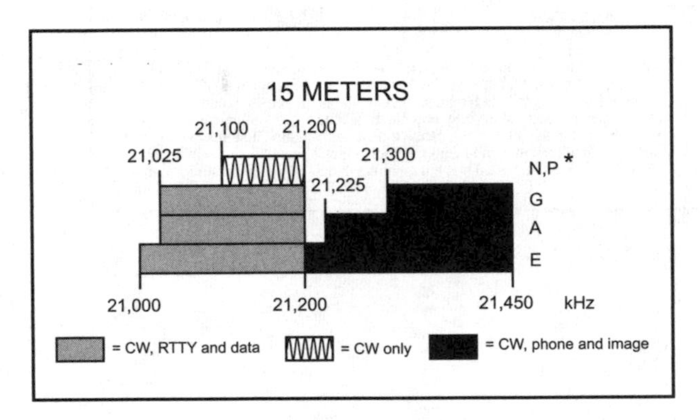


**E1A06 Which frequency bands contain at least one segment authorized to only control operators holding an Amateur Extra Class operator license?**

A. 80, 75, 40, 20 and 15 meters
B. 80, 40, and 20 meters
C. 75, 40, 30 and 10 meters
D. 160, 80, 40 and 20 meters

**A** Amateur Extra Class licensees have exclusive operating privileges in the 80, 75, 40, 20 and 15-meter bands. If you look at the frequency allocations, you will see that the 160, 30 and 10-meter bands have no Amateur Extra exclusive segments. [97.301]

**E1A07 Within the 20-meter band, what is the amount of spectrum authorized to only control operators holding an Amateur Extra Class operator license?**

A. 25 kHz
B. 50 kHz
C. None
D. 25 MHz

**B** Amateur Extra Class licensees have exclusive transmitting privileges from 14.000 to 14.025 MHz and exclusive operating privileges from 14.150 to 14.175 MHz. This makes a total of 50 kHz. [97.301]

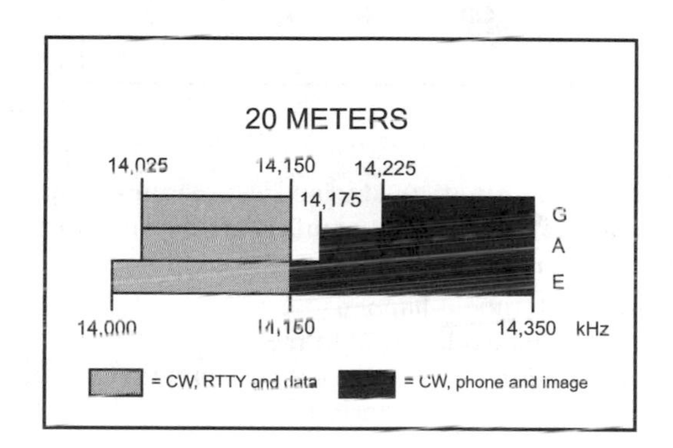


**E1A08 Which frequency bands contain two segments authorized to only control operators holding an Amateur Extra Class operator license, CEPT radio-amateur Class 1 license or Class 1 IARP?**

A. 80/75, 20 and 15 meters
B. 40, 30 and 20 meters
C. 30, 20 and 17 meters
D. 30, 20 and 12 meters

**A** Amateur Extra Class licensees have exclusive privileges in the combined 80/75, 20 and 15-meter bands. They have no exclusive privileges in the 30-meter band.

The CEPT radio-amateur Class 1 license and the Class 1 IARP provide a mechanism for visiting amateurs to obtain operating privileges in another country that participates in the respective agreements. CEPT is the European Conference of Posts and Telecommunications. CITEL is the Inter-American Telecommunication Commission. The IARP is issued under the CITEL/Amateur Convention. Later in this chapter, you'll see more questions on this topic. [97.301]

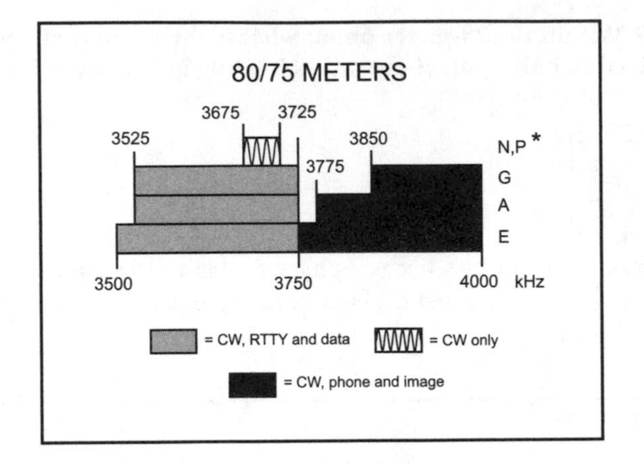


**E1A09 What must an amateur station licensee do if a spurious emission from the station causes harmful interference to the reception of another radio station?**

A. Pay a fine each time it happens
B. Submit a written explanation to the FCC
C. Forfeit the station license if it happens more than once
D. Eliminate or reduce the interference

**D** The FCC rules state, "All spurious emissions from a station transmitter must be reduced to the greatest extent practicable. If any spurious emission, including chassis or power line radiation, causes harmful interference to the reception of another radio station, the licensee of the interfering amateur station is required to take steps to eliminate the interference, in accordance with good engineering practice." [97.307(c)]

**E1A10 This question has been withdrawn.**

**E1A11 This question has been withdrawn.**

**E1A12 What is the maximum mean power permitted to any spurious emission from a transmitter or external RF power amplifier transmitting at a mean power greater than 25 watts on an amateur service VHF band?**

A. 60 dB below the mean power of the fundamental emission
B. 40 dB below the below the mean power of fundamental emission
C. 10 microwatts
D. 25 microwatts

**A** The rule for VHF bands has a different standard than that used for the HF bands. The standard for the VHF bands when running more than 25 W is that spurious emissions must be attenuated at least 60 dB. [97.307(e)]

**E1A13 What is the maximum mean power permitted for any spurious emission from a transmitter having a mean power of 25 W or less on an amateur service VHF band?**

A. The lesser of 25 microwatts or 40 dB below the mean power of the fundamental emission
B. The lesser of 50 microwatts or 40 dB below the mean power of the fundamental emission
C. 20 microwatts
D. 50 microwatts

**A** This is related to the previous question but now you are transmitting at a power not exceeding 25 W. An attenuation of 60 dB at 25 W would give a power level of 25 microwatts. The rule is that spurious emissions must be no more than the lesser of 25 mW or 40 dB below the mean power of the fundamental emission. [97.307(e)]

**E1A14 If a packet bulletin board station in a message forwarding system inadvertently forwards a message that is in violation of FCC rules, who is accountable for the rules violation?**

A. The control operator of the packet bulletin board station
B. The control operator of the originating station and conditionally the first forwarding station
C. The control operators of all the stations in the system
D. The control operators of all the stations in the system not authenticating the source from which they accept communications

**B** The packet relay system is based on trusting that the original messages are proper and legal. Obviously control operators must be responsible for their communications. That's why the rules state, "For stations participating in a message forwarding system, the control operator of the station originating a message is primarily accountable for any violation of the rules in this Part contained in the message."

The rules also state that the control operator of the first forwarding station must either authenticate the identity of the station from which it accepts a communication or accept accountability for any violation of the rules contained in messages it retransmits. [97.219(b), (d)]

**E1A15 If your packet bulletin board station inadvertently forwards a communication that violates FCC rules, what is the first action you should take?**

A. Discontinue forwarding the communication as soon as you become aware of it
B. Notify the originating station that the communication does not comply with FCC rules
C. Notify the nearest FCC Enforcement Bureau office
D. Discontinue forwarding all messages

**A** The FCC wants a problem fixed as quickly as possible. The rules say, "Except as noted in paragraph (d) of this section, for stations participating in a message forwarding system, the control operators of forwarding stations that retransmit inadvertently communications that violate the rules in this Part are not accountable for the violative communications. They are, however, responsible for discontinuing such communications once they become aware of their presence." [97.219(c)]

**E1A16 For each ITU Region, how is each frequency band allocated internationally to the amateur service designated?**

A. Primary service or secondary service
B. Primary service
C. Secondary service
D. Co-secondary service

**A** The amateur service can have either primary or secondary status, depending upon the band. There is no "co-secondary" service in the allocation tables. [97.303]

**E1A17 Why might the FCC modify an amateur station license?**

A. To relieve crowding in certain bands
B. To better prepare for a time of national emergency
C. To enforce a radio quiet zone within one mile of an airport
D. To promote the public interest, convenience and necessity

**D** The FCC may modify a station license either for a limited time or for the duration of the license term. One of the two reasons for this that are given in the rules is, " . . . will promote the public interest, convenience and necessity." Such modification will not become final until the licensee is notified in writing. There is an appeal process. [97.27]

**E1A18 What are the sharing requirements for an amateur station transmitting in the 30-meter band?**

A. It must not cause harmful interference to stations in the fixed service authorized by other nations
B. There are no sharing requirements
C. Stations in the fixed service authorized by other nations must not cause harmful interference to amateur stations in the same country
D. Stations in the fixed service authorized by other nations must not cause harmful interference to amateur stations in another country

**A** The FCC rule says, "No amateur station transmitting in the 30 meter band shall cause harmful interference to stations authorized by other nations in the fixed service. The licensee of the amateur station must make all necessary adjustments, including termination of transmissions, if harmful interference is caused." [97.303(d)]

**E1A19 If an amateur station is installed on board a ship and is separate from the ship radio installation, what condition must be met before the station may transmit?**

A. Its operation must be approved by the master of the ship
B. Its antenna must be separate from the main ship antennas, transmitting only when the main radios are not in use
C. It must have a power supply that is completely independent of the main ship power supply
D. Its operator must have an FCC Marine endorsement on his or her amateur operator license

**A** The only additional requirement that the FCC imposes in this hypothetical situation is that the operation must be approved by the master of the ship. [97.11]

**E1A20 What is the definition of the term telemetry?**

A. A one-way transmission of measurements at a distance from the measuring instrument
B. A two-way interactive transmission
C. A two-way single channel transmission of data
D. A one-way transmission to initiate, modify or terminate functions of a device at a distance

**A** This is a definition right out of the FCC rules, which define telemetry as, "A one-way transmission of measurements at a distance from the measuring instrument." [97.3(a)(45)]

**E1A21 What is the definition of the term telecommand?**

A. A one way transmission of measurements at a distance from the measuring instrument
B. A two-way interactive transmission
C. A two-way single channel transmission of data
D. A one-way transmission to initiate, modify or terminate functions of a device at a distance

**D** Here's another one straight from the rules. Part 97 defines telecommand as a one-way transmission to initiate, modify, or terminate functions of a device at a distance. [97.3(a)(43)]

**E1A22 When may an amateur station transmit special codes intended to obscure the meaning of messages?**

A. Never under any circumstances
B. Only when a Special Temporary Authority has been obtained from the FCC
C. Only when an Amateur Extra Class operator is the station control operator
D. When sending telecommand messages to a station in space operation

**D** As you studied for the Technician and General licenses, you learned that the transmission of special codes was something that was not allowed. Those questions were in the context of two-way communications. There is one major exception made in the Amateur Service and that is for control links to satellites. Often the telecommand transmissions are coded to keep folks from hacking into the satellite. This is not two-way communication, and the FCC explicitly allows the coding to protect the satellite. [97.211(b)]

## E1B Station restrictions: restrictions on station locations; restricted operation; teacher as control operator; station antenna structures; definition and operation of remote control and automatic control; control link

**E1B01 Which of the following factors might restrict the physical location of an amateur station apparatus or antenna structure?**

A. The land may have environmental importance; or it is significant in American history, architecture or culture
B. The location's political or societal importance
C. The location's geographical or horticultural importance
D. The location's international importance, requiring consultation with one or more foreign governments before installation

**A** As you may already know, environmental or historical significance may limit land use in some cases. This includes where someone can install an antenna. That's why FCC reflects this concern in Part 97. [97.13(a)]

**E1B02 Outside of what distance from an FCC monitoring facility may an amateur station be located without concern for protecting the facility from harmful interference?**

A. 1 mile
B. 3 miles
C. 10 miles
D. 30 miles

**A** The Part 97 rule calls for a 1600-meter (1-mile) protection zone. [97.13(b)]

**E1B03 What must be done before an amateur station is placed within an officially designated wilderness area or wildlife preserve, or an area listed in the National Register of Historical Places?**

A. A proposal must be submitted to the National Park Service
B. A letter of intent must be filed with the National Audubon Society
C. An Environmental Assessment must be submitted to the FCC
D. A form FSD-15 must be submitted to the Department of the Interior

**C** You only have to deal with FCC. Fortunately, and to simplify matters, you do not have to deal with other governmental or non-governmental agencies. [97.13(a)]

**E1B04 If an amateur station causes interference to the reception of a domestic broadcast station with a receiver of good engineering design, on what frequencies may the operation of the amateur station be restricted?**

A. On the frequency used by the domestic broadcast station
B. On all frequencies below 30 MHz
C. On all frequencies above 30 MHz
D. On the frequency or frequencies used when the interference occurs

**D** Only by avoiding the frequency or frequencies used when the interference occurs would one reduce the interference, and that's reflected in the rules. Since the amateur station cannot operate on broadcast frequencies, that idea is a bit silly. [97.121(a)]

**E1B05 When may an amateur operator accept compensation for serving as the control operator of an amateur station used in a classroom?**

A. Only when the amateur operator does not accept pay during periods of time when the amateur station is used
B. Only when the classroom is in a correctional institution
C. Only when the amateur operator is paid as an incident of a teaching position during periods of time when the station is used by that teacher as a part of classroom instruction at an educational institution
D. Only when the station is restricted to making contacts with similar stations at other educational institutions

**C** The rules say, "A control operator may accept compensation as an incident of a teaching position during periods of time when an amateur station is used by that teacher as a part of classroom instruction at an educational institution." [97.113(c)]

**E1B06 Who may accept compensation for serving as a control operator in a classroom at an educational institution?**

A. Any licensed amateur operator
B. Only an amateur operator accepting such pay as an incident of a teaching position during times when the station is used by that teacher as a part of classroom instruction
C. Only teachers at correctional institutions
D. Only students at educational or correctional institutions

**B** This is similar to the previous question so you should be able to spot the correct answer—the one consistent with Part 97. [97.113(c)]

**E1B07 If an amateur antenna structure is located in a valley or canyon, what height restrictions apply?**

A. The structure must not extend more than 200 feet above average height of terrain
B. The structure must be no higher than 200 feet above the ground level at its site
C. There are no height restrictions since the structure would not be a hazard to aircraft in a valley or canyon
D. The structure must not extend more than 200 feet above the top of the valley or canyon

**B** The rule says, "200 feet above ground level at the site." That makes it a lot easier to determine the limit. Can you imagine the difficulty of trying to calculate the height of average terrain? [97.15(a)]

**E1B08 What limits must local authorities observe when legislating height and dimension restrictions for an amateur station antenna structure?**

A. FAA regulations specify a minimum height for amateur antenna structures located near airports
B. FCC regulations specify a 200 foot minimum height for amateur antenna structures
C. State and local restrictions of amateur antenna structures are not allowed
D. Such regulation must reasonably accommodate amateur service communications and must constitute the minimum practicable regulation to accomplish the state or local authorities legitimate purpose

**D** The magic rule is the famous PRB-1, which is correctly summarized in the correct answer. [97.15(b)]

**E1B09 If you are installing an amateur radio station antenna at a site within 5 miles from a public use airport, what additional rules apply?**

A. You must evaluate the height of your antenna based on the FCC Part 17 regulations
B. No special rules apply if your antenna structure will be less than 200 feet in height
C. You must file an Environmental Impact Statement with the Environmental Protection Agency before construction begins
D. You must obtain a construction permit from the airport zoning authority

**A** Don't be fooled because they always seem to refer to Part 97. For this question, you'll also need to consult Part 17. [97.15(a)]

**E1B10 What is meant by a remotely controlled station?**

A. A station operated away from its regular home location
B. Control of a station from a point located other than at the station transmitter
C. A station operating under automatic control
D. A station controlled indirectly through a control link

**D** All of these choices may sound like they could fit the definition, but they don't. The key phrase here is operation through a "control link"—only the use of a control link is critical. The rule says that remote control is "The use of a control operator who indirectly manipulates the operating adjustments in the station through a control link to achieve compliance with the FCC Rules." [97.3(a)(38)]

**E1B11 Which of the following amateur stations may not be operated under automatic control?**

A. Remote control of model aircraft
B. Beacon station
C. Auxiliary station
D. Repeater station

**A** For this question, you must identify the type of operation that may *not* be controlled automatically. The rules specifically state, "Only stations specifically designated elsewhere in this Part may be automatically controlled." The Part 97 rules allow automatic control of beacon, auxiliary and repeater stations. [97.109(d), 97.201(d), 97.203(d), 97.205(d)]

**E1B12 What is meant by automatic control of a station?**

A. The use of devices and procedures for control so that the control operator does not have to be present at the control point
B. A station operating with its output power controlled automatically
C. Remotely controlling a station such that a control operator does not have to be present at the control point at all times
D. The use of a control link between a control point and a locally controlled station

**A** The FCC definition of automatic control says, "The use of devices and procedures for control of a station when it is transmitting so that compliance with the FCC Rules is achieved without the control operator being present at a control point." [97.3(a)(6), 97.109(d)]

**E1B13 How do the control operator responsibilities of a station under automatic control differ from one under local control?**

A. Under local control there is no control operator
B. Under automatic control the control operator is not required to be present at the control point
C. Under automatic control there is no control operator
D. Under local control a control operator is not required to be present at a control point

**B** By definition, the control operator of a station operating under automatic control is not required to be physically located at the control point. There must always be a control operator. Local control, as the name implies, requires that the control operator is physically present at the control point. [97.3(a)(6), 97.109]

**E1B14 What is a control link?**

A. A device that automatically controls an unattended station
B. An automatically operated link between two stations
C. The means of control between a control point and a remotely controlled station
D. A device that limits the time of a station's transmission

**C** From a previous question you might be able to spot the right answer. The point to remember is that a control link is associated with a remotely controlled station. [97.3(a)(38)]

**E1B15 What is the term for apparatus to effect remote control between the control point and a remotely controlled station?**

A. A tone link
B. A wire control
C. A remote control
D. A control link

**D** Once again, the words come out of the official definition. You should be able to spot the right choice based on the previous question. [97.3(a)(38)]

## E1C Reciprocal operating: reciprocal operating authority; purpose of reciprocal agreement rules; alien control operator privileges; identification (Note: This includes CEPT and IARP)

**E1C01 What is an FCC authorization for alien reciprocal operation?**

A. An FCC authorization to the holder of an amateur license issued by certain foreign governments to operate an amateur station in the US
B. An FCC permit to allow a US licensed amateur to operate in a foreign nation except Canada
C. An FCC permit allowing a foreign licensed amateur to handle third-party traffic between the US and the amateur's own nation
D. An FCC agreement with another country allowing the passing of third-party traffic between amateurs of the two nations

**A** Only the correct answer reflects the rule in Part 97. The FCC cannot authorize amateurs to operate in another country. Here's what the rule says: "Reciprocal operating authority. A non-citizen of the United States (alien) holding an amateur service authorization granted by the alien's government is authorized to be the control operator of an amateur station located at places where the amateur service is regulated by the FCC, provided there is in effect a multilateral or bilateral reciprocal operating arrangement, to which the United States and the alien's government are parties, for amateur service operation on a reciprocal basis." [97.5(c), (d), (e), 97.107]

**E1C02 Who is authorized for alien reciprocal operation in places where the FCC regulates the amateur service?**

A. Anyone holding a valid amateur service license issued by a foreign government
B. Any non-US citizen holding an amateur service license issued by their government with which the US has a reciprocal operating arrangement
C. Anyone holding a valid amateur service license issued by a foreign government with which the US has a reciprocal operating arrangement
D. Any non-US citizen holding a valid amateur license issued by a foreign government, as long as the person is a citizen of that country

**B** Since the question deals with alien permission, not just anyone can have an authorization. US citizens are eligible to hold foreign licenses, but they do not qualify for alien reciprocal operation in the US. The other key is that the alien must have an amateur service license issued by a foreign government with which the US has a reciprocal operating arrangement. [97.107]

**E1C03 What are the frequency privileges authorized for alien reciprocal operation?**

A. Those authorized to a holder of the equivalent US amateur operator license
B. Those that the alien has in his or her own country
C. Those authorized to the alien by his country of citizenship, but not to exceed those authorized to Amateur Extra Class operators
D. Those approved by the International Amateur Radio Union

**C** Most of the choices may seem reasonable at first reading. However, since you are dealing with reciprocal permissions, only the one that includes both the foreign privileges plus the restrictions placed by the US license structure is right. The words are taken directly from the rules. [97.107]

**E1C04 What indicator must a Canadian amateur station include with the assigned call sign in the station identification announcement when operating in the US?**

A. No indicator is required
B. The grid-square locator number for the location of the station must be included after the call sign
C. The permit number and the call-letter district number of the station location must be included before the Canadian-assigned call sign
D. The letter-numeral indicating the station location after the Canadian call sign and the closest city and state once during the communication

**D** The agreement between the US and Canada specifies that Canadian stations operating in the US (and US stations operating in Canada) must give their station identification by using their home call sign followed by a designator to indicate the station location. For example, VE3HOH/W3 often operates from eastern Pennsylvania. In addition, once during a communication, stations operating under reciprocal operating authority must also give the approximate geographical location by giving the name of the nearest city or town from where they are operating. [97.119(g)]

**E1C05 When may a US citizen holding a foreign amateur service license be authorized for alien reciprocal operation in places where the FCC regulates the amateur service?**

A. Never; US citizens are not eligible for alien reciprocal operation
B. When the US citizen also holds citizenship in the foreign country
C. When the US citizen was born in the foreign country
D. When the US citizen has no current FCC amateur service license

**A** As stated earlier, the alien reciprocal permission applies only to non-US citizens. [97.107]

**E1C06 Which of the following would disqualify a foreign amateur operator from being authorized for alien reciprocal operation in places where the FCC regulates the amateur service?**

A. Not being a citizen of the country that issued the amateur service license
B. Having citizenship in their own country but not US citizenship
C. Holding only an amateur license issued by their own country but holding no FCC amateur service license grant
D. Holding an amateur service license issued by their own country authorizing privileges beyond Amateur Extra Class operator privileges

**A** Another requirement for obtaining FCC authorization for alien reciprocal operation is that the foreign amateur operator must be a citizen of the country that issued the amateur service license. [97.107]

**E1C07 What special document is required before a Canadian citizen holding a Canadian amateur service license may reciprocal operate in the US?**

A. A written FCC authorization for alien reciprocal operation
B. No special document is required
C. The citizen must have an FCC-issued validation of their Canadian license
D. The citizen must have an FCC-issued Certificate of US License Grant without Examination to operate for a period longer than 10 days

**B** Canadian citizens who are licensed amateurs and who wish to operate in the US do not need an FCC authorization or any other document. The US and Canadian governments have an agreement that allows amateurs in each country to operate in the other country using only their own amateur license. [97.107]

**E1C08 What operating privileges does a properly licensed alien amateur have in the US, if the US and the alien amateur's home country have a multilateral or bilateral reciprocal operating agreement?**

A. All privileges of their home license
B. All privileges of an Amateur Extra Class operator license
C. Those authorized by their home license, not to exceed the operating privileges of an Amateur Extra Class operator license
D. Those granted by the home license that match US privileges authorized to amateur operators in ITU Region 1

**C** The operating privileges granted under an FCC authorization for alien reciprocal operation are limited by: (1) The terms of the agreement between the alien's government and the United States; (2) The operating terms and conditions of the amateur service license granted by the alien's government; (3) The applicable rules, but not to exceed the control operator privileges of an FCC-granted Amateur Extra Class operator license. [97.107(b)]

**E1C09 From which locations may a licensed alien amateur operator be the control operator of an amateur station?**

A. Only locations within the boundaries of the 50 United States
B. Only locations listed as the primary station location on an FCC amateur service license
C. Only locations on ground within the US and its territories; no shipboard or aeronautical mobile operation is permitted
D. Any location where the amateur service is regulated by the FCC

**D** The rule states, "The person named in the station license grant or who is authorized for alien reciprocal operation by §97.107 of this Part may use, in accordance with the applicable rules of this Part, the transmitting apparatus under the physical control of the person at places where the amateur service is regulated by the FCC." [97.5(c)]

**E1C10 Which of the following operating arrangements allow an FCC licensed US citizen to operate in many European countries and alien amateurs from many European countries to operate in the US?**

A. CEPT agreement
B. IARP agreement
C. ITU agreement
D. All of these choices are correct

**A** As you saw earlier, CEPT is the European Conference of Posts and Telecommunications. The US is a participant in the CEPT Recommendation, which allows US amateurs to operate in certain European countries. It also allows amateur from many European countries to operate in the US. [97.5(d)]

**E1C11 Which of the following multilateral or bilateral operating arrangements allow an FCC licensed US citizen and many Central and South American amateur operators to operate in each other's countries?**

A. CEPT agreement
B. IARP agreement
C. ITU agreement
D. All of these choices are correct

**B** The IARP is the International Amateur Radio Permit, which covers countries in the Americas. The agreement came out of CITEL (Inter-American Telecommunication Commission). [97.5(e)]

**E1C12 What additional station identification, in addition to his or her own call sign, does an alien operator supply when operating in the US under an FCC authorization for alien reciprocal operation?**

A. No additional operation is required
B. The grid-square locator closest to his or her present location is included before the call
C. The serial number of the permit and the call-letter district number of the station location is included before the call
D. The letter-numeral indicating the station location in the US included before their call and the closest city and state given once during the communication

**D** The identification requirement consists of "an indicator consisting of the appropriate letter-numeral designating the station location, which must be included before the call sign that was issued to the station by the country granting the license . . . At least once during each intercommunication, the identification announcement must include the geographical location as nearly as possible by city and state, commonwealth or possession." As you saw earlier, the rule for Canadian operators is slightly different, so don't be confused. [97.119(g)]

## E1D Radio Amateur Civil Emergency Service (RACES): definition; purpose; station registration; station license required; control operator requirements; control operator privileges; frequencies available; limitations on use of RACES frequencies; points of communication for RACES operation; permissible communications

**E1D01** **What is the Radio Amateur Civil Emergency Service (RACES)?**

A. A radio service using amateur service frequencies on a regular basis for communications that can reasonably be furnished through other radio services
B. A radio service using amateur stations for civil defense communications during periods of local, regional, or national civil emergencies
C. A radio service using amateur service frequencies for broadcasting to the public
D. A radio service using local government frequencies by Amateur Radio operators for emergency communications

**B** RACES is, "A radio service using amateur stations for civil defense communications during periods of local, regional or national civil emergencies." [97.3(a)(37)]

**E1D02** **What is the purpose of RACES?**

A. To provide civil-defense communications during emergencies
B. To provide emergency communications for boat or aircraft races
C. To provide routine and emergency communications for athletic races
D. To provide routine and emergency military communications

**A** RACES exists to allow amateur stations to provide civil defense communications during periods of local, regional or national civil emergencies. [97.3(a)(37)]

**E1D03 With what organization must an amateur station be registered before participating in RACES?**

A. The Amateur Radio Emergency Service
B. The US Department of Defense
C. A civil defense organization
D. The FCC Enforcement Bureau

**C** All that is required is registration with a civil defense organization. The rule says, "No station may transmit in RACES unless it is an FCC-licensed primary, club, or military recreation station and it is certified by a civil defense organization as registered with that organization, or it is an FCC-licensed RACES station. No person may be the control operator of a RACES station, or may be the control operator of an amateur station transmitting in RACES unless that person holds a FCC-issued amateur operator license and is certified by a civil defense organization as enrolled in that organization." [97.407(a)]

**E1D04 Which amateur stations may be operated in RACES?**

A. Only those licensed to Amateur Extra class operators
B. Any FCC-licensed amateur station except a station licensed to a Technician class operator
C. Any FCC-licensed amateur station certified by the responsible civil defense organization for the area served
D. Any FCC licensed amateur station participating in the Military Affiliate Radio System (MARS)

**C** Building upon the previous question, RACES operation requires proper registration and an amateur license of any grade. [97.407(a)]

**E1D05 What frequencies are authorized normally to an amateur station participating in RACES?**

A. All amateur service frequencies otherwise authorized to the control operator
B. Specific segments in the amateur service MF, HF, VHF and UHF bands
C. Specific local government channels
D. Military Affiliate Radio System (MARS) channels

**A** The key to this question is the phrase "authorized normally" in the question statement. The frequencies that can be used are determined by the control operator license. In normal mode, there are no reserved frequencies for RACES operation. [97.407(b)]

**E1D06 What are the frequencies authorized to an amateur station participating in RACES during a period when the President's War Emergency Powers are in force?**

A. All frequencies in the amateur service authorized to the control operator
B. Specific segments in the amateur service MF, HF, VHF and UHF bands
C. Specific local government channels
D. Military Affiliate Radio System (MARS) channels

**B** This question differs from the previous one because they are now speaking of special circumstances of national emergency. If there is an emergency that causes the President of the United States to invoke the War Emergency Powers under the Communications Act of 1934, there may be limits placed on the frequencies available for RACES operation. [97.407]

**E1D07 What frequencies are normally available for RACES operation?**

A. Only those authorized to the civil defense organization
B. Only those authorized to federal government communications
C. Only the top 25 kHz of each amateur service band
D. All frequencies authorized to the amateur service

**D** If RACES operation provides no additional privileges, it also imposes no additional restrictions. The other choices either are untrue restrictions or would allow operation outside of the amateur bands. [97.407(b)]

**E1D08 What type of emergency can cause limits to be placed on the frequencies available for RACES operation?**

A. An emergency during which the President's War Emergency Powers are invoked
B. An emergency in only one of the United States would limit RACES operations to a single HF band
C. An emergency confined to a 25-mile area would limit RACES operations to a single VHF band
D. An emergency involving no immediate danger of loss of life

**A** The rule allow for limits to be placed on the frequencies available for RACES operation in an emergency during which the President's War Emergency Powers are invoked. [97.407(b)]

**E1D09 Who may be the control operator of a RACES station?**

A. Anyone holding an FCC-issued amateur operator license other than Novice
B. Only an Amateur Extra Class operator licensee
C. Anyone who holds an FCC-issued amateur operator license and is certified by a civil defense organization
D. Any person certified as a RACES radio operator by a civil defense organization and who hold an FCC issued GMRS license

**C** Based on the previous questions, you should be able to identify the requirements as being an FCC-issued amateur operator license and certification by a civil defense organization. [97.407(a)]

**E1D10 With which stations may amateur stations participating in RACES communicate?**

A. Any amateur station
B. Amateur stations participating in RACES and specific other stations authorized by the responsible civil defense official
C. Any amateur station or a station in the Disaster Communications Service
D. Any Citizens Band station that is also registered in RACES

**B** When amateur stations are participating in RACES, they may communicate with other amateur stations participating in RACES and other specific stations that are authorized by the responsible civil defense official. [97.407(c), (d)]

**E1D11 What communications are permissible in RACES?**

A. Any type of communications when there is no emergency
B. Any Amateur Radio Emergency Service communications
C. National defense or immediate safety of people and property and communications authorized by the area civil defense organization
D. National defense and security or immediate safety of people and property communications authorized by the President

**C** Only certain types of communications are permitted in RACES and these must be authorized by the area civil defense organization. Permitted types of communications include national defense and immediate safety of people and property. Authorized training drills and tests are also permitted. [97.407(e)]

## E1E Amateur Satellite Service: definition; purpose; station license required for space station; frequencies available; telecommand operation: definition; eligibility; telecommand station (definition); space telecommand station; special provisions; telemetry: definition; special provisions; space station: definition; eligibility; special provisions; authorized frequencies (space station); notification requirements; earth operation: definition; eligibility; authorized frequencies (Earth station)

**E1E01 What is the amateur-satellite service?**

A. A radio navigation service using satellites for the purpose of self-training, intercommunication and technical studies carried out by amateurs
B. A spacecraft launching service for amateur-built satellites
C. A service using amateur stations on satellites for the purpose of self-training, intercommunication and technical investigations
D. A radio communications service using stations on Earth satellites for weather information gathering

**C** The rules define the amateur-satellite service as, "A radiocommunication service using stations on Earth satellites for the same purpose as those of the amateur service." So what do the rules say about the amateur service? It is defined as, "A radiocommunication service for the purpose of self-training, intercommunication and technical investigations carried out by amateurs, that is, duly authorized persons interested in radio technique solely with a personal aim and without pecuniary interest." [97.3(a)(3)]

**E1E02 What is a space station in the amateur-satellite service?**

A. An amateur station located more than 50 km above the Earth's surface
B. An amateur station designed for communications with other amateur stations by means of Earth satellites
C. An amateur station that transmits communications to initiate, modify or terminate functions of an Earth station
D. An amateur station designed for communications with other amateur stations by reflecting signals off objects in space

**A** You do not need to work for NASA to own a space station! The FCC rules define a space station as an amateur station operating more than 50 km above the earth. Your problem is how to get there. [97.3(a)(40)]

**E1E03 What is a telecommand station in the amateur-satellite service?**

A. An amateur station that transmits communications to initiate, modify or terminate functions of a space station
B. An amateur station located on the Earth's surface for communications with other Earth stations by means of Earth satellites
C. An amateur station located more than 50 km above the Earth's surface
D. An amateur station that transmits telemetry consisting of measurements of upper atmosphere data from space

**A** You need to know the definition for telecommand station, which is: "An amateur station that transmits communications to initiate, modify, or terminate functions of a space station." [97.3(a)(44)]

**E1E04 What is an earth station in the amateur-satellite service?**

A. An amateur station within 50 km of the Earth's surface for communications with Amateur stations by means of objects in space
B. An amateur station that is not able to communicate using amateur satellites
C. An amateur station that transmits telemetry consisting of measurement of upper atmosphere data from space
D. Any amateur station on the surface of the Earth

**A** The key here is to notice that the questions deal with stations participating in the satellite service. An earth station is an amateur station located on, or within 50 km of the Earth's surface intended for communications with space stations or with other Earth stations by means of one or more other objects in space. [97.3(a)(16)]

**E1E05 Which of the following types of communications may space stations transmit?**

A. Automatic retransmission of signals from Earth stations and other space stations
B. One-way communications
C. Telemetry consisting of specially coded messages
D. All of these choices are correct

**D** If you look at the pertinent rule, you'll see that automatic retransmission, one-way communications and specially coded telemetry are permitted for space stations. [97.207]

**E1E06 Which amateur stations are eligible to operate as a space station?**

A. Any except those of Technician Class operators
B. Only those of General, Advanced or Amateur Extra Class operators
C. Only those of Amateur Extra Class operators
D. Any FCC-licensed amateur station

**D** This may be surprising to you but any valid amateur license holder is eligible to be the control operator of a space station. However that individual is subject to the privileges of the class of operator license held. [97.207(a)]

**E1E07 What special provision must a space station incorporate in order to comply with space station requirements?**

A. The space station must be capable of effecting a cessation of transmissions by telecommand whenever so ordered by the FCC
B. The space station must cease all transmissions after 5 years
C. The space station must be capable of changing its orbit whenever such a change is ordered by NASA
D. The station call sign must appear on all sides of the spacecraft

**A** A space station must be capable of ceasing transmissions when ordered to do so by the FCC. As a matter of interest, several amateur satellites have enjoyed an operational life that exceeded 5 years. [97.207(b)]

**E1E08 When must the licensee of a space station give the FCC International Bureau the first written pre-space notification?**

A. Any time before initiating the launch countdown for the spacecraft
B. No less than 3 months after initiating construction of the space station
C. No less that 12 months before launch of the space station platform
D. No less than 27 months prior to initiating space station transmissions

**D** Before you begin operation of a space station, you must make two written pre-space station notifications to the FCC International Bureau. The first notification is required no less than 27 months prior to initiating space station transmissions. [97.207(g)(1)]

**E1E09 Which amateur service HF bands have frequencies authorized to space stations?**

A. Only 40 m, 20 m, 17 m, 15 m, 12 m and 10 m
B. Only 40 m, 20 m, 17 m, 15 m and 10 m bands
C. 40 m, 30 m, 20 m, 15 m, 12 m and 10 m bands
D. All HF bands

**A** Part 97 authorizes space station operation at HF in the 17, 15, 12 and 10-meter bands. It also authorizes operation in parts of the 40 and 20-meter bands. [97.207(c)]

**E1E10 Which VHF amateur service bands have frequencies available for space stations?**

A. 2 meters
B. 2 meters and 1.25 meters
C. 6 meters, 2 meters, and 1.25 meters
D. 6 meters and 2 meters

**A** At VHF only 2 meters has frequencies authorized for use by space stations. [97.207(c)(2)]

**E1E11 Which amateur service UHF bands have frequencies available for a space station?**

A. 70 cm, 23 cm, 13 cm
B. 70 cm
C. 70 cm and 33 cm
D. 33 cm and 13 cm

**A** Now the question moves up to UHF where the 70, 23, and 13-cm bands have frequencies authorized for space stations. [97.207(c)(2)]

**E1E12 Which amateur stations are eligible to be telecommand stations?**

A. Any amateur station designated by NASA
B. Any amateur station so designated by the space station licensee
C. Any amateur station so designated by the ITU
D. All of these choices are correct

**B** The rule says, "Any amateur station designated by the licensee of a space station is eligible to transmit as a telecommand station for that space station, subject to the privileges of the class of operator license held by the control operator." [97.211(a)]

**E1E13 What unique privilege is afforded a telecommand station?**

A. A telecommand station may transmit command messages to the space station using codes intended to obscure their meaning
B. A telecommand station may transmit music to the space station
C. A telecommand station may transmit with a PEP output of 5000 watts
D. A telecommand station is not required to transmit its call sign at the end of the communication

**A** Because satellite operators wish to make sure that an unauthorized operator does not "hack" into the satellite, the FCC makes a reasonable accommodation and allows the operators to encode the telecommand signals. [97.211(b)]

**E1E14 What is the term for space-to-Earth transmissions used to communicate the results of measurements made by a space station?**

A. Data transmission
B. Frame check sequence
C. Telemetry
D. Space-to-Earth telemetry indicator (SETI) transmissions

**C** Based on earlier questions; you might spot the correct answer right away. Telemetry is a form of data transmission but data transmission is a more general term so it is not the right choice. It might help to remember that telemetry comes from two words that mean measurement from a distance. Do you think the QPC (Question Pool Committee) smiled as they included the reference to SETI (Search for Extra-Terrestrial Intelligence)? [97.207(f)]

**E1E15 Which amateur stations are eligible to operate as Earth stations?**

A. Any amateur station whose licensee has filed a pre-space notification with the FCC International Bureau
B. Only those of General, Advanced or Amateur Extra Class operators
C. Only those of Amateur Extra Class operators
D. Any amateur station, subject to the privileges of the class of operator license held by the control operator

**D** Your license class is not an impediment to operate an earth station. Any licensee can do it, but is limited to the privileges of the class of operator license held by the control operator. [97.209(a)]

## E1F Volunteer Examiner Coordinators (VECs): definition; VEC qualifications; VEC agreement; scheduling examinations; coordinating VEs; reimbursement for expenses; accrediting VEs; question pools; Volunteer Examiners (VEs): definition; requirements; accreditation; reimbursement for expenses; VE conduct; preparing an examination; examination elements; definition of code and written elements; preparation responsibility; examination requirements; examination credit; examination procedure; examination administration; temporary operating authority

**E1F01 Who may prepare an Element 4 amateur operator license examination?**

A. The VEC Question Pool Committee, which selects questions from the appropriate VEC question pool
B. A VEC that selects questions from the appropriate FCC bulletin
C. An Extra class VE that selects questions from the appropriate FCC bulletin
D. An Extra class VE or a qualified supplier who selects questions from the appropriate VEC question pool

**D** Volunteer examiners may prepare written exams for all classes of Amateur Radio operator license. However, only an Amateur Extra class licensee may prepare an Element 4 exam. The rules say that exams, "must be prepared, or obtained from a supplier, by the administering VEs according to instructions from the coordinating VEC." The rules also state, "Each question set administered to an examinee must utilize questions taken from the applicable question pool." [97.507(a), (b), (c), 97.523]

**E1F02 Where are the questions listed that must be used in all written US amateur license examinations?**

A. In the instructions that each VEC gives to their VEs
B. In an FCC-maintained question pool
C. In the VEC-maintained question pool
D. In the appropriate FCC Report and Order

**C** The Volunteer Examiner Coordinators' Question Pool Committee (QPC) maintains and publishes the question pools for amateur radio license examinations. The FCC does not maintain the question pools. [97.507(b), 97.523]

**E1F03** **Who is responsible for maintaining the question pools from which all amateur license examination questions must be taken?**

A. All of the VECs
B. The VE team
C. The VE question pool team
D. The FCC Wireless Telecommunications Bureau

**A** All VECs are required to cooperate in maintaining one question pool for each written examination element, which they do through their question pool committee (QPC). That single question pool assures an equal treatment of all examinees. The FCC does not maintain the questions. [97.523]

**E1F04** **Who must select from the VEC question pool the set of questions that are administered in an Element 3 examination?**

A. Only a VE holding an Amateur Extra Class operator license grant
B. The VEC coordinating the examination session
C. A VE holding an FCC-issued Amateur Extra or Advanced Class operator license grant
D. The FCC Enforcement Bureau

**C** Element 3 corresponds to the General Class license exam, and the VE must have a higher-class license to select and administer the exam. [97.507(a)(1)]

**E1F05** **This question has been withdrawn.**

**E1F06 What is the purpose of an amateur operator telegraphy examination?**

A. It determines the examinee's level of commitment to the amateur service
B. All of these choices are correct
C. It proves that the examinee has the ability to send correctly by hand and to receive correctly by ear texts in the International Morse Code
D. It helps preserve the proud tradition of radiotelegraphy skill in the amateur service

**C** According to the rules, "A telegraphy examination must be sufficient to prove that the examinee has the ability to send correctly by hand and to receive correctly by ear texts in the international Morse code at not less than the prescribed speed . . ." [97.503(a)]

**E1F07 What is the purpose of an Element 4 examination?**

A. It proves the examinee has the qualifications necessary to perform properly the duties of an Amateur Extra Class operator
B. It proves the examinee is qualified as an electronics technician
C. It proves the examinee is an electronics expert
D. It proves that the examinee is an expert radio operator

**A** The Element 4 written examination is designed to prove that the examinee possesses the operational and technical qualifications required to perform properly the duties of an Amateur Extra Class operator. It's great to be a technical expert in radio and electronics, but that's not what the exam is about. [97.503(b)]

**E1F08 What is a Volunteer-Examiner Coordinator?**

A. A person who has volunteered to administer amateur operator license examinations
B. A person who has volunteered to prepare amateur operator license examinations
C. An organization that has entered into an agreement with the FCC to coordinate amateur operator license examinations
D. The person that has entered into an agreement with the FCC to be the VE session manager

**C** A Volunteer Examiner Coordinator is an organization—not a person. The organization enters into an agreement with the FCC to be a VEC. See the next question. [97.521]

**E1F09 What is an accredited Volunteer Examiner?**

A. An amateur operator who is approved by three or more fellow volunteer examiners to administer amateur license examinations
B. An amateur operator who is approved by a VEC to administer amateur operator license examinations
C. An amateur operator who administers amateur license examinations for a fee
D. An amateur operator who is approved by an FCC staff member to administer amateur operator license examinations

**B** The accreditation process is simply the steps that each VEC takes to ensure that their VEs meet all the FCC requirements to serve in the Volunteer Examiner program. [97.3(a)(48), 97.509, 97.525]

**E1F10 What is a VE Team?**

A. A group of at least three VEs who administer examinations for an amateur operator license
B. The VEC staff
C. One or two VEs who administer examinations for an amateur operator license
D. A group of FCC Volunteer Enforcers who investigate Amateur Rules violations

**A** The rules state that, "Each examination for an amateur operator license must be administered by a team of at least 3 VEs at an examination session coordinated by a VEC." It is that group of at least three Volunteer Examiners that forms the VE team. [97.509]

**E1F11 Which persons seeking to be VEs cannot be accredited?**

A. Persons holding less than an Advanced Class operator license
B. Persons less than 21 years of age
C. Persons who have ever had an amateur operator or amateur station license suspended or revoked
D. Persons who are employees of the federal government

**C** The FCC has left the qualifications to be a VE fairly open. Most amateurs can become a VE without much difficulty. However, the rules specifically exclude any person whose amateur station license or amateur operator license has ever been revoked or suspended. A VE must be at least 18 years of age. [97.509(b)(4)]

**E1F12** **What is the VE accreditation process?**

A. Each General, Advanced and Amateur Extra Class operator is automatically accredited as a VE when the license is granted
B. The amateur operator must pass a VE examination administered by the FCC Enforcement Bureau
C. The prospective VE obtains accreditation from a VE team
D. Each VEC ensures that its Volunteer Examiner applicants meet FCC requirements to serve as VEs

**D** The FCC has delegated this task to the VECs. A VEC has entered into an agreement with the FCC. In turn the VECs accredit VEs. [97.509(b)(1), 97.525]

**E1F13** **Where must the VE team be stationed while administering an examination?**

A. All administering VEs must all be present and observing the examinees throughout the entire examination
B. The VEs must leave the room after handing out the exam(s) to allow the examinees to concentrate on the exam material
C. The VEs may be elsewhere provide at least one VE is present and is observing the examinees throughout the entire examination
D. The VEs may be anywhere as long as they each certify in writing that examination was administered properly

**A** Each administering VE must be present and observing the examinees throughout the entire examination. That means every member of the team. The administering VEs are responsible for the proper conduct and necessary supervision of each examination. They can't do that if they're not physically present and actively observing. [97.509(c)]

**E1F14** **Who is responsible for the proper conduct and necessary supervision during an amateur operator license examination session?**

A. The VEC coordinating the session
B. The FCC
C. The administering VEs
D. The VE session manager

**C** The administering VEs are responsible for the proper conduct and necessary supervision of each examination. It is not just the responsibility of the VE in charge. [97.509(c)]

**E1F15 What should a VE do if a candidate fails to comply with the examiner's instructions during an amateur operator license examination?**

A. Warn the candidate that continued failure to comply will result in termination of the examination
B. Immediately terminate the candidate's examination
C. Allow the candidate to complete the examination, but invalidate the results
D. Immediately terminate everyone's examination and close the session

**B** The FCC is very explicit on this point. Discipline will be maintained. The rule says, "The administering VEs must immediately terminate the examination upon failure of the examinee to comply with their instructions." [97.509(c)]

**E1F16 What special procedures must a VE team follow for an examinee with a physical disability?**

A. A special procedure that accommodates the disability
B. A special procedure specified by the coordinating VEC
C. A special procedure specified by a physician
D. None; the VE team does not have to provide special procedures

**A** The VE team must accommodate an examinee whose physical disabilities require a special examination procedure. However, they may require a physician's certification indicating the nature of the disability before determining which, if any, special procedures must be used. [97.509(k)]

**E1F17 To which of the following examinees may a VE not administer an examination?**

A. The VE's close relatives as listed in the FCC rules
B. Acquaintances of the VE
C. Friends of the VE
D. There are no restrictions as to whom a VE may administer an examination

**A** Part 97 only restricts VEs from administering examinations to close relatives. It defines these as a spouse, children, grandchildren, stepchildren, parents, grandparents, stepparents, brothers, sisters, stepbrothers, stepsisters, aunts, uncles, nieces, nephews, and in-laws. [97.509(d)]

**E1F18 What may be the penalty for a VE who fraudulently administers or certifies an examination?**

A. Revocation of the VE's amateur station license grant and the suspension of the VE's amateur operator license grant
B. A fine of up to $1000 per occurrence
C. A sentence of up to one year in prison
D. All of these choices are correct

**A** If you go to Part 97 you will find, "No VE may administer or certify any examination by fraudulent means or for monetary or other consideration including reimbursement in any amount in excess of that permitted. Violation of this provision may result in the revocation of the grant of the VE's amateur station license and the suspension of the grant of the VE's amateur operator license." [97.509(e)]

**E1F19 What must the VE team do with your test papers when you have finished this examination?**

A. The VE team must collect them for grading at a later date
B. The VE team must collect and send them to the coordinating VEC for grading
C. The VE team must collect and grade them immediately
D. The VE team must collect and send them to the FCC for grading

**C** Upon completion of each examination element, the VE team is required under the FCC rules to immediately grade the examinee's answers. Further, it is the VE team that is responsible for determining the correctness of the examinee's answers. [97.509(h)]

**E1F20 What action must the coordinating VEC complete within 10 days of collecting the information from an examination session?**

A. Screen collected information
B. Resolve all discrepancies and verify that the VEs' certifications are properly completed
C. For qualified examinees, forward electronically all required data to the FCC
D. All of these choices are correct

**D** Within 10 days of collection, the rules require the coordinating VEC to: Screen collected information, resolve all discrepancies and verify that the VE's certifications are properly completed, and for qualified examinees, forward electronically all required data to the FCC. [97.519(b)]

**E1F21 What must the VE team do if an examinee scores a passing grade on all examination elements needed for an upgrade or new license?**

A. Photocopy all examination documents and forwards them to the FCC for processing
B. Notify the FCC that the examinee is eligible for a license grant
C. Issue the examinee the new or upgrade license
D. Three VEs must certify that the examinee is qualified for the license grant and that they have complied with the VE requirements

**D** According to the rules, when the examinee has been credited for all examination elements required for the operator license sought, three VEs must certify that the examinee is qualified for the license grant and that the VEs have complied with these administering VE requirements. [97.509(i)]

**E1F22 What must the VE team do if the examinee does not score a passing grade on the examination?**

A. Return the application document to the examinee and inform the examinee of the grade
B. Return the application document to the examinee
C. Inform the examinee that he or she did not pass
D. Explain how the incorrect questions should have been answered

**A** When the examinee does not score a passing grade on an examination element, the administering VEs must return the application document to the examinee and inform the examinee of the grade. The VE team is not supposed to inform the candidates which answers were incorrect on the exams. [97.509(j)]

**E1F23 What are the consequences of failing to appear for readministration of an examination when so directed by the FCC?**

A. The licensee's license will be cancelled and a new license will be issued that is consistent with examination elements not invalidated
B. The licensee must pay a monetary fine
C. The licensee is disqualified from any future examination for an amateur operator license grant
D. The person may be sentenced to incarceration

**A** The rule says that the FCC may: Cancel the operator/primary station license of any licensee who fails to appear for readministration of an examination when directed by the FCC, or who does not successfully complete any required element that is readministered. In an instance of such cancellation, the person will be granted an operator/primary station license consistent with completed examination elements that have not been invalidated by not appearing for, or by failing, the examination upon readministration. [97.519(d)(3)]

**E1F24 What are the types of out-of-pocket expenses for which the FCC rules authorize a VE and VEC to accept reimbursement?**

A. Preparing, processing, administering and coordinating an examination for an amateur radio license
B. Teaching an amateur operator license examination preparation course
C. None; a VE must never accept any type of reimbursement
D. Providing amateur operator license examination preparation training materials

**A** Earlier, you saw that VEs could not charge for exams. However, the fee charged covers out-of-pocket and other administrative fees—a subtle difference. The rule says, "VEs and VECs may be reimbursed by examinees for out-of-pocket expenses incurred in preparing, processing, administering, or coordinating an examination for an amateur operator license." [97.527]

**E1F25 How much reimbursement may the VE team and VEC accept for preparing, processing, administering and coordinating an examination?**

A. Actual out-of-pocket expenses
B. Up to the national minimum hourly wage times the number of hours spent providing the services
C. Up to the maximum fee per examinee announced by the FCC annually
D. As much as the examinee is willing to donate

**A** If you become a VE, do not expect to get rich from your hobby. You can't charge the maximum fee unless you have expenses in that amount or more. You may not keep any fees other than those to pay for actual out-of-pocket expenses. [97.509(e), 97.527]

**E1F26 What amateur operator license examination credit must be given for a valid Certificate of Successful Completion of Examination (CSCE)?**

A. Only the written elements the CSCE indicates the examinee passed within the previous 365 days
B. Only the telegraphy elements the CSCE indicates the examinee passed within the previous 365 days
C. Each element the CSCE indicates the examinee passed within the previous 365 days
D. None

**C** The rule says that the administering VEs must give credit for each element the CSCE indicates the examinee passed within the previous 365 days. [97.505(a)(6)]

**E1F27 For what period of time does a Technician class licensee, who has just been issued a CSCE for having passed a 5 WPM Morse code examination, have authority to operate on the Novice/ Technician HF subbands?**

A. 365 days from the examination date as indicated on the CSCE
B. 1 year from the examination date as indicated on the CSCE
C. Indefinitely, so long as the Technician license remains valid
D. 5 years plus a 5-year grace period from the examination date as indicated on the CSCE

**C** This is the one case where the CSCE does not become unusable after one year. That's because the Technician Plus license class was eliminated in 2000 and the CSCE is now used to show that the operator has passed the Morse code examination. [97.301(e)]

**E1F28 What period of time does a Technician class licensee, who has just been issued a CSCE for having passed a 5 WPM Morse code examination, have in order to use this credit toward a license upgrade?**

A. 365 days from the examination date as indicated on the CSCE
B. 15 months from the examination date as indicated on the CSCE
C. There is no time limit, so long as the Technician license remains valid
D. 5 years plus a 5-year grace period from the examination date as indicated on the CSCE

**A** For upgrades, the CSCE is valid for only one year. This may appear to be an inconsistency in the FCC rules, but this is for a different case than the previous question. Here, the operator is going for an upgrade and not just staying with the Technician class license. [97.505(a)(6)]

## E1G Certification of external RF power amplifiers and external RF power amplifier kits; Line A; National Radio Quiet Zone; business communications; definition and operation of spread spectrum; auxiliary station operation

**E1G01 What does it mean if an external RF amplifier is listed on the FCC database as certificated for use in the amateur service?**

A. An RF amplifier of that model may be used in any radio service
B. That particular RF amplifier model may be marketed for use in the amateur service
C. All similar models of RF amplifiers produced by other manufacturers may be marketed
D. All models of RF amplifiers produced by that manufacturer may be marketed

**B** Certification is for a specific model and manufacturer. Certification means that it may be marketed for use in the amateur service. [97.315(c)]

**E1G02 Which of the following is one of the standards that must be met by an external RF power amplifier if it is to qualify for a grant of Certification?**

A. It must have a time-delay to prevent it from operating continuously for more than ten minutes
B. It must satisfy the spurious emission standards when driven with at least 50 W mean RF power (unless a higher drive level is specified)
C. It must not be capable of modification without voiding the warranty
D. It must exhibit no more than 6 dB of gain over its entire operating range

**B** The FCC rules state "To receive a grant of certification, the amplifier must satisfy the spurious emission . . . when . . . driven with at least 50 W mean RF input power (unless higher drive level is specified)." [97.317(a)(3)]

**E1G03 Under what condition may an equipment dealer sell an external RF power amplifier capable of operation below 144 MHz if it has not been granted FCC certification?**

A. It was purchased in used condition from an amateur operator and is sold to another amateur operator for use at that operator's station
B. The equipment dealer assembled it from a kit
C. It was imported from a manufacturer in a country that does not require certification of RF power amplifiers
D. It was imported from a manufacturer in another country, and it was certificated by that country's government

**A** There are three conditions that must be satisfied. First, the amplifier must be in "used condition." Second, it must be purchase from an amateur operator and sold to another amateur operator. (The wording allows an equipment dealer to be involved.) Third, the amplifier must be for use at the purchasing operator's station. [97.315(b)(5)]

**E1G04 Which of the following geographic descriptions approximately describes Line A?**

A. A line roughly parallel to, and south of, the US-Canadian border
B. A line roughly parallel to, and west of, the US Atlantic coastline
C. A line roughly parallel to, and north of, the US-Mexican border and Gulf coastline
D. A line roughly parallel to, and east of, the US Pacific coastline

**A** If you operate on the 70-cm band in the northern states, you need to know about Line A which parallels the US-Canadian border. [97.3(a)(32)]

**E1G05 Amateur stations may not transmit in which frequency segment if they are located north of Line A?**

A. 21.225-21.300 MHz
B. 53-54 MHz
C. 222-223 MHz
D. 420-430 MHz

**D** Line A is important because there is a restriction at UHF. The rules say, "No amateur station shall transmit from north of Line A in the 420-430 MHz segment." [97.303(f)(1)]

**E1G06** **What is the National Radio Quiet Zone?**

A. An area in Puerto Rico surrounding the Arecibo Radio Telescope
B. An area in New Mexico surrounding the White Sands Test Area
C. An Area in Maryland, West Virginia and Virginia surrounding the National Radio Astronomy Observatory
D. An area in Florida surrounding Cape Canaveral

**C** The National Radio Quiet Zone protects the radio astronomy facilities for the National Radio Astronomy Observatory in Green Bank, WV and the Naval Research Laboratory at Sugar Grove, WV. It is composed of parts of the states of Maryland, West Virginia and Virginia. [97.3(a)(32)]

**E1G07** **What type of automatically controlled amateur station must not be established in the National Radio Quiet Zone before the licensee gives written notification to the National Radio Astronomy Observatory?**

A. Beacon station
B. Auxiliary station
C. Repeater station
D. Earth station

**A** Before establishing an automatically controlled beacon in the National Radio Quiet Zone or before changing the transmitting frequency, transmitter power, antenna height or directivity, the station licensee must give written notification thereof to the Interference Office of the National Radio Astronomy Observatory. [97.203(e)]

**E1G08** **When may the control operator of a repeater accept payment for providing communication services to another party?**

A. When the repeater is operating under portable power
B. When the repeater is operating under local control
C. During Red Cross or other emergency service drills
D. Under no circumstances

**D** This falls into the area of prohibited transmissions. Specifically prohibited are: "Communications for hire or for material compensation, direct or indirect, paid or promised, except as otherwise provided in these rules." There is no exception in the rules for repeater control operator services. [97.113(a)(2)]

**E1G09 When may an amateur station send a message to a business?**

A. When the total money involved does not exceed $25
B. When the control operator is employed by the FCC or another government agency
C. When transmitting international third-party communications
D. When neither the amateur nor his or her employer has a pecuniary interest in the communications

**D** This also falls into the area of prohibited transmissions. The rule prohibits, "Communications in which the station licensee or control operator has a pecuniary interest, including communications on behalf of an employer." [97.113(a)(3)]

**E1G10 Which of the following types of amateur operator-to-amateur operator communication are prohibited?**

A. Communications transmitted for hire or material compensation, except as otherwise provided in the rules
B. Communication that has a political content
C. Communication that has a religious content
D. Communication in a language other English

**A** The rules say, "No amateur station shall transmit . . . communications for hire or for material compensation, direct or indirect, paid or promised, except as otherwise provided in these rules." [97.113(a)(2)]

**E1G11 What is the term for emissions using bandwidth-expansion modulation?**

A. RTTY
B. Image
C. Spread spectrum
D. Pulse

**C** Spread-spectrum emissions use a bandwidth much larger than that needed by traditional modulation schemes. The spreading is not related to the modulation content. The rules call this, "bandwidth-expansion modulation." [97.3(c)(8)]

**E1G12** **FCC-licensed amateur stations may use spread spectrum (SS) emissions to communicate under which of the following conditions?**

A. When the other station is in an area regulated by the FCC
B. When the other station is in a country permitting SS communications
C. When the transmission is not used to obscure the meaning of any communication
D. All of these choices are correct

**D** All of the statements are correct. Here's the rule: "SS emission transmissions by an amateur station are authorized only for communications between points within areas where the amateur service is regulated by the FCC and between an area where the amateur service is regulated by the FCC and an amateur station in another country that permits such communications. SS emission transmissions must not be used for the purpose of obscuring the meaning of any communication." [97.311(a)]

**E1G13** **Under any circumstance, what is the maximum transmitter power for an amateur station transmitting emission type SS communications?**

A. 1 W
B. 1.5 W
C. 100 W
D. 1.5 kW

**C** The SS transmitter power must not exceed 100 W under any circumstances. [97.311(d)]

**E1G14** **What of the following is a use for an auxiliary station?**

A. To provide a point-to-point communications uplink between a control point and its associated remotely controlled station
B. To provide a point-to-point communications downlink between a remotely controlled station and its control point
C. To provide a point-to-point control link between a control point and its associated remotely controlled station
D. All of these choices are correct

**D** All of the choices are correct. Amateurs are allowed to use auxiliary stations to provide a point-to-point communications uplink and a downlink between a remotely controlled station and its control point. An auxiliary station can also be used to provide a point-to-point control link between a control point and its associated remotely controlled station. [97.3(a)(7), 97.109(c), 97.201]

# Operating Procedures

There will be five questions on your Extra class examination from the Operating Procedures subelement. These five questions will be taken from the five groups of questions labeled E2A through E2E.

## E2A Amateur Satellites: orbital mechanics; frequencies available for satellite operation; satellite hardware; satellite operations

**E2A01** **What is the direction of an ascending pass for an amateur satellite?**

A. From west to east
B. From east to west
C. From south to north
D. From north to south

**C** If the satellite is moving from south to north as it passes over your area, then it makes an ascending pass.

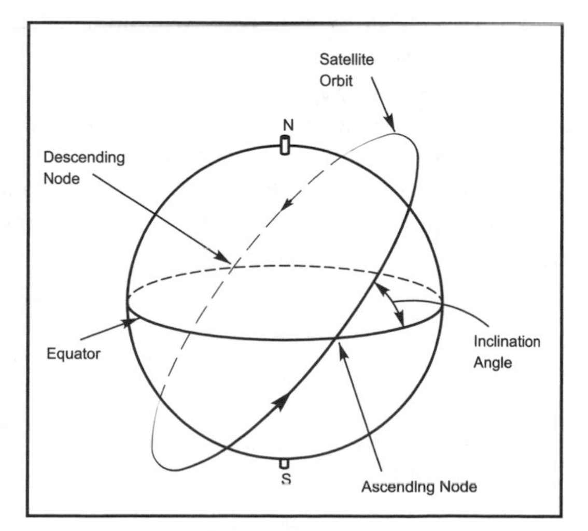


**This drawing illustrates some basic satellite-orbit terminology.**

**E2A02 What is the direction of a descending pass for an amateur satellite?**

A. From north to south
B. From west to east
C. From east to west
D. From south to north

**A** If the satellite is moving from north to south as it passes over your area, then it makes an descending pass.

**E2A03 What is the period of an amateur satellite?**

A. The point of maximum height of a satellite's orbit
B. The point of minimum height of a satellite's orbit
C. The amount of time it takes for a satellite to complete one orbit
D. The time it takes a satellite to travel from perigee to apogee

**C** The period of a satellite is the time it takes that satellite to complete one orbit.

**E2A04 What are the receiving and retransmitting frequency bands used for Mode V/H in amateur satellite operations?**

A. Satellite receiving on Amateur bands in the range of 21 to 30 MHz and retransmitting on 144 to 148 MHz
B. Satellite receiving on 435 to 438 MHz and retransmitting on 144 to 148 MHz
C. Satellite receiving on 435 to 438 MHz and retransmitting on Amateur bands in the range of 21 to 30 MHz
D. Satellite receiving on 144 to 148 MHz and retransmitting on Amateur bands in the range of 21 to 30 MHz

**D** Satellites used for two-way communication generally use one amateur band to receive signals from Earth and another to transmit back down. The amateur satellites use a variety of uplink (Earth to satellite) and downlink (satellite to Earth) band combinations. These band combinations are called operating modes, and should not be confused with SSB, RTTY or CW. The operating modes of a satellite simply refer to the uplink and downlink frequency bands that the satellite uses. The table summarizes the modes that you'll need to remember.

**Table 2-1**
**Satellite Operating Modes**

| *Mode* | *Satellite Receive* | *Satellite Transmit* |
|---|---|---|
| V/H | VHF (144 - 146 MHz) | HF (21 - 30 MHz) |
| U/V | UHF (435 - 438 MHz) | VHF (144 - 146 MHz) |
| V/U | VHF (144 - 146 MHz) | UHF (435 - 438 MHz) |
| L/U | L-Band (1.26 - 1.27 GHz) | UHF (435 - 438 MHz) |

**E2A05 What are the receiving and retransmitting frequency bands used for Mode U/V in amateur satellite operations?**

A. Satellite receiving on Amateur bands in the range of 21 to 30 MHz and retransmitting on 144 to 148 MHz
B. Satellite receiving on 435 to 438 MHz and retransmitting on 144 to 148 MHz
C. Satellite receiving on 435 to 438 MHz and retransmitting on Amateur bands in the range of 21 to 30 MHz
D. Satellite receiving on 144 to 148 MHz and retransmitting on Amateur bands in the range of 21 to 30 MHz

**B** The U/V designation means that the satellite receives on UHF (435 to 438 MHz) and transmits on VHF (144 to 148 MHz).

**E2A06 What are the receiving and retransmitting frequency bands used for Mode V/U in amateur satellite operations?**

A. Satellite receiving on 435 to 438 MHz and retransmitting on 144 to 148 MHz
B. Satellite receiving on 144 to 148 MHz and retransmitting on Amateur bands in the range of 21 to 30 MHz
C. Satellite receiving on 144 to 148 MHz and retransmitting on 435 to 438 MHz
D. Satellite receiving on 435 to 438 MHz and transmitting on 21 to 30 MHz

**C** The V/U designation means that the satellite receives on VHF (144 to 148 MHz) and transmits on UHF (435 to 438 MHz).

**E2A07 What are the receiving and retransmitting frequency bands used for Mode L/U in amateur satellite operations?**

A. Satellite receiving on 435 to 438 MHz and retransmitting on 21 to 30 MHz
B. Satellite receiving on Amateur bands in the range of 21 to 30 MHz and retransmitting on 435 to 438 MHz
C. Satellite receiving on 435 to 438 MHz and retransmitting on 1.26 to 1.27 GHz
D. Satellite receiving on 1.26 to 1.27 GHz and retransmitting on 435 to 438 MHz

**D** The L/U designation means that the satellite receives on L-Band (1.26 to 1.27 GHz) and transmits on UHF (435 to 438 MHz).

**E2A08 What is a linear transponder?**

A. A repeater that passes only linear or CW signals
B. A device that receives and retransmits signals of any mode in a certain passband
C. An amplifier that varies its output linearly in response to input signals
D. A device that responds to satellite telecommands and is used to activate a linear sequence of events

**B** By convention, transponder is the name given to a linear translator that is installed in a satellite. It is somewhat like a repeater in that both receive signals and retransmit them. A repeater does that for signals of a single mode on a single frequency. By contrast, a transponder's receive passband includes enough spectrum for many channels. The satellite transponder translates (or frequency converts) all signals—regardless of mode—in its passband, amplifies them and retransmits them in the new frequency range.

**E2A09 What is the name of the effect that causes the downlink frequency of a satellite to vary by several kHz during a low-earth orbit?**

A. The Kepler effect
B. The Bernoulli effect
C. The Einstein effect
D. The Doppler effect

**D** Doppler shift or Doppler effect is the name given to describe the way the downlink frequency of a satellite varies by several kHz during a low-eàrth orbit. Doppler shift is caused by the relative motion between you and the satellite. In operation, as the satellite is moving toward you, the frequency of a downlink signal appears to be increased by a small amount. When the satellite passes overhead and begins to move away from you, there will be a sudden frequency drop of a few kilohertz, in much the same was as the tone of a car horn or train whistle drops as the vehicle moves past you.

**E2A10 Why may the received signal from an amateur satellite exhibit a fairly rapid pulsed fading effect?**

A. Because the satellite is rotating
B. Because of ionospheric absorption
C. Because of the satellite's low orbital altitude
D. Because of the Doppler effect

**A** Satellite designers usually spin a satellite to improve its pointing stability. Of course the satellite antennas spin too, and this results in a fairly rapid pulsed fading effect. This effect is called spin modulation.

**E2A11 What type of antenna can be used to minimize the effects of spin modulation and Faraday rotation?**

A. A nonpolarized antenna
B. A circularly polarized antenna
C. An isotropic antenna
D. A log-periodic dipole array

**B** Circularly polarized antennas of the proper sense will minimize the effects of spin modulation that you read about in the explanation to the previous question.

The polarization of a radio signal passing through the ionosphere does not remain constant. A "horizontally polarized" signal leaving a satellite will not be horizontally polarized after it passes through the ionosphere on its way to Earth. That signal will in fact seem to be changing polarization at a receiving station. This effect is called Faraday rotation. The best way to deal with Faraday rotation is to use circularly polarized antennas for transmitting and receiving

**E2A12 How may the location of a satellite at a given time be predicted?**

A. By means of the Doppler data for the specified satellite
B. By subtracting the mean anomaly from the orbital inclination
C. By adding the mean anomaly to the orbital inclination
D. By means of the Keplerian elements for the specified satellite

**D** Johannes Kepler described the planetary orbits of our solar system. The laws and mathematical formulas that he developed may be used to calculate the location of a satellite at a given time. If you know the values of a set of measurements about the satellite orbit, called "Keplerian elements," you can do the calculation. These days, most folks use computer software to do the calculations.

## E2B Television: fast scan television (FSTV) standards; slow scan television (SSTV) standards; facsimile (fax) communications

**E2B01 How many times per second is a new frame transmitted in a fast-scan television system?**

A. 30
B. 60
C. 90
D. 120

**A** A picture is divided sequentially into pieces for transmission or viewing; this process is called scanning. A total of 525 scan lines comprise a frame (complete picture) in the US television system. Thirty frames are generated each second.

**E2B02 How many horizontal lines make up a fast-scan television frame?**

A. 30
B. 60
C. 525
D. 1050

**C** A total of 525 horizontal lines make up a fast-scan television frame (complete picture).

**E2B03 How is the interlace scanning pattern generated in a fast-scan television system?**

A. By scanning the field from top to bottom
B. By scanning the field from bottom to top
C. By scanning from left to right in one field and right to left in the next
D. By scanning odd numbered lines in one field and even numbered ones in the next

**D** The fast-scan TV frame consists of two fields of 262½ lines each. The odd numbered lines are scanned in one field and the even numbered ones are scanned in the next. The half line is the secret to the interlaced scan pattern. This is illustrated in the drawing.

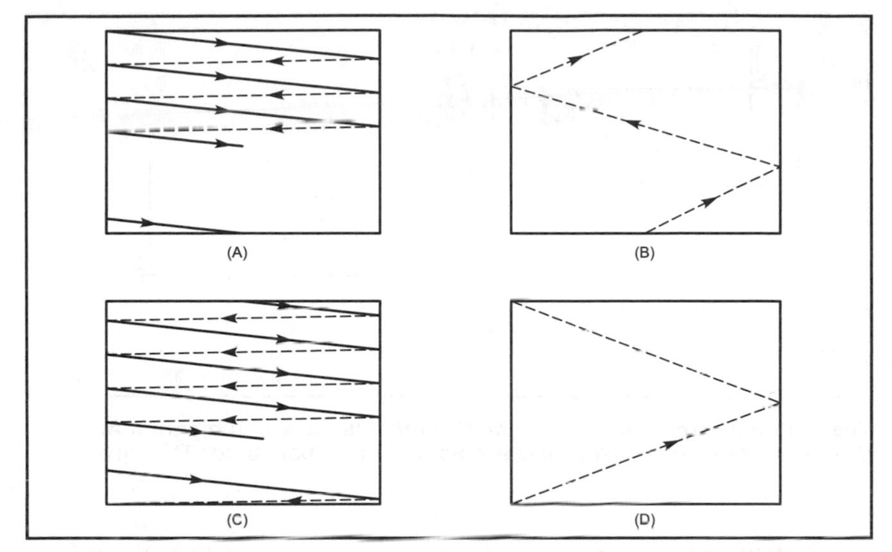


**This diagram shows the interlaced scanning used in TV. In field one, 262½ lines are scanned (A). At the end of field one, the electron scanning beam is returned to the top of the picture area (B). Scanning lines in field two (C) fall between the lines of field one. At the end of field two, the scanning beam is again returned to the top where scanning continues with field one (D).**

**E2B04 What is blanking in a video signal?**

A. Synchronization of the horizontal and vertical sync pulses
B. Turning off the scanning beam while it is traveling from right to left and from bottom to top
C. Turning off the scanning beam at the conclusion of a transmission
D. Transmitting a black and white test pattern

**B** Blanking is blacker than black. Its function is to turn off the scanning beam while the beam is traveling from right to left and from bottom to top. The blanking signal occurs at the end of each scan line and at the end of each scan field.

**E2B05 What is the bandwidth of a vestigial sideband AM fast-scan television transmission?**

A. 3 kHz
B. 10 kHz
C. 25 kHz
D. 6 MHz

**D** The spectrum of a vestigial sideband AM fast-scan television transmission is approximately 6 MHz wide. Vestigial means that only a part of one sideband is present.

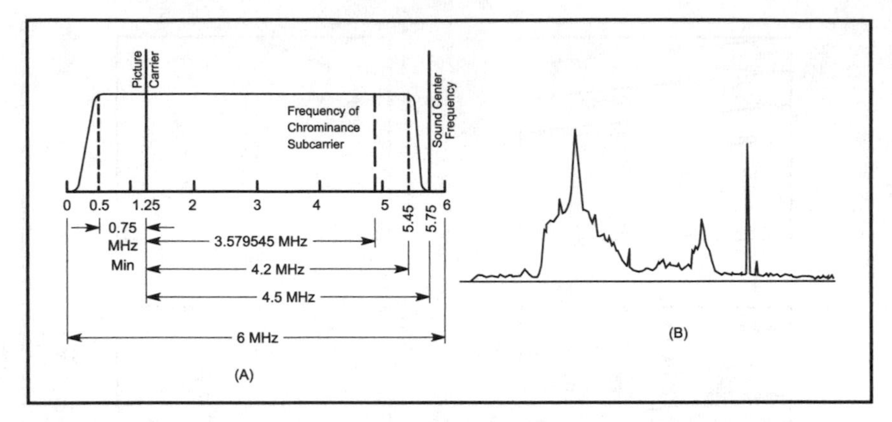


**The frequency spectrum of a color TV signal is shown in diagram A. Part B represents a spectrum analyzer display of a typical color TV signal.**

**E2B06 What is the standard video level, in percent PEV, for black in amateur fast scan television?**

A. 0%
B. 12.5%
C. 70%
D. 100%

**C** PEV is peak envelope voltage and corresponds to levels as seen on an oscilloscope. To assure that the picture locks, sync signals are the highest level output and white is the lowest. The standard video level, in percent PEV, for black in amateur fast scan television is 70%. See the table.

## Table 2-2

## Standard Video Levels

| | *% PEV* |
|---|---|
| Zero carrier | 0 |
| White | 12.5 |
| Black | 70 |
| Blanking | 75 |
| Sync tip | 100 |

**E2B07 What is the standard video level, in percent PEV, for blanking in amateur fast scan television?**

A. 0%
B. 12.5%
C. 75%
D. 100%

**C** This is related to the previous question. Blanking is "blacker than black," and the standard value is 75%. You can see this in the table.

**E2B08 Which of the following is NOT a common method of transmitting accompanying audio with amateur fast-scan television?**

A. Amplitude modulation of the video carrier
B. Frequency-modulated sub-carrier
C. A separate VHF or UHF audio link
D. Frequency modulation of the video carrier

**A** The video carrier is already amplitude modulated by the video signal. For that reason, if you amplitude modulate the video carrier with audio it will interfere with the video reception. The other techniques work well, and are used for transmitting accompanying audio with amateur fast-scan television.

**E2B09 What is facsimile?**

A. The transmission of characters by radioteletype that form a picture when printed
B. The transmission of still pictures by slow-scan television
C. The transmission of video by amateur television
D. The transmission of printed pictures for permanent display on paper

**D** Facsimile is the transmission of printed pictures for permanent display on paper. The key to remembering this is that in facsimile a picture is physically printed on paper.

**E2B10 What is the modern standard scan rate for a fax image transmitted by an amateur station?**

A. 240 lines per minute
B. 50 lines per minute
C. 150 lines per second
D. 60 lines per second

**A** The modern standard scan rate for a fax image transmitted by an amateur station is 240 lines per minute. This represents a good compromise between resolution and image transmission time.

**E2B11 What is the approximate transmission time per frame for a fax picture transmitted by an amateur station at 240 lpm?**

A. 6 minutes
B. 3.3 minutes
C. 6 seconds
D. 1/60 second

**B** To answer this question, you'll need to know that the typical fax picture comprises 800 lines. From the question, you know that 240 lines per minute is the transmission speed. The time required to transmit the picture is 800 lines ÷ 240 lines/Minute = 3.3 minutes.

**E2B12 What information is sent by slow-scan television transmissions?**

A. Baudot or ASCII characters that form a picture when printed
B. Pictures for permanent display on paper
C. Moving pictures
D. Still pictures

**D** It takes 8 seconds to transmit a slow-scan television frame in black and white. Color frames require even more time. For that reason SSTV is only suitable for sending still pictures.

**E2B13 How many lines are commonly used in each frame on an amateur slow-scan color television picture?**

A. 30 to 60
B. 60 or 100
C. 128 or 256
D. 180 or 360

**C** Color SSTV standards specify either 128 or 256 lines per frame depending on the format that you chose.

**E2B14 What is the audio frequency for black in an amateur slow-scan television picture?**

A. 2300 Hz
B. 2000 Hz
C. 1500 Hz
D. 120 Hz

**C** The audio frequency for black in an amateur slow-scan television picture is 1500 Hz.

**E2B15 What is the audio frequency for white in an amateur slow-scan television picture?**

A. 120 Hz
B. 1500 Hz
C. 2000 Hz
D. 2300 Hz

**D** The audio frequency for white in an amateur slow-scan television picture is 2300 Hz.

**E2B16 What is the standard video level, in percent PEV, for white in an amateur fast-scan television transmission?**

A. 0%
B. 12.5%
C. 70%
D. 100%

**B** In Table 2-2 you saw that white in an amateur fast-scan television transmission is 12.5% of the PEV (peak envelope voltage).

**E2B17 Which of the following is NOT a characteristic of FMTV (Frequency-Modulated Amateur Television) as compared to vestigial sideband AM television?**

A. Immunity from fading due to limiting
B. Poor weak signal performance
C. Greater signal bandwidth
D. Greater complexity of receiving equipment

**A** You are looking for the false statement. FMTV, like other FM transmission systems, has no immunity from fading due to limiting in the FM receiver. The other statements are true characteristics of FMTV as compared to vestigial sideband AM television.

**E2B18 What is the approximate bandwidth of a slow-scan TV signal?**

A. 600 Hz
B. 2 kHz
C. 2 MHz
D. 6 MHz

**B** As you saw earlier, white is indicated by a tone of 2300 Hz and other portions are represented by lower tones. The entire SSTV signal is transmitted through an SSB transmitter. The bandwidth of an SSTV signal is approximately 2 kHz.

**E2B19 Which of the following systems is used to transmit high-quality still images by radio?**

A. AMTOR
B. Baudot RTTY
C. AMTEX
D. Facsimile

**D** Only facsimile is designed specifically for image transmission. The other modes listed are text or character based and cannot transmit high-quality still images by radio.

**E2B20** **What special restrictions are imposed on fax transmissions?**

A. None; they are allowed on all amateur frequencies
B. They are restricted to 7.245 MHz, 14.245 MHz, 21.345, MHz, and 28.945 MHz
C. They are allowed in phone band segments if their bandwidth is no greater than that of a voice signal of the same modulation type
D. They are not permitted above 54 MHz

**C** Fax transmissions are allowed in phone band segments if their bandwidth is no greater than that of a voice signal of the same modulation type.

## E2C Contest and DX operating; spread-spectrum transmissions; automatic HF forwarding; selecting your operating frequency

**E2C01** **When operating during a contest, which of these standards should you generally follow?**

A. Always listen before transmitting, be courteous and do not cause harmful interference to other communications
B. Always reply to other stations calling CQ at least as many times as you call CQ
C. When initiating a contact, always reply with the call sign of the station you are calling followed by your own call sign
D. Always include your signal report, name and transmitter power output in any exchange with another station

**A** In all your operating, you should always listen before transmitting, be courteous and not cause harmful interference to other communications. This is true even for the most competitive contester on the band. In contest operation, you'll want to keep your calls short and transmit only the required information for the contest exchange and for proper (legal) station identification.

**E2C02 What is one of the main purposes for holding on-the-air operating contests?**

A. To test the dollar-to-feature value of station equipment during difficult operating circumstances
B. To enhance the communicating and operating skills of amateur operators in readiness for an emergency
C. To measure the ionosphere's capacity for refracting RF signals under varying conditions
D. To demonstrate to the FCC that amateur station operation is possible during difficult operating circumstances

**B** On-the-air operating contests are held mainly to enhance the communicating and operating skills of the amateur operators that participate in these events and to improve their readiness to operate during an emergency.

**E2C03 Which of the following is typical of operations during an international amateur DX contest?**

A. Calling CQ is always done on an odd minute and listening is always done on an even minute
B. Contacting a DX station is best accomplished when the WWV K index is above a reading of 8
C. Some DX operators use split frequency operations (transmitting on a frequency different from the receiving frequency)
D. DX contacts during the day are never possible because of known band attenuation from the sun

**C** Some DX operators use split frequency operations (transmitting on a frequency different from their receiving frequency) during an international amateur DX contest. This technique is required on 40-meter phone where stations in different regions have different (non-overlapping) frequency privileges.

**E2C04 If a DX station asks for your grid square locator, what should be your reply?**

A. The square of the power fed to the grid of your final amplifier and your current city, state and country
B. The DX station's call sign followed by your call sign and your RST signal report
C. The subsection of the IARU region in which you are located based upon dividing the entire region into a grid of squares 10 km wide
D. Your geographic Maidenhead grid location (e.g., FN31AA) based on your current latitude and longitude

**D** In the Maidenhead grid square system, the Earth is divided into "squares" that are 2° of longitude by 1° of latitude. Each square is designated by two letters and two numbers. These grid squares can be divided further into smaller segments, described by two more letters. During casual operation or a contest you may be asked for your grid square locator. If so, the other operator wants to know your geographic Maidenhead grid location (e.g., FN31aa).

**E2C05 What does a Maidenhead grid square refer to?**

A. A two-degree longitude by one-degree latitude square, as part of a world wide numbering system
B. A one-degree longitude by one degree latitude square, beginning at the South Pole
C. An antenna made of wire grid used to amplify low-angle incoming signals while reducing high-angle incoming signals
D. An antenna consisting of a screen or grid positioned directly beneath the radiating element

**A** A Maidenhead grid square refers to a two-degree longitude by one-degree latitude square, which is part of a worldwide numbering system.

**E2C06 During a VHF/UHF contest, in which band section would you expect to find the highest level of contest activity?**

A. At the top of each band, usually in a segment reserved for contests
B. In the middle of each band, usually on the national calling frequency
C. In the weak signal segment of the band, with most of the activity near the calling frequency
D. In the middle of the band, usually 25 kHz above the national calling frequency

**C** In VHF/UHF contests, while some of the action takes place on FM, much of the activity is on SSB or CW. You'll find most of the contest activity in the weak signal segment of the band, with most of the activity near the calling frequency.

**E2C07 If you are in the US calling a station in Texas on a frequency of 1832 kHz and a station replies that you are in the window, what does this mean?**

A. You are operating out of the band privileges of your license
B. You are calling at the wrong time of day to be within the window of frequencies that can be received in Texas at that time
C. You are transmitting in a frequency segment that is reserved for international DX contacts by gentlemen's agreement
D. Your modulation has reached an undesirable level and you are interfering with another contact

**C** The point of this question is that certain frequencies are set aside by common agreement for DX use. In this case, "in the window," means that you are transmitting in a frequency segment that is reserved for international DX contacts by gentlemen's agreement.

**E2C08 Why are received spread-spectrum signals so resistant to interference?**

A. Signals not using the spectrum-spreading algorithm are suppressed in the receiver
B. The high power used by a spread-spectrum transmitter keeps its signal from being easily overpowered
C. The receiver is always equipped with a special digital signal processor (DSP) interference filter
D. If interference is detected by the receiver it will signal the transmitter to change frequencies

**A** A spread-spectrum signal increases the bandwidth of transmitted information according to a well defined pattern. The receiver despreads the information according to, and synchronous with, the same pattern. If interference is not synchronized with the original spread spectrum signal, it will not appear after despreading at the receiver. In other words, signals not using the spectrum-spreading algorithm are suppressed in the receiver.

**E2C09 How does the spread-spectrum technique of frequency hopping (FH) work?**

A. If interference is detected by the receiver it will signal the transmitter to change frequencies
B. If interference is detected by the receiver it will signal the transmitter to wait until the frequency is clear
C. A pseudo-random binary bit stream is used to shift the phase of an RF carrier very rapidly in a particular sequence
D. The frequency of the transmitted signal is changed very rapidly according to a particular sequence also used by the receiving station

**D** FH spread spectrum is a form of spreading in which the center frequency of a conventional carrier is altered many times per second in accordance with a list of frequency channels. The same frequency list is used by the receiving station which "hops" in sync with the transmitter.

**E2C10 While participating in an HF contest, how should you attempt to contact a station calling CQ and stating that he is listening on another specific frequency?**

A. By sending your full call sign on the listening frequency specified
B. By sending only the suffix of your call sign on the listening frequency
C. By sending your full call sign on the frequency on which you heard the station calling CQ
D. By sending only the suffix of your call sign on the frequency on which you heard the station calling CQ

**A** In this case the contester is operating in split mode where the operator calls on one frequency and listens on another. You should send your full call sign on the operator's listening frequency so that he can hear and answer you.

**E2C11 When operating SSB in a VHF contest, how should your attempt to contact a station calling CQ while a pileup of other stations are also trying to contact the same station?**

A. By sending your full call sign after the distant station transmits QRZ
B. By sending only the last letters of your call sign after the distant station transmits QRZ
C. By sending your full call sign and grid square as soon as you hear the distant station transmit QRZ
D. By sending the call sign of the distant station three times, the words "this is", then your call sign three times

**A** When the other operator sends "QRZ?" it means, "Who is calling me?" This is your cue to call by sending your full call sign. Sending only part of your call sign is not a proper way to identify your station.

**E2C12 In North America during low sunspot activity, signals from Europe become weak and fluttery across an entire HF band two to three hours after sunset, what might help to contact other European DX stations?**

A. Switch to a higher frequency HF band, because the MUF has increased
B. Switch to a lower frequency HF band because the MUF has decreased
C. Wait 90 minutes or so for the signal degradation to pass
D. Wait 24 hours before attempting another communication on the band

**B** The "weak and fluttery after sunset" condition indicates that the band conditions are deteriorating. You can continue to operate by changing frequencies. In this case, you'll want to operate at a lower frequency because the MUF has moved lower as well.

## E2D Operating VHF / UHF digital modes: packet clusters; digital bulletin boards; Automatic Position Reporting System (APRS)

**E2D01 What does CMD: mean when it is displayed on the video monitor of a packet station?**

A. The TNC is ready to exit the packet terminal program
B. The TNC is in command mode, ready to receive instructions from the keyboard
C. The TNC will exit to the command mode on the next keystroke
D. The TNC is in KISS mode running TCP/IP, ready for the next command

**B** When "CMD" is displayed on your packet station video monitor, the TNC is in command mode, ready to receive instructions from the keyboard.

**E2D02 What is a Packet Cluster Bulletin Board?**

A. A packet bulletin board devoted primarily to serving a special interest group
B. A group of general-purpose packet bulletin boards linked together in a cluster
C. A special interest cluster of packet bulletin boards devoted entirely to packet radio computer communications
D. A special interest telephone/modem bulletin board devoted to amateur DX operations

**A** Many amateurs interested in chasing DX and operating in contests enjoy using their local packet cluster system and the packet cluster bulletin board. A packet cluster normally is devoted to serving a special interest group, such as DXers or contesters. These systems allow many stations to connect to the cluster and to communicate with each other. It has nothing to do with forming clusters of bulletin boards.

**E2D03 In comparing HF and 2-meter packet Operations, which of the following is NOT true?**

A. HF packet typically uses an FSK signal with a data rate of 300 bauds; 2-meter packet uses an AFSK signal with a data rate of 1200 bauds
B. HF packet and 2-meter packet operations use the same code for information exchange
C. HF packet is limited to Amateur Extra class amateur licensees; 2-meter packet is open to all but Novice Class amateur licensees
D. HF packet operations are limited to CW/Data-only band segments; 2-meter packet is allowed wherever FM operations are allowed

**C** Here you are looking for a false statement. The only false statement is that HF packet is limited to Amateur Extra Class amateur licensees.

**E2D04 What is the purpose of a digital store and forward on an Amateur satellite?**

A. To stockpile packet TNCs and other digital hardware to be distributed to RACES operators in the event of an emergency
B. To relay messages across the country via a network of HF digital stations
C. To store messages in an amateur satellite for later download by other stations
D. To store messages in a packet digipeater for relay via the Internet

**C** Digital communications satellites provide non-real time computer-to-computer communications. These satellites work like temporary mail boxes in space. You upload a message or a file to a satellite and it is stored for a time (could be days or weeks) until someone else—possibly on the other side of the world—downloads it. Messages or files can be sent to an individual recipient or everyone. Such communications are called store and-forward.

**E2D05 Which of the following techniques is normally used by low-earth orbiting digital satellites to relay messages around the world?**

A. Digipeating
B. Store and forward
C. Multi-satellite relaying
D. Node hopping

**B** Since low-earth orbiting (LEO) satellites cannot see large segments of the world at once, messages are sent via store-and-forward mode which allows recipients to pick up their messages from the satellite "mail box" as the satellite flies overhead. See also the explanation to the previous question.

**E2D06 What is the common 2-meter APRS frequency?**

A. 144.20 MHz
B. 144.39 MHz
C. 145.02 MHz
D. 146.52 MHz

**B** The common 2-meter APRS frequency is 144.39 MHz.

**E2D07 Which of the following digital protocols does APRS use?**

A. AX.25
B. 802.11
C. PACTOR
D. AMTOR

**A** The APRS system is based on the amateur AX.25 packet protocol.

**E2D08 Which of the following types of packet frames is used to transmit APRS beacon data?**

A. Connect frames
B. Disconnect frames
C. Acknowledgement frames
D. Unnumbered Information frames

**D** To simplify the communication between stations, an APRS beacon is transmitted as an unnumbered information (UI) frame. The stations in an APRS network are not "connected" in the normal packet radio sense. The beacon frames are not directed to a specific station, and receiving stations do not acknowledge correct receipt of the frames.

**E2D09 Under clear communications conditions, which of these digital communications modes has the fastest data throughput?**

A. AMTOR
B. 170-Hz shift, 45 baud RTTY
C. PSK31
D. 300-baud packet

**D** For fastest throughput under clear communications conditions (assumed to be error-free transmission), the highest data rate is needed. Of the choices given, 300-baud packet has the highest data rate and, therefore, the fastest data throughput.

**E2D10 How can an APRS station be used to help support a public service communications activity, such as a walk-a-thon?**

A. An APRS station with an emergency medical technician can automatically transmit medical data to the nearest hospital
B. APRS stations with General Personnel Scanners can automatically relay the participant numbers and time as they pass the check points
C. An APRS station with a GPS unit can automatically transmit information to show the station's position along the course route
D. All of these choices are correct

**C** At this point, it is good to remember that APRS stands for Automatic Position Reporting System. Positions of fixed stations can be entered directly into software. Mobile APRS stations equipped with a GPS unit can automatically transmit information to show the station's position. This capability can be useful in support of a public service communications activity, such as a walk-a-thon.

**E2D11 Which of the following data sources are needed to accurately transmit your geographical location over the APRS network?**

A. The NMEA-0183 formatted data from a Global Positioning System (GPS) satellite receiver
B. The latitude and longitude of your location, preferably in degrees, minutes and seconds, entered into the APRS computer software
C. The NMEA-0183 formatted data from a LORAN navigation system
D. All of these choices are correct

**D** Each of the statements is correct.

## E2E Operating HF digital modes

**E2E01 What is the most common method of transmitting data emissions below 30 MHz?**

A. DTMF tones modulating an FM signal
B. FSK (frequency-shift keying) of an RF carrier
C. AFSK (audio frequency-shift keying) of an FM signal
D. Key-operated on/off switching of an RF carrier

**B** The most common method of transmitting data emissions below 30 MHz is by FSK (frequency-shift keying) of an RF carrier.

**E2E02 What do the letters FEC mean as they relate to AMTOR operation?**

A. Forward Error Correction
B. First Error Correction
C. Fatal Error Correction
D. Final Error Correction

**A** The telecommunications industry uses FEC as a standard acronym for Forward Error Correction. In AMTOR Mode B (the FEC mode), each character is sent twice. The receiving station checks each character for the correct mark/space ratio. This provides some assurance of correct reception, but it is not fool proof.

**E2E03 How is Forward Error Correction implemented?**

A. By transmitting blocks of 3 data characters from the sending station to the receiving station, which the receiving station acknowledges
B. By transmitting a special FEC algorithm which the receiving station uses for data validation
C. By transmitting extra data that may be used to detect and correct transmission errors
D. By varying the frequency shift of the transmitted signal according to a predefined algorithm

**C** This is a general question about Forward Error Correction systems. These systems do not require receiving stations to transmit an acknowledgement to the sending station. FEC is implemented by transmitting extra data that may be used to detect and correct transmission errors.

**E2E04 If an oscilloscope is connected to a TNC or terminal unit and is displaying two crossed ellipses, one of which suddenly disappears, what would this indicate about the observed signal?**

A. The phenomenon known as selective fading has occurred
B. One of the signal filters has saturated
C. The receiver should be retuned, as it has probably moved at least 5 kHz from the desired receive frequency
D. The mark and space signal have been inverted and the receiving equipment has not yet responded to the change

**A** Most RTTY software uses a pair of ellipses to indicate tuning accuracy. Each ellipse represents one of the two tones being sent. With the propagation effect known as selective fading, a small region of the radio spectrum undergoes a deep fade as if a narrow filter has been applied to it. This is what can make one of the ellipses on the terminal unit display disappear.

**E2E05 What is the name for a bulletin transmission system that includes a special header to allow receiving stations to determine if the bulletin has been previously received?**

A. ARQ mode A
B. FEC mode B
C. AMTOR
D. AMTEX

**D** Some AMTOR bulletin-transmission systems include a special message header that allows the receiving system to determine if the bulleting has been received previously. This system is commonly known as NAVTEX because it was first developed for use with transmissions to ships at sea. The amateur adaptation of this system is called AMTEX.

**E2E06 What is the most common data rate used for HF packet communications?**

A. 48 bauds
B. 110 bauds
C. 300 bauds
D. 1200 bauds

**C** The most common data rate used for HF packet communications is 300 bauds.

**E2E07 What is the typical bandwidth of a properly modulated MFSK16 signal?**

A. 31 Hz
B. 316 Hz
C. 550 Hz
D. 2 kHz

**B** MFSK16 uses 16 tones, which are sent one at a time at 15.625 bauds. Because the 16 tones are spaced 15.625 Hz apart, a properly modulated MFSK16 signal has a bandwidth of 316 Hz.

**E2E08 Which of the following HF digital modes can be used to transfer binary files?**

A. Hellschreiber
B. PACTOR
C. RTTY
D. AMTOR

**B** PACTOR was developed to combine the best features of packet radio and AMTOR. Since PACTOR carries binary data, you can use this mode to transfer binary data files directly between stations. The other mode choices are not suitable for this purpose.

**E2E09 This question has been withdrawn.**

**E2E10 This question has been withdrawn.**

**E2E11 What is the Baudot code?**

A. A code used to transmit data only in modern computer-based data systems using seven data bits
B. A binary code consisting of eight data bits
C. An alternate name for Morse code
D. The International Telegraph Alphabet Number 2 (ITA2) which uses five data bits

**D** Traditional RTTY communication uses the Baudot code. This digital code, also called the International Telegraph Alphabet Number 2 (ITA2), uses five data bits to represent each character, with additional start and stop bits to indicate the beginning and end of each character.

**E2E12 Which of these digital communications modes has the narrowest bandwidth?**

A. AMTOR
B. 170-Hz shift, 45 baud RTTY
C. PSK31
D. 300-baud packet

**C** PSK31 uses a data rate of 31.25 bits per second. This results in an RF signal that has a bandwidth of only 31.25 Hz! This is by far the narrowest bandwidth of any digital communications mode.

# Radio Wave Propagation

There will be three questions on your Extra class examination from the Radio Wave Propagation subelement. These three questions will be taken from the three groups of questions labeled E3A through E3C.

## E3A Earth-Moon-Earth (EME or moonbounce) communications; meteor scatter

**E3A01 What is the maximum separation between two stations communicating by moonbounce?**

A. 500 miles maximum, if the moon is at perigee
B. 2000 miles maximum, if the moon is at apogee
C. 5000 miles maximum, if the moon is at perigee
D. Any distance as long as the stations have a mutual lunar window

**D** Two stations must be able to simultaneously see the moon to communicate by reflecting VHF or UHF signals off the lunar surface. Those stations may be separated by nearly 180° of arc on the Earth's surface—a distance of more than 11,000 miles. There is no specific maximum distance between two stations to communicate via moonbounce, as long as they have a mutual lunar window. In other words, the moon must be above the "radio horizon" where both stations can "see" it at the same time.

**E3A02 What characterizes libration fading of an earth-moon-earth signal?**

A. A slow change in the pitch of the CW signal
B. A fluttery irregular fading
C. A gradual loss of signal as the sun rises
D. The returning echo is several hertz lower in frequency than the transmitted signal

**B** Libration fading is multipath scattering of the radio waves from the very large (2000-mile diameter) and rough Moon surface combined with the relative short-term motion between Earth and Moon. Libration fading of an EME signal is characterized in general as fluttery, rapid, irregular fading not unlike that observed in tropospheric-scatter propagation. Fading can be very deep, 20 dB or more, and the maximum fading will depend on the operating frequency. You can see this in the drawing.

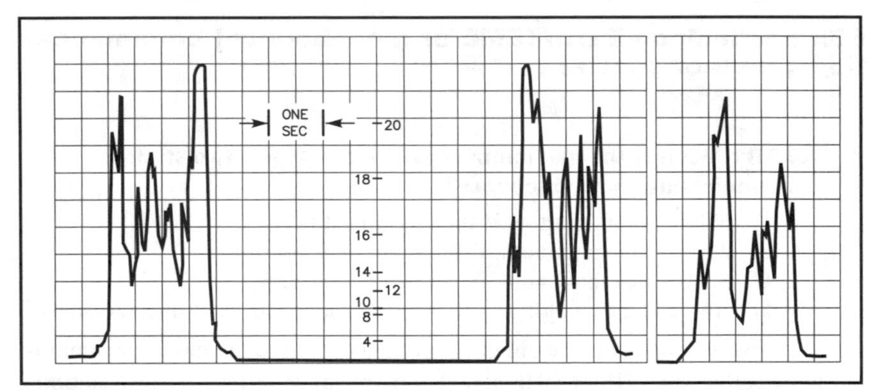


**This graph is a chart recording of 1296-MHz moon echoes received at W2NFA.**

**E3A03 When scheduling EME contacts, which of these conditions will generally result in the least path loss?**

A. When the moon is at perigee
B. When the moon is full
C. When the moon is at apogee
D. When the MUF is above 30 MHz

**A** The moon's orbit is slightly elliptical, with the closest distance (perigee) being 225,000 miles and the furthest (apogee) being 252,000 miles. EME path loss is typically 2 dB less at perigee.

**E3A04 What type of receiving system is desirable for EME communications?**

A. Equipment with very low power output
B. Equipment with very low dynamic range
C. Equipment with very low gain
D. Equipment with very low noise figures

**D** A low-noise receiving setup is essential for successful EME work. Since many of the signals to be copied on EME are barely, but not always, out of the noise, a low-noise receiver is a must. At 144 MHz a noise figure of under 0.5 dB will make cosmic noise the limiting factor of what you're able to hear. You can achieve this with inexpensive modern devices. At UHF, you'll want the lowest noise figure you can attain. With GaAsFET devices, you should be able to build a preamplifier with a 0.5 dB noise figure.

**E3A05 What transmit and receive time sequencing is normally used on 144 MHz when attempting an earth-moon-earth contact?**

A. Two-minute sequences, where one station transmits for a full two minutes and then receives for the following two minutes
B. One-minute sequences, where one station transmits for one minute and then receives for the following one minute
C. Two-and-one-half minute sequences, where one station transmits for a full 2.5 minutes and then receives for the following 2.5 minutes
D. Five-minute sequences, where one station transmits for five minutes and then receives for the following five minutes

**A** For 144-MHz contacts, a two-minute calling sequence is used. The eastern-most station transmits first for two full minutes, and then that station receives for two full minutes while the western-most station transmits.

**E3A06 What transmit and receive time sequencing is normally used on 432 MHz when attempting an EME contact?**

A. Two-minute sequences, where one station transmits for a full two minutes and then receives for the following two minutes
B. One-minute sequences, where one station transmits for one minute and then receives for the following one minute
C. Two and one half minute sequences, where one station transmits for a full 2.5 minutes and then receives for the following 2.5 minutes
D. Five minute sequences, where one station transmits for five minutes and then receives for the following five minutes

**C** For UHF EME contacts, operators use two and a half-minute calling sequences. The eastern-most station transmits first, for two and a half minutes. Then the eastern station listens for the next two and a half minutes, while the western-most station transmits.

**E3A07 What frequency range would you normally tune to find EME stations in the 2-meter band?**

A. 144.000 - 144.001 MHz
B. 144.000 - 144.100 MHz
C. 144.100 - 144.300 MHz
D. 145.000 - 145.100 MHz

**B** Most EME contacts are made in the weak-signal portion of the bands. On 2 meters, this is 144.000 to 144.100 MHz. EME contacts are generally made by prearranged schedule, although some contacts are made at random. The larger stations, especially on 144 and 432 MHz where there is a good amount of activity, often call CQ during evenings and weekends when the moon is at perigee, and listen for random replies.

**E3A08 What frequency range would you normally tune to find EME stations in the 70-cm band?**

A. 430.000 - 430.150 MHz
B. 430.100 - 431.100 MHz
C. 431.100 - 431.200 MHz
D. 432.000 - 432.100 MHz

**D** As on 2 meters, EME contacts are made in the weak-signal portion of the band. That means 432.000 to 432.100 MHz.

**E3A09 When a meteor strikes the earth's atmosphere, a cylindrical region of free electrons is formed at what layer of the ionosphere?**

A. The E layer
B. The F1 layer
C. The F2 layer
D. The D layer

**A** Meteor trails are formed at approximately the altitude of the ionospheric E layer, 50 to 75 miles above the Earth. This is illustrated in the drawing. As a meteor speeds through the upper atmosphere, it begins to burn or vaporize as it collides with air molecules. This action creates heat and light and leaves a trail of free electrons and positively charged ions behind as the meteor races along. Trail size is directly dependent on meteor size and speed. A typical meteor is the size of a grain of sand. A particle this size creates a trail about 3 feet in diameter and 12 miles or longer, depending on speed.

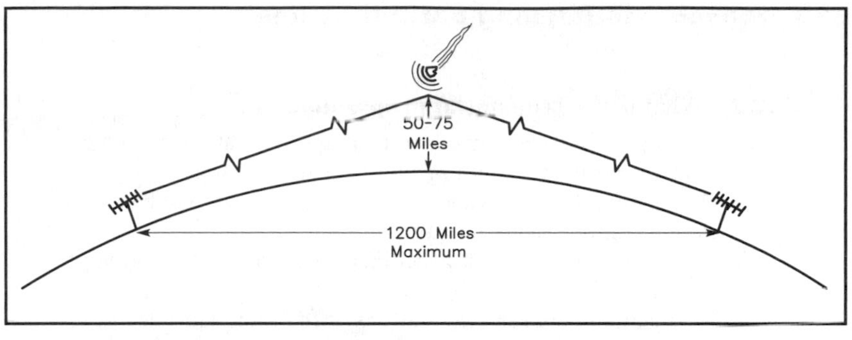


**Meteor-scatter communication makes extended-range VHF communications possible.**

**E3A10 Which range of frequencies is well suited for meteor-scatter communications?**

A. 1.8 - 1.9 MHz
B. 10 - 14 MHz
C. 28 - 148 MHz
D. 220 - 450 MHz

**C** The electron density in a typical meteor trail will strongly affect radio waves between 28 and 148 MHz. Signal frequencies as low as 20 MHz and as high as 432 MHz will be usable for meteor-scatter communication at times.

**E3A11 What transmit and receive time sequencing is normally used on 144 MHz when attempting a meteor-scatter contact?**

A. Two-minute sequences, where one station transmits for a full two minutes and then receives for the following two minutes
B. One-minute sequences, where one station transmits for one minute and then receives for the following one minute
C. 15-second sequences, where one station transmits for 15 seconds and then receives for the following 15 seconds
D. 30-second sequences, where one station transmits for 30 seconds and then receives for the following 30 seconds

**C** The secret to successful meteor-scatter communication is short transmissions. The accepted convention for timing transmissions breaks each minute into four 15-second periods. The station at the western end of the path transmits during the first and third period of each minute. During the second and fourth 15-second periods, the eastern station transmits.

## E3B Transequatorial; long path; gray line

**E3B01 What is transequatorial propagation?**

A. Propagation between two points at approximately the same distance north and south of the magnetic equator
B. Propagation between two points at approximately the same latitude on the magnetic equator
C. Propagation between two continents by way of ducts along the magnetic equator
D. Propagation between two stations at the same latitude

**A** Transequatorial propagation (TE) is a form of F-layer ionospheric propagation that was discovered by amateurs. TE allows hams on either side of the magnetic equator to communicate with each other. As the signal frequency increases the communication zones become more restricted to those equidistant from, and perpendicular to, the magnetic equator.

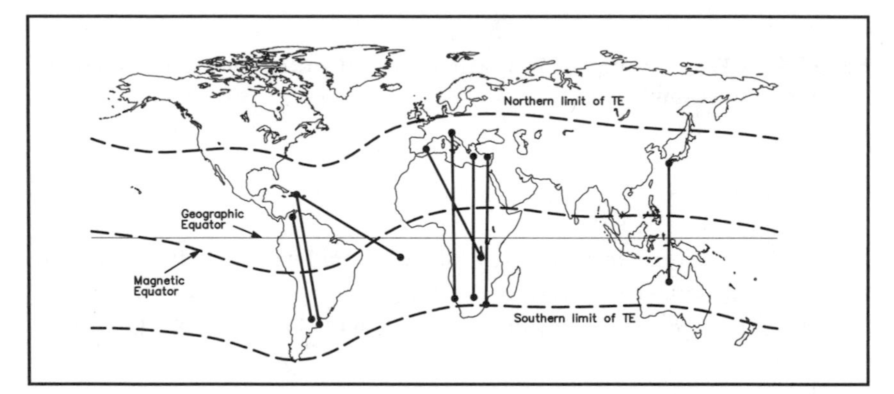


**This world map shows TE paths worked by amateurs on 144 MHz. Notice the symmetrical distribution of stations with respect to the magnetic equator.**

**E3B02 What is the approximate maximum range for signals using transequatorial propagation?**

A. 1000 miles
B. 2500 miles
C. 5000 miles
D. 7500 miles

**C** TE range extends to approximately 5000 miles—2500 miles on each side of the magnetic equator.

**E3B03** **What is the best time of day for transequatorial propagation?**

A. Morning
B. Noon
C. Afternoon or early evening
D. Late at night

**C** Ionization levels that support TE are forming during the morning, are well established by noon and may last until after midnight. The best (peak) time is in the afternoon and early evening hours.

**E3B04** **What type of propagation is probably occurring if an HF beam antenna must be pointed in a direction 180 degrees away from a station to receive the strongest signals?**

A. Long-path
B. Sporadic-E
C. Transequatorial
D. Auroral

**A** Propagation between any two points on the Earth's surface is usually by the shortest direct route, which is a great-circle path between the two points. A great circle is an imaginary line, or ring, drawn around the Earth, formed by a plane passing through the center of the Earth. Unless the two points are opposite each other one way will be shorter than the other will, and this is the usual propagation path. The longer path may be useful for communications when conditions are favorable. Under those conditions, you'll have to point a beam antenna in the direction of the long path.

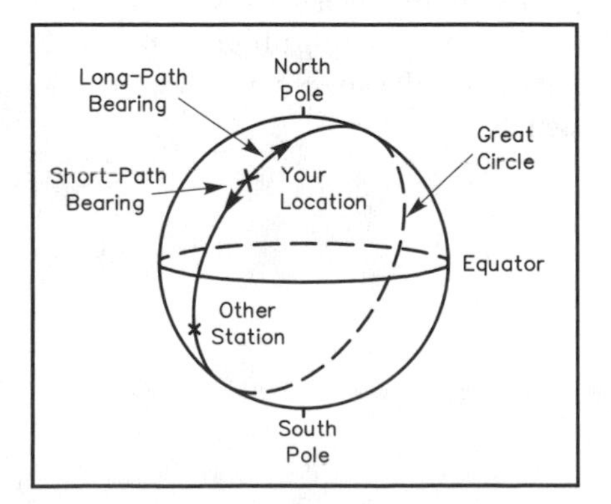


**This sketch of the earth shows a great circle drawn between two stations. The short-path and long-path bearings are shown from the Northern Hemisphere station.**

**E3B05 On what amateur bands can long-path propagation provide signal enhancement?**

A. 160 to 40 meters
B. 30 to 10 meters
C. 160 to 10 meters
D. 6 meters to 2 meters

**C** Long-path propagation can occur on any band that provides ionospheric propagation. That means you might hear this type of signal enhancement on the 160 to 10-meter bands.

**E3B06 What amateur band consistently yields long-path enhancement using a modest antenna of relatively high gain?**

A. 80 meters
B. 20 meters
C. 10 meters
D. 6 meters

**B** You can consistently make use of long-path enhancement on the 20-meter band. All it takes is a modest beam antenna with a relatively high gain compared to a dipole, such as a three-element Yagi or two-element Quad.

**E3B07 What is the typical reason for hearing an echo on the received signal of a station in Europe while directing your HF antenna toward the station?**

A. The station's transmitter has poor frequency stability
B. The station's transmitter is producing spurious emissions
C. Auroral conditions are causing a direct and a long-path reflected signal to be received
D. There are two signals being received, one from the most direct path and one from long-path propagation

**D** If you are in North America, and hear an echo on signals from European stations when your antenna is pointing toward Europe, the echo may be coming in by long-path propagation. Because the signals have to travel much further on the long path, they will be delayed compared to the short-path signals.

**E3B08 What type of propagation is probably occurring if radio signals travel along the terminator between daylight and darkness?**

A. Transequatorial
B. Sporadic-E
C. Long-path
D. Gray-line

**D** The gray line is a band around the Earth that separates daylight from darkness. Astronomers call this line the terminator. Propagation along the gray line is very efficient.

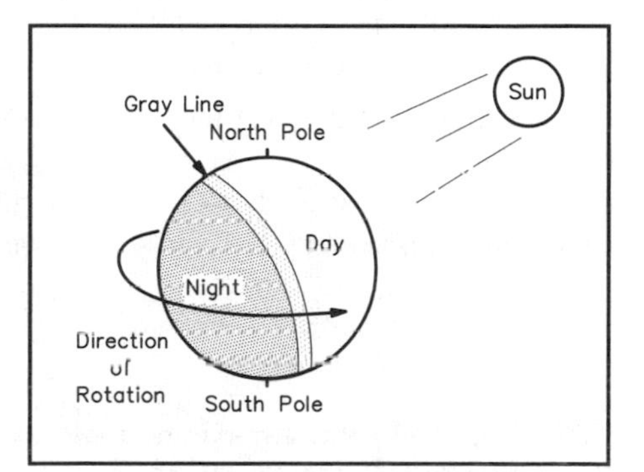


**The gray line is a transition region between daylight and darkness. One side of the Earth is coming into sunrise, and the other side is just past sunset.**

**E3B09 At what time of day is gray-line propagation most prevalent?**

A. Twilight, at sunrise and sunset
B. When the sun is directly above the location of the transmitting station
C. When the sun is directly overhead at the middle of the communications path between the two stations
D. When the sun is directly above the location of the receiving station

**A** Look for gray-line propagation at twilight, around sunrise and sunset.

**E3B10 What is the cause of gray-line propagation?**

A. At midday the sun, being directly overhead, superheats the ionosphere causing increased refraction of radio waves
B. At twilight solar absorption drops greatly while atmospheric ionization is not weakened enough to reduce the MUF
C. At darkness solar absorption drops greatly while atmospheric ionization remains steady
D. At mid afternoon the sun heats the ionosphere, increasing radio wave refraction and the MUF

**B** Propagation along the gray line is very efficient. One major reason for this is that the D-layer, which absorbs HF signals, disappears rapidly on the sunset side of the gray line, and it has not yet built up on the sunrise side. By contrast, the much higher F-layer forms earlier and lasts much longer.

**E3B11** **What communications are possible during gray-line propagation?**

A. Contacts up to 2,000 miles only on the 10-meter band
B. Contacts up to 750 miles on the 6- and 2-meter bands
C. Contacts up to 8,000 to 10,000 miles on three or four HF bands
D. Contacts up to 12,000 to 15,000 miles on the 2 meter and 70 centimeter bands

**C** Gray-line propagation contacts up to 8,000 to 10,000 miles are possible. The three or four lowest-frequency amateur bands (160, 80, 40 and 30 meters) are the most likely to experience gray-line enhancement, because they are the most affected by D-layer absorption.

## E3C Auroral propagation; selective fading; radio-path horizon; take-off angle over flat or sloping terrain; earth effects on propagation

**E3C01** **What effect does auroral activity have upon radio communications?**

A. The readability of SSB signals increases
B. FM communications are clearer
C. CW signals have a clearer tone
D. CW signals have a fluttery tone

**D** Auroral propagation occurs when VHF radio waves are reflected from ionization associated with an auroral curtain. The reflecting properties of an aurora vary rapidly, so signals received via this mode are badly distorted by multipath effects. CW is the most effective mode for auroral work. CW signals have a fluttery tone. The tone is so badly distorted that it is most often a buzzing or hissing sound rather than a pure tone.

**E3C02** **What is the cause of auroral activity?**

A. A high sunspot level
B. A low sunspot level
C. The emission of charged particles from the sun
D. Meteor showers concentrated in the northern latitudes

**C** Aurora results from a large-scale interaction between the magnetic field of the Earth and electrically charged particles arriving from the sun. During times of enhanced solar activity, electrically charged particles are ejected from the surface of the sun. These particles form a solar wind, which travels through space. If this solar wind travels toward Earth, the charged particles may interact with the magnetic field around the Earth causing an aurora.

**E3C03 Where in the ionosphere does auroral activity occur?**

A. At F-region height
B. In the equatorial band
C. At D-region height
D. At E-region height

**D** Auroral activity is caused by ionization at an altitude of about 70 miles above Earth. This is very near the altitude (height) of the ionospheric E layer.

**E3C04 Which emission mode is best for auroral propagation?**

A. CW
B. SSB
C. FM
D. RTTY

**A** Signals received by auroral propagation are badly distorted. For that reason, CW is the most effective mode for auroral work. While SSB may be usable at 6 meters when signals are strong and the operator speaks slowly and distinctly, it is rarely useable at 2 meters or higher frequencies.

**E3C05 What causes selective fading?**

A. Small changes in beam heading at the receiving station
B. Phase differences between radio-wave components of the same transmission, as experienced at the receiving station
C. Large changes in the height of the ionosphere at the receiving station ordinarily occurring shortly after either sunrise or sunset
D. Time differences between the receiving and transmitting stations

**B** Selective fading is a type of fading that occurs when the wave path from a transmitting station to a receiving station varies with very small changes in frequency. It is possible for components of the same signal that are only a few kilohertz apart (such as a carrier and the sidebands in an AM signal) to be acted upon differently by the ionosphere, causing modulation sidebands to arrive at the receiver out of phase. Selective fading occurs because of phase differences between radio-wave components of the same transmission, as experienced at the receiving station. The result is distortion that may range from mild to severe.

**E3C06 How does the bandwidth of a transmitted signal affect selective fading?**

A. It is more pronounced at wide bandwidths
B. It is more pronounced at narrow bandwidths
C. It is the same for both narrow and wide bandwidths
D. The receiver bandwidth determines the selective fading effect

**A** In general, the distortion from selective fading is more pronounced for signals with wider bandwidths. It is worse with FM than it is with AM. SSB and CW signals, which have a narrower bandwidth, are affected less by selective fading.

**E3C07 How much farther does the VHF/UHF radio-path horizon distance exceed the geometric horizon?**

A. By approximately 15% of the distance
B. By approximately twice the distance
C. By approximately one-half the distance
D. By approximately four times the distance

**A** The radio horizon is approximately 15% farther than the geometric horizon. Under normal conditions, the structure of the atmosphere near the Earth causes radio waves to bend into a curved path that keeps them nearer to the Earth than true straight-line travel would.

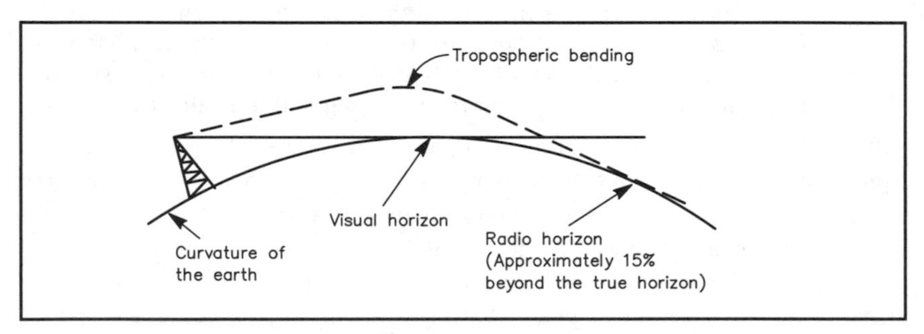


**Under normal conditions tropospheric bending causes VHF and UHF radio wave to be returned to Earth beyond the visible horizon.**

**E3C08 For a 3-element beam antenna with horizontally mounted elements, how does the main lobe takeoff angle vary with height above flat ground?**

A. It increases with increasing height
B. It decreases with increasing height
C. It does not vary with height
D. It depends on E-region height, not antenna height

**B** In general, the radiation takeoff angle from a Yagi antenna with horizontally mounted elements decreases as the antenna height increases above flat ground. If you raise the height of your antenna, the takeoff angle will decrease.

**E3C09 What is the name of the high-angle wave in HF propagation that travels for some distance within the F2 region?**

A. Oblique-angle ray
B. Pedersen ray
C. Ordinary ray
D. Heaviside ray

**B** Radio waves may at times propagate for some distance through the F region of the ionosphere. Studies have shown that a signal radiated at a medium elevation angle sometimes reaches the Earth at a greater distance than a lower-angle wave. This higher-angle wave, called the Pedersen ray, is believed to penetrate the F region farther than lower-angle rays. In the less densely ionized upper edge of the region, the amount of refraction is less, nearly equaling the curvature of the region itself as it encircles the Earth. The drawing shows how the Pedersen ray could provide propagation beyond the normal single-hop distance.

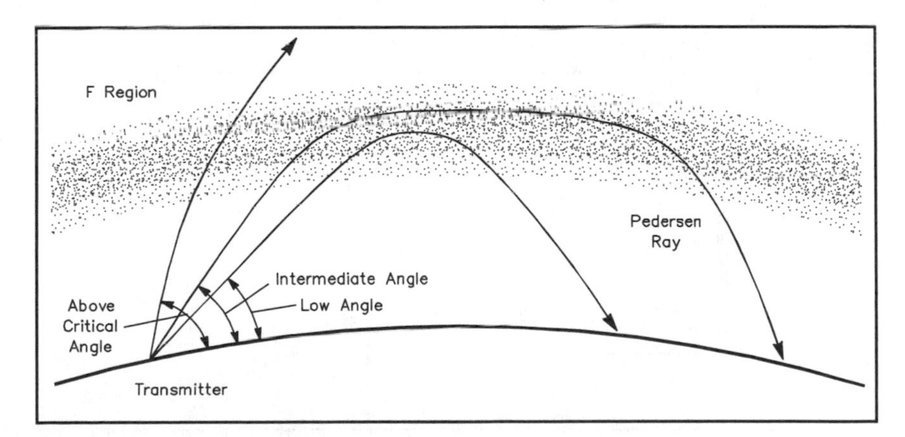


**This diagram shows a radio wave entering the F region at an intermediate angle, which penetrates higher than normal into the F region and then follows that region for some distance before being bent enough to return to Earth. A signal that travels for some distance through the F region is called a Pedersen ray.**

**E3C10 What effect is usually responsible for propagating a VHF signal over 500 miles?**

A. D-region absorption
B. Faraday rotation
C. Tropospheric ducting
D. Moonbounce

**C** VHF propagation is usually limited to distances of approximately 500 miles. At times, however, VHF communications are possible with stations up to 2000 or more miles away. Certain weather conditions cause ducts in the troposphere, simulating propagation within a waveguide. Such ducts cause VHF radio waves to follow the curvature of the Earth for hundreds, or thousands, of miles. This form of propagation is called tropospheric ducting.

**E3C11 For a 3-element beam antenna with horizontally mounted elements, how does the main lobe takeoff angle vary with the downward slope of the ground (moving away from the antenna)?**

A. It increases as the slope gets steeper
B. It decreases as the slope gets steeper
C. It does not depend on the ground slope
D. It depends of the F-region height

**B** A horizontal Yagi antenna installed above a slope will have a lower takeoff angle in the downward direction of the slope than a similar Yagi mounted above flat Earth. The steeper the slope, the lower the takeoff angle will be.

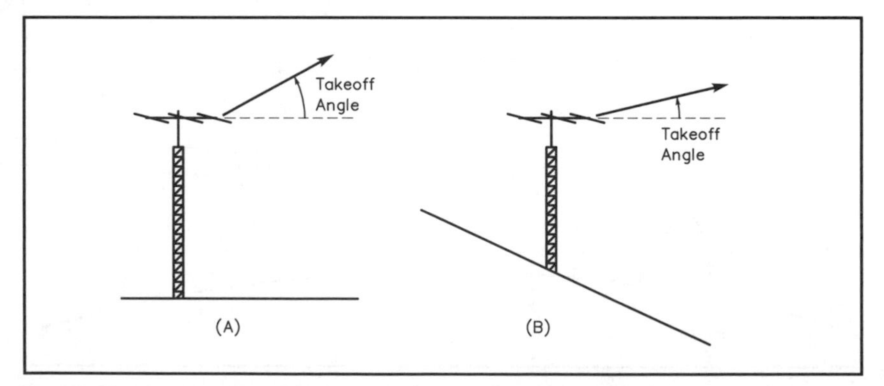


**Part A illustrates the takeoff angle for radio waves leaving a Yagi antenna with horizontal elements over flat ground. Higher antenna elevations result in smaller takeoff angles. Part B shows the takeoff angle for a similar antenna over sloping ground. For steeper slopes away from the front of the antenna, the takeoff angle gets smaller.**

**E3C12 In the northern hemisphere, in which direction should a directional antenna be pointed to take maximum advantage of auroral propagation?**

A. South
B. North
C. East
D. West

**B** Auroras occur over the magnetic poles. In the northern hemisphere, stations point their antennas north and "bounce" their signals off the auroral zone. Operators may have to move their antennas slightly for best results.

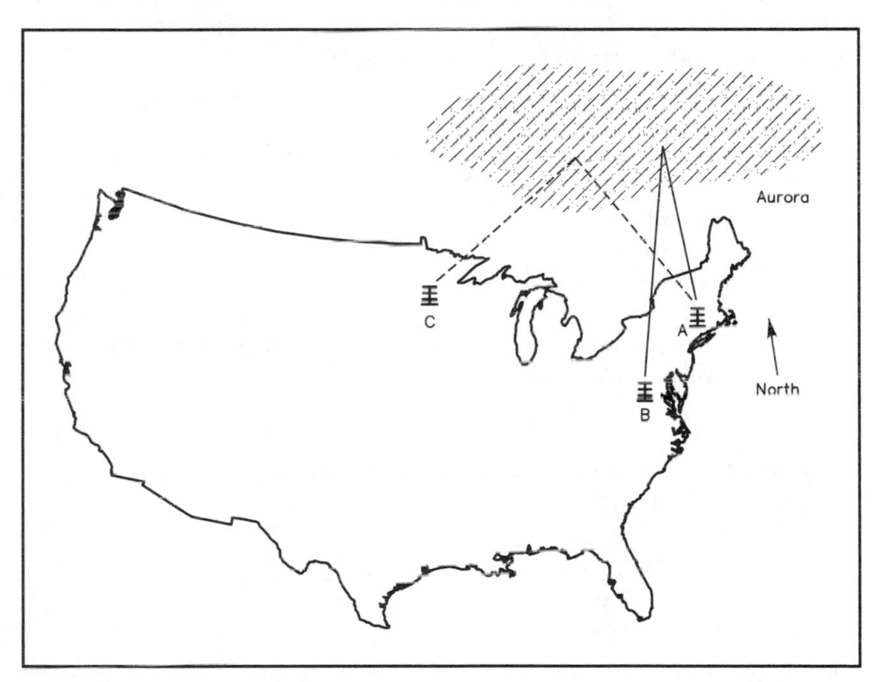


**To work the aurora, stations point their antennas north. Station A may have to beam west of north to work station C.**

**E3C13 As the frequency of a signal is increased, how does its ground wave propagation change?**

A. It increases
B. It decreases
C. It stays the same
D. Radio waves don't propagate along the earth's surface

**B** Ground-wave propagation refers to diffraction of vertically polarized waves. Ground-wave propagation is most noticeable on the AM broadcast band and the 160-meter and 80-meter amateur bands. Practical ground-wave communications distances on these bands often extend to 120 miles or more. Ground-wave loss increases significantly with higher frequencies, so its effects are not noticeable even at 40 meters. Although the term ground-wave propagation is often applied to any short-distance communication, the actual mechanism is unique to the lower frequencies.

**E3C14 What typical polarization does ground-wave propagation have?**

A. Vertical
B. Horizontal
C. Circular
D. Elliptical

**A** As described in the previous question, all ground-wave propagation uses vertical polarization.

**E3C15 Why does the radio-path horizon distance exceed the geometric horizon?**

A. E-region skip
B. D-region skip
C. Auroral skip
D. Radio waves may be bent

**D** Under normal conditions, the structure of the atmosphere near the Earth causes radio waves to bend into a curved path. That effect keeps the radio waves nearer to the Earth than true straight-line travel would.

Subelement **E4**

# Amateur Radio Practices

There will be five questions on your Extra Class examination from the Amateur Radio Practices subelement. These five questions will be taken from the five groups of questions labeled E4A through E4E.

## E4A Test equipment: spectrum analyzers (interpreting spectrum analyzer displays; transmitter output spectrum), logic probes (indications of high and low states in digital circuits; indications of pulse conditions in digital circuits)

**E4A01 How does a spectrum analyzer differ from a conventional time-domain oscilloscope?**

A. A spectrum analyzer measures ionospheric reflection; an oscilloscope displays electrical signals
B. A spectrum analyzer displays signals in the time domain; an oscilloscope displays signals in the frequency domain
C. A spectrum analyzer displays signals in the frequency domain; an oscilloscope displays signals in the time domain
D. A spectrum analyzer displays radio frequencies; an oscilloscope displays audio frequencies

**C** Use a spectrum analyzer to view signals in the frequency domain and an oscilloscope to view them in the time domain. For both instruments the vertical axis is signal amplitude. The difference comes on the horizontal axis. The spectrum analyzer displays frequency along the horizontal axis, and the oscilloscope displays time.

**E4A02 What parameter does the horizontal axis of a spectrum analyzer display?**

A. Amplitude
B. Voltage
C. Resonance
D. Frequency

**D** The spectrum analyzer shows frequency on the horizontal axis.

**This diagram shows how the complex signal at A can viewed in the time domain (oscilloscope) or the frequency domain (spectrum analyzer). At B this information is shown as it would appear on an oscilloscope. The two signals are shown separately here, although the actual oscilloscope display would only show the bold line that represents $f_1 + 2f_1$. At C, the same information is shown as it would appear on a spectrum analyzer screen.**

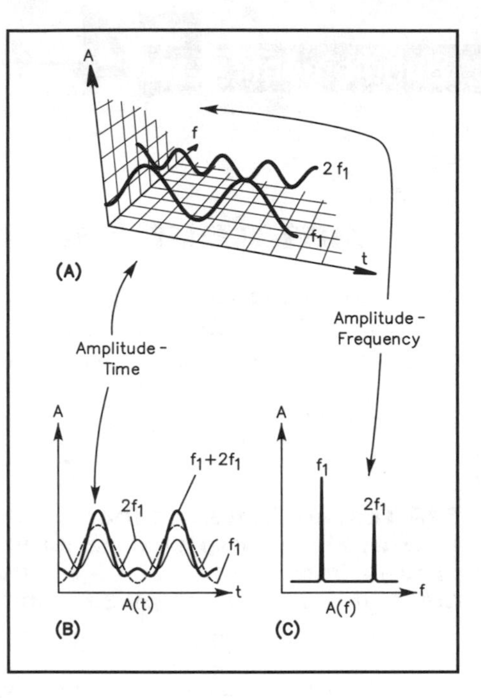


**E4A03 What parameter does the vertical axis of a spectrum analyzer display?**

A. Amplitude
B. Duration
C. Frequency
D. Time

**A** The vertical axis of the spectrum analyzer shows signal amplitude.

**E4A04 Which test instrument is used to display spurious signals from a radio transmitter?**

A. A spectrum analyzer
B. A wattmeter
C. A logic analyzer
D. A time-domain reflectometer

**A** A spectrum analyzer is the best instrument for displaying spurious signals. The other instruments listed here are not suited for that purpose.

**E4A05 Which test instrument is used to display intermodulation distortion products in an SSB transmission?**

A. A wattmeter
B. A spectrum analyzer
C. A logic analyzer
D. A time-domain reflectometer

**B** This question is similar to the previous one in that we are looking at a frequency domain measurement so the spectrum analyzer is the correct choice.

**E4A06 Which of the following is NOT something that could be determined with a spectrum analyzer?**

A. The degree of isolation between the input and output ports of a 2 meter duplexer
B. Whether a crystal is operating on its fundamental or overtone frequency
C. The speed at which a transceiver switches from transmit to receive when being used for packet radio
D. The spectral output of a transmitter

**C** For this question, you are looking for a wrong answer among three correct ones. An oscilloscope would be used to measure the speed at which a transceiver switches from transmit to receive when being used for packet radio. You can't make that measurement with a spectrum analyzer, and thus it represents the correct choice. The other measurements can be made with a spectrum analyzer.

**E4A07 What is an advantage of using a spectrum analyzer to observe the output from a VHF transmitter?**

A. There are no advantages; an inexpensive oscilloscope can display the same information
B. It displays all frequency components of the transmitted signal
C. It displays a time-varying representation of the modulation envelope
D. It costs much less than any other instrumentation useful for such measurements

**B** Because a spectrum analyzer displays amplitude along the frequency axis, it displays all frequency components of the transmitted signal.

**E4A08 What advantage does a logic probe have over a voltmeter for monitoring the status of a logic circuit?**

A. It has many more leads to connect to the circuit than a voltmeter
B. It can be used to test analog and digital circuits
C. It can read logic circuit voltage more accurately than a voltmeter
D. It is smaller and shows a simplified readout

**D** A typical logic probe is smaller than the typical voltmeter. Further, the voltmeter has to indicate voltage levels with a meter or digital display. By contrast, the logic probe only has to show high and low logic levels. Some logic probes also have an indicator to show the presence of pulses.

**E4A09 Which test instrument is used to directly indicate high and low digital voltage states?**

A. An ohmmeter
B. An electroscope
C. A logic probe
D. A Wheatstone bridge

**C** A logic probe is used to directly indicate high and low digital voltage states.

**E4A10 What can a logic probe indicate about a digital logic circuit?**

A. A short-circuit fault
B. An open-circuit fault
C. The resistance between logic modules
D. The high and low logic states

**D** A logic probe measures and displays digital logic states.

**E4A11 Which of the following test instruments can be used to indicate pulse conditions in a digital logic circuit?**

A. A logic probe
B. An ohmmeter
C. An electroscope
D. A Wheatstone bridge

**A** By now you should be able to spot the logic probe as the correct choice. Did you get it right?

**E4A12 Which of the following procedures should you follow when connecting a spectrum analyzer to a transmitter output?**

A. Use high quality coaxial lines
B. Attenuate the transmitter output going to the spectrum analyzer
C. Use a signal divider
D. Match the antenna to the load

**B** Most spectrum analyzers cannot handle signals stronger than 1 watt. Therefore, a signal coming from the transmitter usually needs to pass through an attenuator before it is applied to the spectrum analyzer input.

## E4B Frequency measurement devices (i.e., frequency counter, oscilloscope Lissajous figures, dip meter); meter performance limitations; oscilloscope performance limitations; frequency counter performance limitations

**E4B01 What is a frequency standard?**

A. A frequency chosen by a net control operator for net operations
B. A device used to produce a highly accurate reference frequency
C. A device for accurately measuring frequency to within 1 Hz
D. A device used to generate wide-band random frequencies

**B** A frequency standard is a device used to produce a highly accurate reference frequency.

**E4B02 What factors limit the accuracy, frequency response and stability of a frequency counter?**

A. Phase comparator slew rate, speed of the logic and time base stability
B. Time base accuracy, speed of the logic and time base stability
C. Time base accuracy, temperature coefficient of the logic and time base reactance
D. Number of digits in the readout, external frequency reference and temperature coefficient of the logic

**B** A frequency counter counts the number of pulses applied to its input during a period of time and displays the results. The time base determines the period for counting pulses, so the accuracy of the time base determines the accuracy of the count. The speed of the logic determines the counter's frequency response. The stability of the time base determines the stability of the frequency counter.

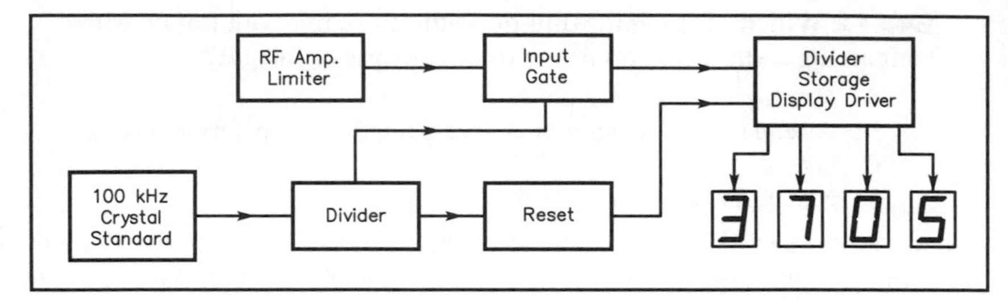


**Block diagram of the basic parts of a frequency counter.**

**E4B03 How can the accuracy of a frequency counter be improved?**

A. By using slower digital logic
B. By improving the accuracy of the frequency response
C. By increasing the accuracy of the time base
D. By using faster digital logic

**C** As you saw in the explanation to the previous question, it is the accuracy of the time base that determines the accuracy of the frequency counter.

**E4B04 If a frequency counter with a specified accuracy of +/– 1.0 ppm reads 146,520,000 Hz, what is the most the actual frequency being measured could differ from the reading?**

A. 165.2 Hz
B. 14.652 kHz
C. 146.52 Hz
D. 1.4652 MHz

**C** Here you have the first of a series of questions where the answer is basically computed the same way. Use the formula

$$\text{Error} = \text{Frequency} \times \text{Accuracy}$$

In this case when you plug in the numbers, you get

$$\text{Error} = 146{,}520{,}000 \text{ Hz} \times \frac{\pm 1}{1{,}000{,}000} = \pm 146.520 \text{ Hz}$$

If you write the frequency in MHz then it will cancel with the ppm. That makes the math a bit easier. Try it on the next problem.

**E4B05 If a frequency counter with a specified accuracy of +/– 0.1 ppm reads 146,520,000 Hz, what is the most the actual frequency being measured could differ from the reading?**

A. 14.652 Hz
B. 0.1 MHz
C. 1.4652 Hz
D. 1.4652 kHz

**A** Use the same formula as you did for the previous question, but use the shortcut this time. You find

$$\text{Error}\left(\text{Hz}\right) = \text{Frequency}\left(\text{MHz}\right) \times \text{Accuracy}\left(\text{ppm}\right) = 146.52 \times \pm 0.1 = \pm 14.652 \text{ Hz}$$

That was a bit easier, wasn't it?

**E4B06 If a frequency counter with a specified accuracy of +/– 10 ppm reads 146,520,000 Hz, what is the most the actual frequency being measured could differ from the reading?**

A. 146.52 Hz
B. 10 Hz
C. 146.52 kHz
D. 1465.20 Hz

**D** Use the same formula and you'll find

$$\text{Error} = 146.52 \text{ MHz} \times \pm 10 \text{ ppm} = \pm 1465.20 \text{ Hz}$$

**E4B07 If a frequency counter with a specified accuracy of +/– 1.0 ppm reads 432,100,000 Hz, what is the most the actual frequency being measured could differ from the reading?**

A. 43.21 MHz
B. 10 Hz
C. 1.0 MHz
D. 432.1 Hz

**D** You know how to use the friendly formula, and when you do you'll find

$$\text{Error} = 432.1 \text{ MHz} \times \pm 1 \text{ ppm} = \pm 432.1 \text{ Hz}$$

It's getting easy, isn't it?

**E4B08 If a frequency counter with a specified accuracy of +/– 0.1 ppm reads 432,100,000 Hz, what is the most the actual frequency being measured could differ from the reading?**

A. 43.21 Hz
B. 0.1 MHz
C. 432.1 Hz
D. 0.2 MHz

**A** Can you do this one in your head? Let's check

$$\text{Error} = 432.1 \text{ MHz} \times \pm 0.1 \text{ ppm} = \pm 43.21 \text{ Hz}$$

You've only got one more of these to do.

**E4B09 If a frequency counter with a specified accuracy of +/– 10 ppm reads 432,100,000 Hz, what is the most the actual frequency being measured could differ from the reading?**

A. 10 MHz
B. 10 Hz
C. 4321 Hz
D. 432.1 Hz

**C** Here you go, and it's the same procedure

$$\text{Error} = 432.1 \text{ MHz} \times \pm 10 \text{ ppm} = \pm 4321 \text{ Hz}$$

**E4B10 If a 100 Hz signal is fed to the horizontal input of an oscilloscope and a 150 Hz signal is fed to the vertical input, what type of Lissajous figure will be displayed on the screen?**

A. A looping pattern with 100 loops horizontally and 150 loops vertically
B. A rectangular pattern 100 mm wide and 150 mm high
C. A looping pattern with 3 loops horizontally and 2 loops vertically
D. An oval pattern 100 mm wide and 150 mm high

**C** The Lissajous figure is a series of loops on an oscilloscope. The number of loops in the vertical and horizontal axes indicates the ratio of the input frequencies. In this case the ratio of the two input signals is 3:2, so you'll see a looping pattern with 3 loops horizontally and 2 loops vertically.

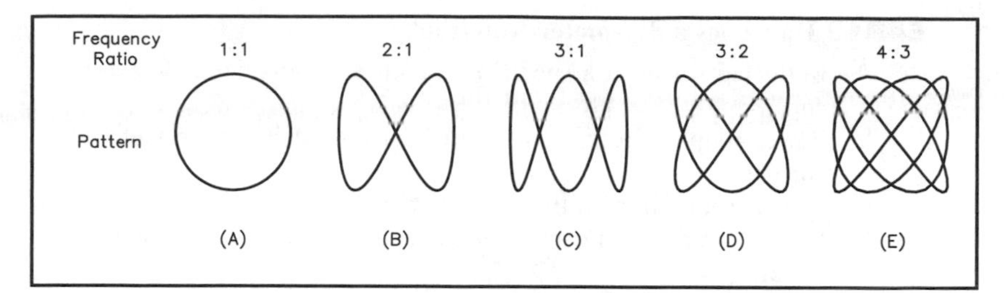


**Lissajous figures as displayed on an oscilloscope. The corresponding frequency ratios between the inputs are shown above each pattern.**

**E4B11 What is a dip-meter?**

A. A field-strength meter
B. An SWR meter
C. A device consisting of a variable frequency LC oscillator and an indicator showing the metered feedback current
D. A marker generator

**C** A dip meter is a variable frequency LC oscillator that is used for measuring resonance in a circuit. When the meter is brought near a circuit resonant at the meter oscillation frequency, that circuit will take some power from the dip meter. Power taken from the oscillator results in a slight drop in the meter reading of the feedback circuit current.

**E4B12 What does a dip-meter do?**

A. It accurately indicates signal strength
B. It measures frequency accurately
C. It measures transmitter output power accurately
D. It gives an indication of the resonant frequency of a nearby circuit

**D** A dip meter gives an indication of the resonant frequency of a nearby circuit.

**E4B13 How does a dip-meter function?**

A. Reflected waves at a specific frequency desensitize a detector coil
B. Power coupled from an oscillator causes a decrease in metered current
C. Power from a transmitter cancels feedback current
D. Harmonics from an oscillator cause an increase in resonant circuit Q

**B** The secret to remembering this answer is to associate "dip" with a decrease in metered current.

**E4B14 What two ways could a dip-meter be used in an amateur station?**

A. To measure resonant frequency of antenna traps and to measure percentage of modulation
B. To measure antenna resonance and to measure percentage of modulation
C. To measure antenna resonance and to measure antenna impedance
D. To measure resonant frequency of antenna traps and to measure a tuned circuit resonant frequency

**D** From looking at this, you should probably gather that a dip meter will measure antenna resonance since this is common to all four choices. In fact, a dip meter is used to measure resonance—as in antenna traps. It won't do those other things.

**E4B15 For best accuracy, how tightly should a dip-meter be coupled with the LC circuit being checked?**

A. As loosely as possible
B. As tightly as possible
C. First loosely, then tightly
D. With a jumper wire between the meter and the circuit to be checked

**A** Although dip meters are relatively easy to use, the touchiest part of their use is coupling the oscillator coil to the circuit being tested. This coupling should be as loose as possible and still provide a definite, but small dip in current when coupled to a circuit resonant at the dip-meter-oscillator frequency.

**E4B16 What factors limit the accuracy, frequency response and stability of an oscilloscope?**

A. Accuracy and linearity of the time base and the linearity and bandwidth of the deflection amplifiers
B. Tube face voltage increments and deflection amplifier voltage
C. Accuracy and linearity of the time base and tube face voltage increments
D. Deflection amplifier output impedance and tube face frequency increments

**A** The accuracy, frequency response and stability of an oscilloscope is determined by the accuracy and linearity of the time base and the linearity and bandwidth of the deflection amplifiers.

**E4B17 What happens in a dip-meter when it is too tightly coupled with the tuned circuit being checked?**

A. Harmonics are generated
B. A less accurate reading results
C. Cross modulation occurs
D. Intermodulation distortion occurs

**B** When a dip-meter it is too tightly coupled with the tuned circuit being checked, a less accurate reading results. Whenever two circuits are coupled, no matter how loosely, each circuit affects the other to some extent. Too tight a coupling almost certainly will yield an inaccurate reading on the dip meter.

**E4B18 What factors limit the accuracy, frequency response and stability of a D'Arsonval-type meter?**

A. Calibration, coil impedance and meter size
B. Calibration, mechanical tolerance and coil impedance
C. Coil impedance, electromagnetic voltage and movement mass
D. Calibration, series resistance and electromagnet current

**B** Since a D'Arsonval meter is one of the analog meters with a mechanical movement, you should expect that the mechanical tolerance would be included as a limiting factor. Calibration and coil impedance are also important factors.

**E4B19 How can the frequency response of an oscilloscope be improved?**

A. By using a triggered sweep and a crystal oscillator as the time base
B. By using a crystal oscillator as the time base and increasing the vertical sweep rate
C. By increasing the vertical sweep rate and the horizontal amplifier frequency response
D. By increasing the horizontal sweep rate and the vertical amplifier frequency response

**D** Time is represented on the horizontal axis of an oscilloscope. Amplitude variations are shown on the vertical axis. Increasing the horizontal sweep rate allows you to see higher frequency components on the screen. Of course, you'll need to increase the vertical amplifier's frequency response to improve the oscilloscope's performance.

## E4C Receiver performance characteristics (i.e., phase noise, desensitization, capture effect, intercept point, noise floor, dynamic range {blocking and IMD}, image rejection, MDS, signal-to-noise-ratio); intermodulation and cross-modulation interference

**E4C01 What is the effect of excessive phase noise in the local oscillator section of a receiver?**

A. It limits the receiver ability to receive strong signals
B. It reduces the receiver sensitivity
C. It decreases the receiver third-order intermodulation distortion dynamic range
D. It allows strong signals on nearby frequencies to interfere with reception of weak signals

**D** One result of receiver phase noise is that as you tune towards a strong signal, the receiver noise floor appears to increase. In other words, you hear an increasing amount of noise in an otherwise quiet receiver as you tune towards the strong signal. This means that strong signals may interfere with the reception of a nearby weak signal.

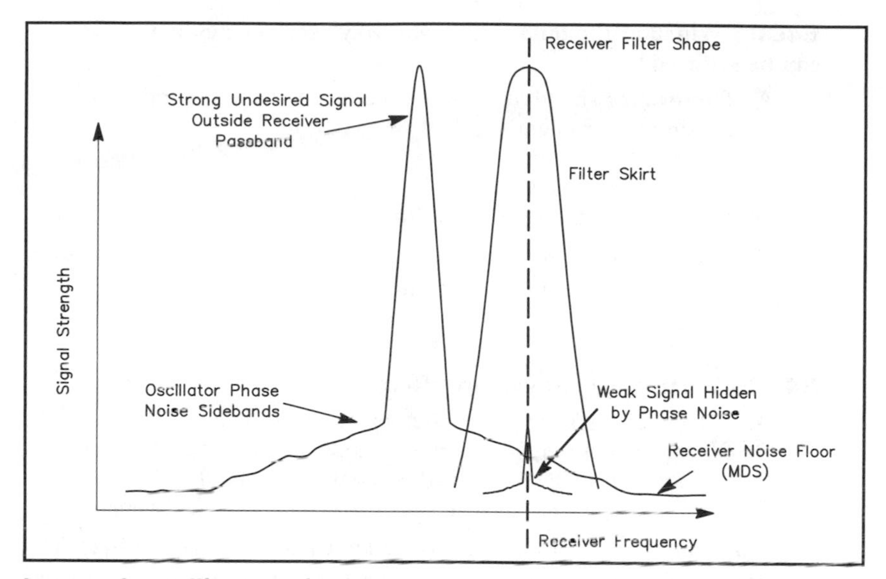


**In a receiver with excessive phase noise, a strong signal near the receiver passband can raise the apparent receiver noise floor in the passband. This increased noise can cover a weak signal that you are trying to receive.**

**E4C02 What is the term for the reduction in receiver sensitivity caused by a strong signal near the received frequency?**

A. Desensitization
B. Quieting
C. Cross-modulation interference
D. Squelch gain rollback

**A** Desensitization is the name given to a reduction in receiver sensitivity that is caused by a strong signal near the received frequency

**E4C03 Which of the following can cause receiver desensitization?**

A. Audio gain adjusted too low
B. Strong adjacent-channel signals
C. Audio bias adjusted too high
D. Squelch gain adjusted too low

**B** Receiver desensitization can occur when a strong signal is close in frequency to the desired signal.

**E4C04 Which of the following is one way receiver desensitization can be reduced?**

A. Improve the shielding between the receiver and the transmitter causing the problem
B. Increase the transmitter audio gain
C. Decrease the receiver squelch level
D. Increase the receiver bandwidth

**A** One way to reduce receiver desensitization is to improve the shielding between the receiver and the transmitter causing the problem.

**E4C05 What is the FM capture effect?**

A. All signals on a frequency are demodulated by an FM receiver
B. All signals on a frequency are demodulated by an AM receiver
C. The strongest signal received is the only demodulated signal
D. The weakest signal received is the only demodulated signal

**C** FM receivers exhibit a characteristic known as the capture effect. The loudest signal received, even if it is only two or three times (3 to 5 dB) stronger than other signals on the same frequency, will be the only signal demodulated. This can be an advantage if you want to receive the strong signal. However, the capture effect can prevent you from hearing a weaker signal in the presence of a stronger one.

**E4C06 What is the term for the blocking of one FM phone signal by another, stronger FM phone signal?**

A. Desensitization
B. Cross-modulation interference
C. Capture effect
D. Frequency discrimination

**C** This is just another was of asking the previous question. You should be able to pick out capture effect as the correct answer.

**E4C07 What is meant by the noise floor of a receiver?**

A. The weakest signal that can be detected under noisy atmospheric conditions
B. The amount of phase noise generated by the receiver local oscillator
C. The minimum level of noise that will overload the receiver RF amplifier stage
D. The weakest signal that can be detected above the receiver internal noise

**D** The noise floor of a receiver represents the level of a signal that equals the noise level generated within the receiver. It is the smallest input-signal level that can be detected, and is determined by the receiver's internal electronics.

**E4C08 What is the blocking dynamic range for a receiver that has an 8-dB noise figure and an IF bandwidth of 500 Hz when the blocking level (1-dB compression point) is –20 dBm?**

A. –119 dBm
B. 119 dB
C. 146 dB
D. –146 dBm

**B** The blocking dynamic range of a receiver is the difference between the noise floor and the blocking level of that same receiver. You are given the blocking level in dBm (dB compared to a milliwatt), but you'll have to compute the level (also in dBm) of the receiver's noise floor. Then you'll take the difference of those two levels.

Start with the theoretically lowest receiver noise floor in a 1-Hz bandwidth, which is –174 dBm. Next, adjust the theoretical minimum for the bandwidth of the receiver. Since the bandwidth 500 times greater (500 Hz instead of 1 Hz), the noise level will be 500 times greater. Expressed in dB, this is 10 log (500) or 27 dB. Add 27 dB to –174 dBm and you get –147 dBm, which is the ideal noise floor for a 500-Hz bandwidth receiver. Ideal is not real world, and you'll need to account for that difference. The noise figure of this receiver is 8 dB so add that to –147 dBm to get –139 dBm for the noise floor of this receiver.

The blocking dynamic range of your receiver is the difference between the noise floor (–139 dBm) and the receiver blocking level (–20 dBm), which is 119 dB. The range is in dB, even though noise floor and blocking level are in dBm. (When you take the difference of the two levels, the reference to 1 milliwatt—dBm—drops out and leaves you with dB.) Also the range will always be expressed as a positive number.

**E4C09 What is meant by the dynamic range of a communications receiver?**

A. The number of kHz between the lowest and the highest frequency to which the receiver can be tuned
B. The maximum possible undistorted audio output of the receiver, referenced to one milliwatt
C. The ratio between the minimum discernible signal and the largest tolerable signal without causing audible distortion products
D. The difference between the lowest-frequency signal and the highest- frequency signal detectable without moving the frequency control

**C** Dynamic range refers to the ability of a receiver to tolerate strong signals. A general definition describes dynamic range as the ratio between the minimum discernible signal and the largest tolerable signal without causing audible distortion products.

**E4C10 What type of problems are caused by poor dynamic range in a communications receiver?**

A. Cross modulation of the desired signal and desensitization from strong adjacent signals
B. Oscillator instability requiring frequent retuning, and loss of ability to recover the opposite sideband, should it be transmitted
C. Cross modulation of the desired signal and insufficient audio power to operate the speaker
D. Oscillator instability and severe audio distortion of all but the strongest received signals

**A** A receiver with poor IMD dynamic range will exhibit cross modulation of the desired signal by strong adjacent signals. One with poor blocking dynamic range will suffer from desensitization.

**E4C11 If you measured the MDS of a receiver, what would you be measuring?**

A. The meter display sensitivity (MDS), or the responsiveness of the receiver S-meter to all signals
B. The minimum discernible signal (MDS), or the weakest signal that the receiver can detect
C. The minimum distorting signal (MDS), or the strongest signal the receiver can detect without overloading
D. The maximum detectable spectrum (MDS), or the lowest to highest frequency range of the receiver

**B** The minimum discernible signal (MDS) of a receiver is defined as the smallest input-signal level that can be detected.

**E4C12 How does intermodulation interference between two repeater transmitters usually occur?**

A. When the signals from the transmitters are reflected out of phase from airplanes passing overhead
B. When they are in close proximity and the signals mix in one or both of their final amplifiers
C. When they are in close proximity and the signals cause feedback in one or both of their final amplifiers
D. When the signals from the transmitters are reflected in phase from airplanes passing overhead

**B** Intermodulation can be a problem in transmitters as well as receivers. This can happen when two transmitters are in close proximity and the signals mix in one or both of their final amplifiers. This can result in severe interference.

**E4C13 How can intermodulation interference between two repeater transmitters in close proximity often be reduced or eliminated?**

A. By using a Class C final amplifier with high driving power
B. By installing a terminated circulator or ferrite isolator in the feed line to the transmitter and duplexer
C. By installing a band-pass filter in the antenna feed line
D. By installing a low-pass filter in the antenna feed line

**B** Circulators and isolators are usually highly effective in eliminating intermodulation between two transmitters. They work like one-way valves, allowing energy to flow from the transmitter to the antenna while greatly reducing energy flow in the opposite direction. One might think that installing some type of filter would cure the problem, but that's not true in this case because the offending transmitter will have a very strong signal in the desired pass band.

**E4C14 If a receiver tuned to 146.70 MHz receives an intermodulation-product signal whenever a nearby transmitter transmits on 146.52 MHz, what are the two most likely frequencies for the other interfering signal?**

A. 146.34 MHz and 146.61 MHz
B. 146.88 MHz and 146.34 MHz
C. 146.10 MHz and 147.30 MHz
D. 73.35 MHz and 239.40 MHz

**A** The strongest IMD frequency components come from the equations

$$f_{IMD} = 2f_1 \pm f_2 \text{ and } f_{IMD} = 2f_2 \pm f_1$$

You are given $f_1 = 146.52$ MHz and $f_{IMD} = 146.70$ MHz. Further, the sums fall into the UHF range. For that reason you'll only need to look at the differences. Solve for $f_2$ and you'll find

$$f_2 = 2f_1 - f_{IMD} = 2 \times 146.52 \text{ MHz} - 146.70 \text{ MHz} = 146.34 \text{ MHz and}$$

$$f_2 = \left(f_1 + f_{IMD}\right)/2 = \left(146.52 \text{ MHz} + 146.70 \text{ MHz}\right)/2 = 146.61 \text{ MHz}$$

**E4C15 If the signals of two transmitters mix together in one or both of their final amplifiers and unwanted signals at the sum and difference frequencies of the original signals are generated, what is this called?**

A. Amplifier desensitization
B. Neutralization
C. Adjacent channel interference
D. Intermodulation interference

**D** Intermodulation interference occurs when the signals of two transmitters mix together in one or both of their final amplifiers and unwanted signals at the sum and difference frequencies of the original signals are generated. The other effects are all real electronic terms but they do not apply here.

**E4C16 What is cross-modulation interference?**

A. Interference between two transmitters of different modulation type
B. Interference caused by audio rectification in the receiver preamp
C. Harmonic distortion of the transmitted signal
D. Modulation from an unwanted signal is heard in addition to the desired signal

**D** The term "cross-modulation" is used when modulation from an unwanted signal is heard in addition to the desired signal.

**E4C17 What causes intermodulation in an electronic circuit?**

A. Too little gain
B. Lack of neutralization
C. Nonlinear circuits or devices
D. Positive feedback

**C** In a linear circuit, the output is a faithful representation of the input. Nonlinearities in either circuits or devices cause distortion. This nonlinearity is the cause of intermodulation in an electronic circuit.

**E4C18 What two factors determine the sensitivity of a receiver?**

A. Dynamic range and third-order intercept
B. Cost and availability
C. Intermodulation distortion and dynamic range
D. Bandwidth and noise figure

**D** The sensitivity or MDS (minimum discernible signal) of a receiver depends on two factors: noise figure and the bandwidth of the system.

**E4C19 What is the limiting condition for sensitivity in a communications receiver?**

A. The noise floor of the receiver
B. The power-supply output ripple
C. The two-tone intermodulation distortion
D. The input impedance to the detector

**A** You are looking for a factor that will limit the ability of a receiver to detect weak signals. From the explanation to the previous question, you know that internal receiver noise and bandwidth determines the sensitivity. In this case, the noise floor will set the lower limit of being able to discern a weak signal.

**E4C20 Selectivity can be achieved in the front-end circuitry of a communications receiver by using what means?**

A. An audio filter
B. An additional RF amplifier stage
C. A preselector
D. An additional IF amplifier stage

**C** The front end of a communications receiver is the circuitry closest to the input jack. This typically includes both selectivity and amplification. An amplifier does not have the ability to choose between wanted and unwanted signals—it must be done by providing selectivity. Selectivity can be achieved in the front-end circuitry of a communications receiver by using a preselector.

**E4C21 What degree of selectivity is desirable in the IF circuitry of an amateur RTTY receiver?**

A. 100 Hz
B. 300 Hz
C. 6000 Hz
D. 2400 Hz

**B** You'll want a filter that's wide enough to pass the mark and space frequencies along with their respective sidebands. These are spaced less than 200 Hz apart in the usual RTTY signal. You'll want a little bit extra bandwidth to allow for tuning error. Don't make it too wide or you let through noise and interference.

**E4C22 What degree of selectivity is desirable in the IF circuitry of a single-sideband phone receiver?**

A. 1 kHz
B. 2.4 kHz
C. 4.2 kHz
D. 4.8 kHz

**B** Intelligibility of a voice signal is mostly contained in the range of 300 Hz to 2700 Hz. While wider filters may increase fidelity (depends on the transmitted signal), they're not necessary and they'll allow more noise and interference to pass.

**E4C23 What is an undesirable effect of using too wide a filter bandwidth in the IF section of a receiver?**

A. Output-offset overshoot
B. Filter ringing
C. Thermal-noise distortion
D. Undesired signals will reach the audio stage

**D** Some operators like to use wide filters when tuning or monitoring a band that is quiet in terms of noise and in terms of the number of transmitting stations. Few want wider filters when the band is active and many stations are transmitting. A filter that is wider than necessary allows extra signals (and noise) to pass through the IF to the detector and on to the audio output.

**E4C24 How should the filter bandwidth of a receiver IF section compare with the bandwidth of a received signal?**

A. It should be slightly greater than the received-signal bandwidth
B. It should be approximately half the received-signal bandwidth
C. It should be approximately twice the received-signal bandwidth
D. It should be approximately four times the received-signal bandwidth

**A** If the IF filter is too wide, it lets in extra noise and interference. If the IF filter is too narrow, it will limit the intelligibility of the desired signal. The correct compromise is an IF bandwidth just slightly larger than the signal bandwidth.

**E4C25 What degree of selectivity is desirable in the IF section of an FM phone receiver?**

A. 1 kHz
B. 2.4 kHz
C. 4.2 kHz
D. 15 kHz

**D** You'll want the filter to be approximately the bandwidth of the FM phone signal, which is 15 kHz.

**E4C26 In a receiver, if the third-order intermodulation products have a power of –70 dBm when using two test tones at –30 dBm, what is the third-order intercept point?**

A. –20 dBm
B. –10 dBm
C. 0 dBm
D. +10 dBm

**B** The third-order intercept point of a receiver is that input level where third-order IMD products equal the desired (first-order) output level. Real-world receivers will be in compression or saturation before the input rises to that level, and for that reason you have to compute the intercept point. You can't measure it directly.

You can see how this works in the drawing. The desired output increases 1 dB for a 1-dB increase of the input. The second-order IMD increases 2 dB, and third order goes up 3 dB for each 1 dB increase in input level.

From the information given, you can calculate the third-order intercept point using the formula:

$$IP_3 = \frac{3 \times P_A - P_{IM_3}}{3-1} = \frac{3 \times \left(-30 \text{ dBm}\right) - \left(-70 \text{ dBm}\right)}{2} = \frac{-20 \text{ dBm}}{2} = -10 \text{ dBm}$$

Where:

$IP_3$ is the third-order intercept point

$P_A$ is the input power of one of the signals on the receiver input

$P_{IM}$ is the power of the intermodulation distortion (IMD) products

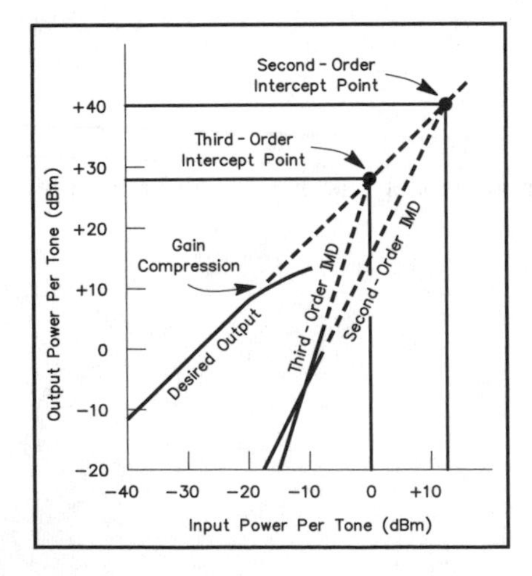


**This graph shows how the output power of the desired signal and the output power of the second and third-order distortion products vary with changes of input power. The input consists of two equal-power sine-wave signals. Higher intercept points represent better receiver IMD performance.**

**E4C27 In a receiver, if the second-order intermodulation products have a power of –70 dBm when using two test tones at –30 dBm, what is the second-order intercept point?**

A. –20 dBm
B. –10 dBm
C. 0 dBm
D. +10 dBm

**D** The second-order intercept point of a receiver is that input level where second-order IMD products equal the desired (first-order) output level. This is much like the previous question, but you're dealing here with second-order IMD. For that reason the formula is a little bit different. In this case it is:

$$IP_2 = \frac{2 \times P_A - P_{IM_2}}{2 - 1} = \frac{2 \times (-30 \text{ dBm}) - (-70 \text{ dBm})}{1} = +10 \text{ dBm}$$

Where:

$IP_2$ is the second-order intercept point
$P_A$ is the input power of one of the signals on the receiver input
$P_{IM}$ is the power of the intermodulation distortion (IMD) products

## E4D Noise suppression: vehicular system noise; electronic motor noise; static; line noise

**E4D01 What is one of the most significant problems associated with reception in HF transceivers?**

A. Ignition noise
B. Doppler shift
C. Radar interference
D. Mechanical vibrations

**A** Automotive ignition noise can be a serious problem for HF receivers.

**E4D02 What is the proper procedure for suppressing electrical noise in a mobile transceiver?**

A. Follow the vehicle manufacturer's recommended procedures
B. Insulate all plane sheet metal surfaces from each other
C. Apply antistatic spray liberally to all non-metallic surfaces
D. Install filter capacitors in series with all DC wiring

**A** Modern automobiles use sophisticated, high-energy, computer controlled, electronic-ignition systems. Solutions to noise problems that were effective for older vehicles may not work at all on a modern auto. In fact, those "fixes" may impair proper engine performance. For that reason, the first rule when installing a mobile transceiver in a modern vehicle is to follow the manufacturer's recommended procedures.

**E4D03 Where should ferrite beads be installed to suppress ignition noise in a mobile transceiver?**

A. In the resistive high-voltage cable
B. Between the starter solenoid and the starter motor
C. In the primary and secondary ignition leads
D. In the antenna lead to the transceiver

**C** To suppress the ignition noise, the ferrite beads need to be installed in the primary and secondary ignition leads.

**E4D04 How can alternator whine be minimized?**

A. By connecting the radio's power leads to the battery by the longest possible path
B. By connecting the radio's power leads to the battery by the shortest possible path
C. By installing a high-pass filter in series with the radio's DC power lead to the vehicle's electrical system
D. By installing filter capacitors in series with the DC power lead

**B** Alternator whine is a common form of conducted interference, and can affect both transmitting and receiving. This kind of noise can be minimized by connecting the radio power leads directly to the battery.

**E4D05 How can conducted and radiated noise caused by an automobile alternator be suppressed?**

A. By installing filter capacitors in series with the DC power lead and by installing a blocking capacitor in the field lead
B. By connecting the radio to the battery by the longest possible path and installing a blocking capacitor in both leads
C. By installing a high-pass filter in series with the radio's power lead and a low-pass filter in parallel with the field lead
D. By connecting the radio's power leads directly to the battery and by installing coaxial capacitors in the alternator leads

**D** Conducted and radiated noise caused by an automobile alternator can be suppressed by connecting the radio's power leads directly to the battery and by installing coaxial capacitors in the alternator leads.

**E4D06 How can noise from an electric motor be suppressed?**

A. Install a ferrite bead on the AC line used to power the motor
B. Install a brute-force, AC-line filter in series with the motor leads
C. Install a bypass capacitor in series with the motor leads
D. Use a ground-fault current interrupter in the circuit used to power the motor

**B** A brute-force, AC-line filter in series with the motor leads can suppress noise from an electric motor

**E4D07 What is a major cause of atmospheric static?**

A. Sunspots
B. Thunderstorms
C. Airplanes
D. Meteor showers

**B** Thunderstorms are a major cause of atmospheric static. The other options presented here are not.

**E4D08 How can it be determined if line-noise interference is being generated within your home?**

A. By checking the power-line voltage with a time-domain reflectometer
B. By observing the AC power line waveform with an oscilloscope
C. By turning off the AC power line main circuit breaker and listening on a battery-operated radio
D. By observing the AC power line voltage with a spectrum analyzer

**C** If there is no line noise when the AC to the home is turned off, then one should look there for the noise source.

**E4D09 What type of signal is picked up by electrical wiring near a radio transmitter?**

A. A common-mode signal at the frequency of the radio transmitter
B. An electrical-sparking signal
C. A differential-mode signal at the AC power line frequency
D. Harmonics of the AC power line frequency

**A** This answer is as easy as it seems. If operating properly, the signal will be at the frequency of the transmitter. "Common mode" means that the electrical wiring is working like an antenna.

**E4D10 Which of the following types of equipment would be least useful in locating power line noise?**

A. An AM receiver with a directional antenna
B. An FM receiver with a directional antenna
C. A hand-held RF sniffer
D. An ultrasonic transducer, amplifier and parabolic reflector

**B** For this one, you are looking for the worst device to use. The FM receiver is the least sensitive to noise, and that makes it the worst option given and therefore the correct answer.

## E4E Component mounting techniques (i.e., surface, dead bug (raised), circuit board; direction finding: techniques and equipment; fox hunting

**E4E01 What circuit construction technique uses leadless components mounted between circuit board pads?**

A. Raised mounting
B. Integrated circuit mounting
C. Hybrid device mounting
D. Surface mounting

**D** Surface mounting uses leadless components mounted between circuit board pads. The other device mounting techniques generally have leads attached to the devices.

**E4E02 What is the main drawback of a wire-loop antenna for direction finding?**

A. It has a bidirectional pattern broadside to the loop
B. It is non-rotatable
C. It receives equally well in all directions
D. It is practical for use only on VHF bands

**A** A wire-loop antenna has a bidirectional pattern. That means that it will not uniquely identify the direction from which a signal is arriving.

**E4E03 What pattern is desirable for a direction-finding antenna?**

A. One which is non-cardioid
B. One with good front-to-back and front-to-side ratio
C. One with good top-to-bottom and side-to-side ratio
D. One with shallow nulls

**B** For direction finding, one wishes to have an antenna with a high directivity or a well-defined null. This occurs when one has an antenna with a good front-to-back ratio and front-to-side ratio.

**E4E04 What is the triangulation method of direction finding?**

A. The geometric angle of ground waves and sky waves from the signal source are used to locate the source

B. A fixed receiving station plots three beam headings from the signal source on a map

C. Beam antenna headings from several receiving stations are used to plot the signal source on a map

D. A fixed receiving station uses three different antennas to plot the location of the signal source

**C** To perform triangulation, one combines azimuth measurements from several diverse physical locations to determine the transmitter location. These azimuths or bearings are typically drawn on a map and where they cross is the location of the transmitter.

**E4E05 Why is an RF attenuator desirable in a receiver used for direction finding?**

A. It narrows the bandwidth of the received signal

B. It eliminates the effects of isotropic radiation

C. It reduces loss of received signals caused by antenna pattern nulls

D. It prevents receiver overload from extremely strong signals

**D** If you think about it, the receiver in the "fox hunt" will need to work with signals over a large power range. Since the receiver may have a limited reception signal range, an attenuator makes a convenient helper in extending the dynamic range of the receiver by attenuating signals from a nearby fox.

**E4E06 What is a sense antenna?**

A. A vertical antenna added to a loop antenna to produce a cardioid reception pattern

B. A horizontal antenna added to a loop antenna to produce a cardioid reception pattern

C. A vertical antenna added to an Adcock antenna to produce a omnidirectional reception pattern

D. A horizontal antenna added to an Adcock antenna to produce a omnidirectional reception pattern

**A** A sense antenna (sometimes called a sensing element) is a vertical antenna that is added to a loop antenna, and together they produce a cardioid reception pattern. This pattern is useful for direction finding.

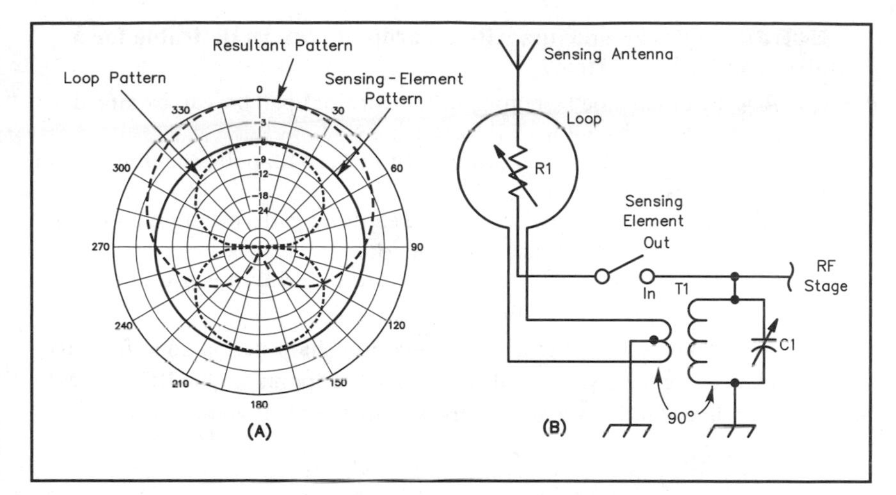


**At A, the directivity pattern of a loop antenna with sensing element. At B is a circuit for combining the signals from the two elements. C1 is adjusted for resonance with T1 at the operating frequency.**

**E4E07 What is a loop antenna?**

A. A large circularly-polarized antenna
B. A small coil of wire tightly wound around a toroidal ferrite core
C. Several turns of wire wound in the shape of a large open coil
D. Any antenna coupled to a feed line through an inductive loop of wire

**C** This question is another one that is as simple as it looks. A loop antenna consists of one or more turns of wire wound in the shape of a large open coil.

**E4E08 How can the output voltage of a loop antenna be increased?**

A. By reducing the permeability of the loop shield
B. By increasing the number of wire turns in the loop and reducing the area of the loop structure
C. By reducing either the number of wire turns in the loop or the area of the loop structure
D. By increasing either the number of wire turns in the loop or the area of the loop structure

**D** The strength of the signal coming from a loop antenna is proportional to the cross-sectional area of the antenna and the number of turns—the voltage increases as either of these parameters increase.

**E4E09** **Why is an antenna with a cardioid pattern desirable for a direction-finding system?**

A. The broad-side responses of the cardioid pattern can be aimed at the desired station
B. The deep null of the cardioid pattern can pinpoint the direction of the desired station
C. The sharp peak response of the cardioid pattern can pinpoint the direction of the desired station
D. The high-radiation angle of the cardioid pattern is useful for short- distance direction finding

**B** An antenna with either a sharp peak or a sharp null is good for direction finding because the peak or null can be used to "point" to the RF source. In the cardioid pattern, there is a deep, narrow null in one direction.

**E4E10** **What type of terrain can cause errors in direction finding?**

A. Homogeneous terrain
B. Smooth grassy terrain
C. Varied terrain
D. Terrain with no buildings or mountains

**C** Errors in direction finding will come from reflections off objects and terrain. Varied terrain will tend to cause multipath (signals seem to arrive from multiple directions). As you can imagine, this can confuse your direction finding efforts.

**E4E11** **What is the amateur station activity known as fox hunting?**

A. Attempting to locate a hidden transmitter by using receivers and direction-finding techniques
B. Attempting to locate a hidden receiver by using receivers and direction- finding techniques
C. Assisting government agents with tracking transmitter collars worn by foxes
D. Assembling stations using generators and portable antennas to test emergency communications skills

**A** Participants in automobiles or on foot use portable receivers and direction-finding techniques to locate hidden transmitters. This fun activity is the sport known as fox hunting.

# Subelement E5

# Electrical Principles

There will be nine questions on your Extra Class examination from the Electrical Principles subelement. These nine questions will be taken from the nine groups of questions labeled E5A through E5I.

## E5A Characteristics of resonant circuits: Series resonance (capacitor and inductor to resonate at a specific frequency); Parallel resonance (capacitor and inductor to resonate at a specific frequency); half-power bandwidth

**E5A01 What can cause the voltage across reactances in series to be larger than the voltage applied to them?**

A. Resonance
B. Capacitance
C. Conductance
D. Resistance

**A** At resonance, the voltage across the inductor and capacitor in a series circuit can be many times greater than the applied voltage. In practical circuits, it can be ten or a hundred times greater. How can this be? The reason is that the voltage across the capacitor is 180 degrees out of phase with the voltage across the inductor. In other words, when the voltage across the capacitor is at a positive peak, the voltage across the inductor is at a negative peak.

**E5A02 What is resonance in an electrical circuit?**

A. The highest frequency that will pass current
B. The lowest frequency that will pass current
C. The frequency at which capacitive reactance equals inductive reactance
D. The frequency at which power factor is at a minimum

**C** At resonance, capacitive reactance equals inductive reactance and vice versa.

**E5A03 What are the conditions for resonance to occur in an electrical circuit?**

A. The power factor is at a minimum
B. Inductive and capacitive reactances are equal
C. The square root of the sum of the capacitive and inductive reactance is equal to the resonant frequency
D. The square root of the product of the capacitive and inductive reactance is equal to the resonant frequency

**B** For resonance to occur, the inductive reactance must equal the capacitive reactance.

**E5A04 When the inductive reactance of an electrical circuit equals its capacitive reactance, what is this condition called?**

A. Reactive quiescence
B. High Q
C. Reactive equilibrium
D. Resonance

**D** Here you have another restatement of the definition of resonance so you probably picked the right choice. At resonance capacitive and inductive reactances are equal.

**E5A05 What is the magnitude of the impedance of a series R-L-C circuit at resonance?**

A. High, as compared to the circuit resistance
B. Approximately equal to capacitive reactance
C. Approximately equal to inductive reactance
D. Approximately equal to circuit resistance

**D** In a series circuit at resonance, the reactance of L and C cancel so all that is left is the circuit resistance.

**E5A06 What is the magnitude of the impedance of a circuit with a resistor, an inductor and a capacitor all in parallel, at resonance?**

A. Approximately equal to circuit resistance
B. Approximately equal to inductive reactance
C. Low, as compared to the circuit resistance
D. Approximately equal to capacitive reactance

**A** Just because the reference has changed to a parallel circuit, the basic principle does not change. In a parallel circuit at resonance, the L and C reactances mostly cancel so all that is left is the circuit resistance.

**E5A07 What is the magnitude of the current at the input of a series R-L-C circuit at resonance?**

A. It is at a minimum
B. It is at a maximum
C. It is DC
D. It is zero

**B** Current in a series circuit is maximum at resonance.

**E5A08 What is the magnitude of the circulating current within the components of a parallel L-C circuit at resonance?**

A. It is at a minimum
B. It is at a maximum
C. It is DC
D. It is zero

**B** The circulating current within the components of a parallel L-C circuit are maximum at resonance. Earlier you saw a similar situation involving the voltage across the components of a series L-C circuit. These currents are not flowing *through* the circuit; they are circulating *within* it. As you will see in the next question, current through the circuit is minimum at resonance. This is possible because the current in the inductance is 180 degrees out of phase with the current in the capacitance. In other words, when one is at a positive peak, the other is at a negative peak.

**E5A09 What is the magnitude of the current at the input of a parallel R-L-C circuit at resonance?**

A. It is at a minimum
B. It is at a maximum
C. It is DC
D. It is zero

**A** At resonance, the input current to a parallel R-L-C circuit is at a minimum. The current will not be zero, because of resistance in the circuit.

**E5A10 What is the relationship between the current through a resonant circuit and the voltage across the circuit?**

A. The voltage leads the current by 90 degrees
B. The current leads the voltage by 90 degrees
C. The voltage and current are in phase
D. The voltage and current are 180 degrees out of phase

**C** At resonance, the current and voltage are in phase. Also at resonance, the reactances are equal and they frequently say that these reactances cancel each other. We'll be seeing more of current and voltage phase shifts caused by reactance later in this chapter.

**E5A11 What is the relationship between the current into (or out of) a parallel resonant circuit and the voltage across the circuit?**

A. The voltage leads the current by 90 degrees
B. The current leads the voltage by 90 degrees
C. The voltage and current are in phase
D. The voltage and current are 180 degrees out of phase

**C** At resonance, the current and voltage are in phase. See the explanation for the previous question.

**E5A12 What is the half-power bandwidth of a parallel resonant circuit that has a resonant frequency of 1.8 MHz and a Q of 95?**

A. 18.9 kHz
B. 1.89 kHz
C. 189 Hz
D. 58.7 kHz

**A** This is the first of several questions dealing with the bandwidth of resonant circuits. The relationship between bandwidth, W, resonant frequency, $f_r$, and quality factor, Q, is:

$$W = \frac{f_r}{Q}$$

Using the numbers in the question you'll find

$$W = \frac{1.8 \times 10^6 \text{ Hz}}{95} = 18.9 \times 10^3 \text{ Hz} = 18.9 \text{ kHz}$$

**E5A13 What is the half-power bandwidth of a parallel resonant circuit that has a resonant frequency of 7.1 MHz and a Q of 150?**

A. 211 kHz
B. 16.5 kHz
C. 47.3 kHz
D. 21.1 kHz

**C** Use the same relationship given the previous question to solve for the bandwidth. This time instead of using Hz, use kHz for the resonant frequency. That will give you the answer directly in kHz. Using the numbers given, compute the bandwidth

$$W = \frac{f_r}{Q} = \frac{7100 \text{ kHz}}{150} = 47.3 \text{ kHz}$$

**E5A14 What is the half-power bandwidth of a parallel resonant circuit that has a resonant frequency of 14.25 MHz and a Q of 150?**

A. 95 kHz
B. 10.5 kHz
C. 10.5 MHz
D. 17 kHz

**A** Can you do this without a calculator or paper and pencil? If you divide the frequency by the Q you'll get a little less than 0.1 MHz. So if you guessed 95 kHz, you'd be correct. Now let's do it using the math formula

$$W = \frac{14.25 \text{ MHz}}{150} = 0.095 \text{ MHz} = 95 \text{ kHz}$$

**E5A15 What is the half-power bandwidth of a parallel resonant circuit that has a resonant frequency of 21.15 MHz and a Q of 95?**

A. 4.49 kHz
B. 44.9 kHz
C. 22.3 kHz
D. 222.6 kHz

**D** Once again use the formula as you did in the previous question. You can probably do this problem without a calculator. Made your guess? Now check your answer.

$$W = \frac{21.15 \text{ MHz}}{95} = 0.2226 \text{ MHz} = 222.6 \text{ kHz}$$

Congratulations. You got it right.

**E5A16 What is the half-power bandwidth of a parallel resonant circuit that has a resonant frequency of 3.7 MHz and a Q of 118?**

A. 22.3 kHz
B. 76.2 kHz
C. 31.4 kHz
D. 10.8 kHz

**C** Keep applying the same formula to compute the bandwidth for parallel circuits. Using the numbers given

$$W = \frac{3700 \text{ kHz}}{118} = 31.4 \text{ kHz}$$

**E5A17 What is the half-power bandwidth of a parallel resonant circuit that has a resonant frequency of 14.25 MHz and a Q of 187?**

A. 22.3 kHz
B. 10.8 kHz
C. 76.2 kHz
D. 13.1 kHz

**C** One last question on computing bandwidth with the same formula. Using the numbers given,

$$W = \frac{14250 \text{ kHz}}{187} = 76.2 \text{ kHz}$$

**E5A18 What is the resonant frequency of a series RLC circuit if R is 47 ohms, L is 50 microhenrys and C is 40 picofarads?**

A. 79.6 MHz
B. 1.78 MHz
C. 3.56 MHz
D. 7.96 MHz

**C** Next, you have a series of questions dealing with series resonant circuits. Remember that resonance occurs when the capacitive and inductive reactances are equal. Series RLC circuits are resonant at

$$f_r = \frac{1}{2\pi\sqrt{L \times C}}$$

Where all values are given in basic units, that is Hertz, Henrys and Farads.

For this problem,

$$f_r = \frac{1}{2\pi\sqrt{50 \times 10^{-6} \times 40 \times 10^{-12}}} = 3558813 \text{ Hz} \approx 3.56 \text{ MHz}$$

Remember that resistance does not determine resonance.

**E5A19 What is the resonant frequency of a series RLC circuit if R is 47 ohms, L is 40 microhenrys and C is 200 picofarads?**

A. 1.99 kHz
B. 1.78 MHz
C. 1.99 MHz
D. 1.78 kHz

**B** Here you have the next question dealing with resonant circuits. Using the same circuit theory and formula, compute the resonant frequency

$$f_r = \frac{1}{2\pi\sqrt{40 \times 10^{-6} \times 200 \times 10^{-12}}} = 1.78 \text{ MHz}$$

Be careful of choice D because it has the correct numbers but the MHz unit is replaced with kHz. You should be able to convert Hz to MHz, right?

**E5A20 What is the resonant frequency of a series RLC circuit if R is 47 ohms, L is 50 microhenrys and C is 10 picofarads?**

A. 3.18 MHz
B. 3.18 kHz
C. 7.12 kHz
D. 7.12 MHz

**D** Here is another question dealing with resonant circuits. Using the same circuit theory, compute the resonant frequency at

$$f_r = \frac{1}{2\pi\sqrt{50 \times 10^{-6} \times 10 \times 10^{-12}}} = 7.12 \text{ MHz}$$

Watch out for choice C because it has the correct numbers but the MHz unit is replaced with kHz.

**E5A21 What is the resonant frequency of a series RLC circuit if R is 47 ohms, L is 25 microhenrys and C is 10 picofarads?**

A. 10.1 MHz
B. 63.7 MHz
C. 10.1 kHz
D. 63.7 kHz

**A** Since this is the same circuit configuration, you should use the same circuit theory to compute the resonant frequency as

$$f_r = \frac{1}{2\pi\sqrt{25 \times 10^{-6} \times 10 \times 10^{-12}}} = 10.1 \text{ MHz}$$

**E5A22 What is the resonant frequency of a series RLC circuit if R is 47 ohms, L is 3 microhenrys and C is 40 picofarads?**

A. 13.1 MHz
B. 14.5 MHz
C. 14.5 kHz
D. 13.1 kHz

**B** You are still solving series resonant circuits as in the previous questions. Use the same formula, and compute the resonant frequency as

$$f_r = \frac{1}{2\pi\sqrt{3 \times 10^{-6} \times 40 \times 10^{-12}}} = 14.5 \text{ MHz}$$

**E5A23 What is the resonant frequency of a series RLC circuit if R is 47 ohms, L is 4 microhenrys and C is 20 picofarads?**

A. 19.9 kHz
B. 17.8 kHz
C. 19.9 MHz
D. 17.8 MHz

**D** Here you have the next question dealing with resonant circuits. Using the same circuit theory and formula, compute the resonant frequency as

$$f_r = \frac{1}{2\pi\sqrt{4 \times 10^{-6} \times 20 \times 10^{-12}}} = 17.8 \text{ MHz}$$

**E5A24 What is the resonant frequency of a series RLC circuit if R is 47 ohms, L is 8 microhenrys and C is 7 picofarads?**

A. 2.84 MHz
B. 28.4 MHz
C. 21.3 MHz
D. 2.13 MHz

**C** Are you catching onto resonant series circuits yet? Using the same formula, compute the resonant frequency as

$$f_r = \frac{1}{2\pi\sqrt{8 \times 10^{-6} \times 7 \times 10^{-12}}} = 21.3 \text{ MHz}$$

**E5A25** **What is the resonant frequency of a series RLC circuit if R is 47 ohms, L is 3 microhenrys and C is 15 picofarads?**

A. 23.7 MHz
B. 23.7 kHz
C. 35.4 kHz
D. 35.4 MHz

**A** This is the last question dealing with resonant circuits in this section. Using the same formula, and compute the resonant frequency as

$$f_r = \frac{1}{2\pi\sqrt{3 \times 10^{-6} \times 15 \times 10^{-12}}} = 23.7 \text{ MHz}$$

## E5B Exponential charge/discharge curves (time constants): definition; time constants in RL and RC circuits

**E5B01** **What is the term for the time required for the capacitor in an RC circuit to be charged to 63.2% of the supply voltage?**

A. An exponential rate of one
B. One time constant
C. One exponential period
D. A time factor of one

**B** In an RC circuit, when the capacitor has no initial charge, it takes one time factor to charge the capacitor to 63.2% of the applied voltage. In the graph, you can see how the voltage across a capacitor rises, with time, when charged through a resistor. The symbol τ is used to indicate a period equal to the time constant.

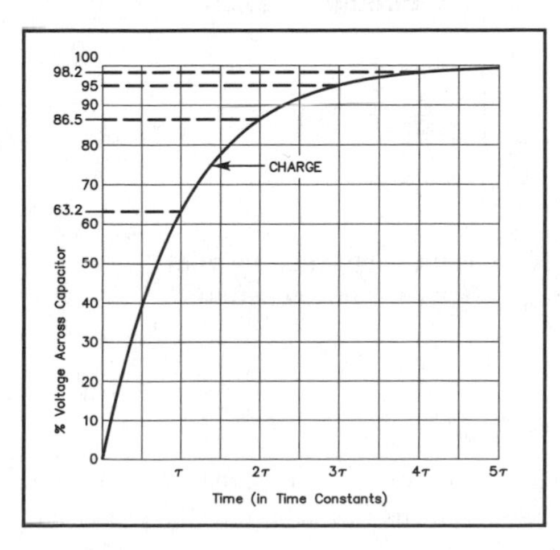


Graph showing the voltage rise across a capacitor, with time, when charged through a resistor.

**E5B02** **What is the term for the time required for the current in an RL circuit to build up to 63.2% of the maximum value?**

A. One time constant
B. An exponential period of one
C. A time factor of one
D. One exponential rate

**A** Current increase through an inductor or voltage increase across a capacitor follows the same pattern. This is the definition of one time constant.

**E5B03** **What is the term for the time it takes for a charged capacitor in an RC circuit to discharge to 36.8% of its initial value of stored charge?**

A. One discharge period
B. An exponential discharge rate of one
C. A discharge factor of one
D. One time constant

**D** Charging or discharging the results are predictable. As the discharge curve shows, this question is the definition of one time constant. The symbol $\tau$ is used to indicate a period equal to the time constant.

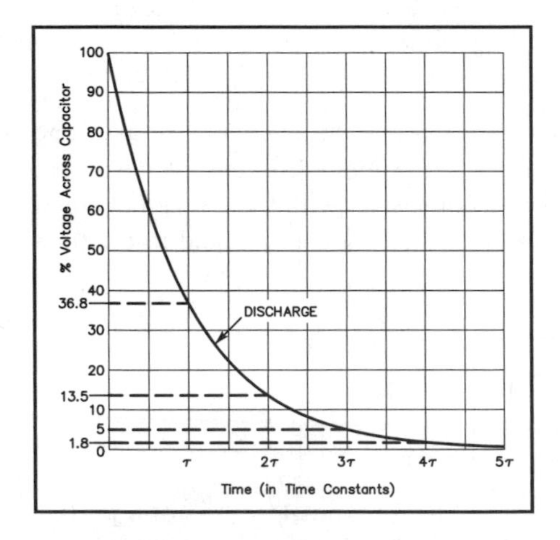


**Graph showing the voltage decrease across a capacitor, with time, when discharged through a resistor.**

**E5B04** **The capacitor in an RC circuit is charged to what percentage of the supply voltage after two time constants?**

A. 36.8%
B. 63.2%
C. 86.5%
D. 95%

**C** Look again at the charging curve. There you can see that after two time constants, the circuit has charged to 86.5% of its full value.

**E5B05 The capacitor in an RC circuit is discharged to what percentage of the starting voltage after two time constants?**

A. 86.5%
B. 63.2%
C. 36.8%
D. 13.5%

**D** This time look at the discharge curve. There you can see that after two time constants, the circuit has discharged to 13.5% of its full value.

**E5B06 What is the time constant of a circuit having two 100-microfarad capacitors and two 470-kilohm resistors all in series?**

A. 47 seconds
B. 101.1 seconds
C. 103 seconds
D. 220 seconds

**A** In this series circuit, the total resistance is the sum of the resistors or 940 kΩ. The total capacitance is 50 µF. Remember to convert all values to basic units, that is resistance in ohms and capacitance in Farads. The time constant is

$$\tau = R \times C = 940 \times 10^{3} \times 50 \times 10^{-6} = 47 \text{ seconds}$$

**E5B07 What is the time constant of a circuit having two 220-microfarad capacitors and two 1-megohm resistors all in parallel?**

A. 47 seconds
B. 101.1 seconds
C. 103 seconds
D. 220 seconds

**D** In this parallel circuit, the total resistance is 500 kΩ. The total capacitance is 440 µF. Convert to basic units and calculate. The time constant is

$$\tau = R \times C = 500 \times 10^{3} \times 440 \times 10^{-6} = 220 \text{ seconds}$$

**E5B08 What is the time constant of a circuit having a 220-microfarad capacitor in series with a 470-kilohm resistor?**

A. 47 seconds
B. 80 seconds
C. 103 seconds
D. 220 seconds

**C** This should be simple now. Can you calculate it?

$\tau = R \times C = 470 \times 10^3 \times 220 \times 10^{-6} = 103$ seconds

**E5B09 How long does it take for an initial charge of 20 V DC to decrease to 7.36 V DC in a 0.01-microfarad capacitor when a 2-megohm resistor is connected across it?**

A. 0.02 seconds
B. 0.08 seconds
C. 450 seconds
D. 1350 seconds

**A** First you'll need to find out how many time constants this amount of discharge represents. Because 7.36 V is 36.8% of 20 V (7.36/20), the circuit has discharged for one time constant. You can see that on the discharge curve. The time constant for this circuit is

$\tau = R \times C = 2 \times 10^6 \times 0.01 \times 10^{-6} = 0.02$ seconds

**E5B10 How long does it take for an initial charge of 20 V DC to decrease to 0.37 V DC in a 0.01-microfarad capacitor when a 2-megohm resistor is connected across it?**

A. 0.02 seconds
B. 0.08 seconds
C. 450 seconds
D. 1350 seconds

**B** Use the same analysis as you did for the previous question. First find out how many time constants the discharge represents. Because 0.37 V is 1.85% of 20 V, the circuit has discharged for four time constants. You can see that on the discharge curve. The time constant for this circuit is

$\tau = R \times C = 2 \times 10^6 \times 0.01 \times 10^{-6} = 0.02$ seconds

The discharge time is four times this value or 0.08 seconds. Don't forget to multiply by four, which is the number of time constants it takes to discharge to 1.85%.

**E5B11 How long does it take for an initial charge of 800 V DC to decrease to 294 V DC in a 450-microfarad capacitor when a 1-megohm resistor is connected across it?**

A. 0.02 seconds
B. 0.08 seconds
C. 450 seconds
D. 1350 seconds

**C** How much help do you need on this question? First you'll need to find out how many time constants the discharge represents. 294 V is 36.8% of 800 V so the circuit has discharged by one time constant. The time constant for the circuit is

$$\tau = R \times C = 1 \times 10^{6} \times 450 \times 10^{-6} = 450 \text{ seconds}$$

## E5C Impedance diagrams: Basic principles of Smith charts; impedance of RLC networks at specified frequencies; PC based impedance analysis (including Smith Charts)

**E5C01 What type of graph can be used to calculate impedance along transmission lines?**

A. A Smith chart
B. A logarithmic chart
C. A Jones chart
D. A radiation pattern chart

**A** The Smith chart was developed for the purpose of graphically calculating impedance along a transmission line. It is unique in that ability.

**E5C02 What type of coordinate system is used in a Smith chart?**

A. Voltage circles and current arcs
B. Resistance circles and reactance arcs
C. Voltage lines and current chords
D. Resistance lines and reactance chords

**B** The mnemonic for this question is R & R: *r*esistance and *r*eactance, ci*r*cles and a*r*cs. Impedance is resistance and reactance these are plotted on a coordinate system that is shown in the drawings. For simplicity, resistance and reactance coordinate systems are shown separately.

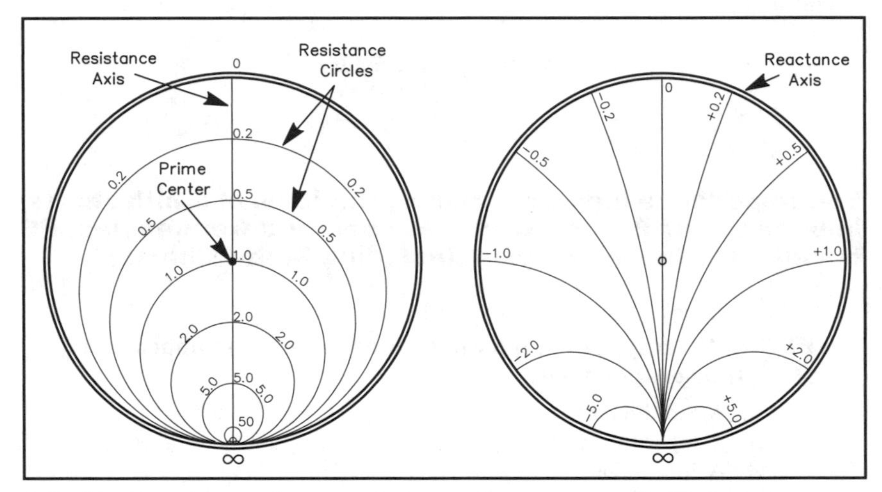


**A Smith Chart has resistance circles and reactance arcs. To help you visualize them, these are shown separately in this drawing.**

**E5C03 What type of calculations can be performed using a Smith chart?**

A. Beam headings and radiation patterns
B. Satellite azimuth and elevation bearings
C. Impedance and SWR values in transmission lines
D. Circuit gain calculations

**C** A Smith chart is not only used to plot impedances, it can also be used to calculate changes in resistance and reactance along a length of transmission line.

**E5C04** **What are the two families of circles that make up a Smith chart?**

A. Resistance and voltage
B. Reactance and voltage
C. Resistance and reactance
D. Voltage and impedance

**C** Since the Smith chart graphs impedances, the correct answer is resistance and reactance. Do you remember R & R?

**E5C05** **What type of chart is shown in Figure E5-1?**

A. Smith chart
B. Free-space radiation directivity chart
C. Vertical-space radiation pattern chart
D. Horizontal-space radiation pattern chart

**A** In Figure E5-1 you'll see a Smith chart.

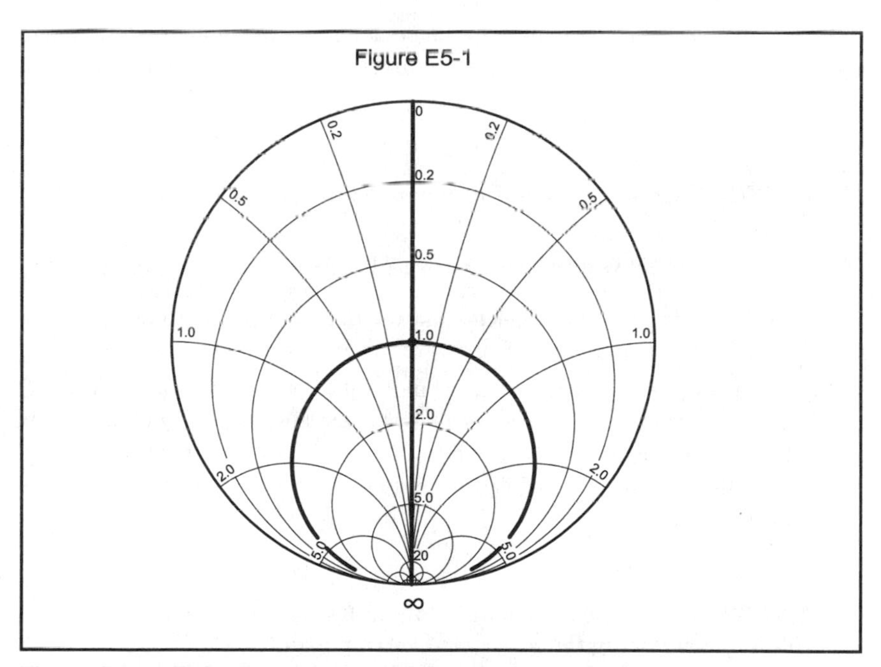


**Figure E5-1—Refer to questions E5C05 through E5C07.**

**E5C06 On the Smith chart shown in Figure E5-1, what is the name for the large outer circle bounding the coordinate portion of the chart?**

A. Prime axis
B. Reactance axis
C. Impedance axis
D. Polar axis

**B** If you noticed that the earlier questions always dealt with resistance and reactance, then you should be able to spot reactance axis as the right choice.

**E5C07 On the Smith chart shown in Figure E5-1, what is the only straight line shown?**

A. The reactance axis
B. The current axis
C. The voltage axis
D. The resistance axis

**D** That straight line is the resistance axis. The previous question asked for the reactance axis. It should not have surprised you to find that this question asks for the resistance axis.

**E5C08 What is the process of normalizing with regard to a Smith chart?**

A. Reassigning resistance values with regard to the reactance axis
B. Reassigning reactance values with regard to the resistance axis
C. Reassigning impedance values with regard to the prime center
D. Reassigning prime center with regard to the reactance axis

**C** The process of assigning resistance values with regard to the value at prime center is called normalizing. To normalize values for a 50-ohm system, divide the resistance by 50. To convert from the chart values back to actual values, multiply by 50. Normalization permits the Smith chart to be used for any impedance value.

**E5C09 What is the third family of circles, which are added to a Smith chart during the process of solving problems?**

A. Standing-wave ratio circles
B. Antenna-length circles
C. Coaxial-length circles
D. Radiation-pattern circles

**A** The correct answer is standing wave ratio circles. Smith chart plots can be used to give a measure of impedance mismatch.

**E5C10 In rectangular coordinates, what is the impedance of a network comprised of a 10-microhenry inductor in series with a 40-ohm resistor at 500 MHz?**

A. $40 + j31{,}400$
B. $40 - j31{,}400$
C. $31{,}400 + j40$
D. $31{,}400 - j40$

**A** Here's a shortcut. You can immediately eliminate C and D because they have the resistive component where the reactive component belongs. Since this is an inductive circuit, the reactive part has a plus sign. You can verify intuition by analysis: for this circuit, the total impedance is the complex sum of the resistive and inductive portions at the operating frequency or

$$Z = R + j2\pi fL = 40 + j \times 2 \times \pi \times 500 \times 10^6 \times 10 \times 10^{-6} = 40 + j31416\ \Omega$$

**E5C11 In polar coordinates, what is the impedance of a network comprised of a 100-picofarad capacitor in parallel with a 4,000-ohm resistor at 500 kHz?**

A. 2490 ohms, $\angle 51.5$ degrees
B. 4000 ohms, $\angle 38.5$ degrees
C. 2490 ohms, $\angle -51.5$ degrees
D. 5112 ohms, $\angle -38.5$ degrees

**C** Since the reactance is capacitive in this circuit; you can immediately eliminate answers that have positive phase angles. Since the circuit is parallel, you are looking for an impedance magnitude that is less than the resistance. Only one choice fits, and you've solved the problem.

How can you prove it, you ask? Okay, let's analyze the problem. The impedance of the resistor and capacitor in parallel is

$$Z = \frac{1}{\frac{1}{R} + \frac{1}{\frac{1}{j2\pi fC}}} = \frac{1}{\frac{1}{R} + j2\pi fC} = \frac{1}{\frac{1}{4000} + j2\pi \times 500 \times 10^3 \times 100 \times 10^{-12}}$$

$$= \frac{1}{0.00025 + j0.000314}\ \Omega$$

You are looking for the final answer in polar coordinates. It will be easier to find the final answer to the previous equation if you convert the denominator to polar coordinates. That is a two-step process. First, determine the absolute magnitude of the impedance, which is the square root of the sum of the squares of the resistance and the reactance. Second, determine the phase angle, which is the angle whose tangent is equal to the reactance divided by the resistance.

Here are the calculations. First absolute impedance (that's what the straight lines mean)

$$|Z| = \frac{1}{\sqrt{(0.00025)^2 + (0.000314)^2}} = \frac{1}{0.0004014}\Omega$$

And the phase angle

$$\theta = \tan^{-1}\left(\frac{0.000314}{0.00025}\right) = 51.5°$$

For the last step, you have to find the reciprocal of these values. The reciprocal of 0.0004014 is approximately 2490, and that is the absolute magnitude of the impedance. To find the reciprocal of the phase angle, you only have to change the sign (multiply by –1). That gives you an impedance of: 2490 ohms, /–51.5 degrees.

**E5C12 Which point on Figure E5-2 best represents the impedance of a series circuit consisting of a 300-ohm resistor, a 0.64-microhenry inductor and a 85-picofarad capacitor at 24.900 MHz?**

A. Point 1
B. Point 3
C. Point 5
D. Point 8

**D** Because the resistance is 300 Ω, you can eliminate all points except 1, 3, and 8 from further consideration. For this circuit, the total impedance is the complex sum of the resistive, capacitive, and inductive portions at the operating frequency or

$$Z = R + j2\pi fL - \frac{j}{2\pi fC}$$

$$= 300 + j \times 2 \times \pi \times 24.9 \times 10^6 \times 0.64 \times 10^{-6} - \frac{j}{2 \times \pi \times 24.9 \times 10^6 \times 85 \times 10^{-12}}$$

$$= 300 + j100 - j75 = 300 + j25$$

Resistance is plotted on the x-axis and reactance is plotted on the y-axis. You'll find the impedance plotted on the graph at point 8.

Here are some facts about this chart that will help with subsequent questions. (1) No actual R-L-C circuits will be found in quadrants II (upper-left) and III (lower-left), because resistors do not have negative resistance. (2) Purely resistive circuits will be found along the *x*-axis, purely inductive reactances lie along the +*y*-axis while purely capacitive reactances lie along the –*y*-axis. (3) If the circuit is in resonance, its impedance will lie along the x-axis since the inductive and capacitive reactances cancel out. (4) If the circuit has a net inductive reactance, it will lie in quadrant I (upper-right), and if the circuit has a net capacitive reactance, it will lie in quadrant IV (lower right). (5) Circuits in quadrant I have positive (leading) phase angles while those in quadrant IV have negative (lagging) phase angles. (6) If the magnitude of the resistance is greater than the magnitude of the net reactance, the phase angle will be less than 45° while if the magnitude of the net reactance is greater than the magnitude of the resistance, the phase angle will be greater than 45°.

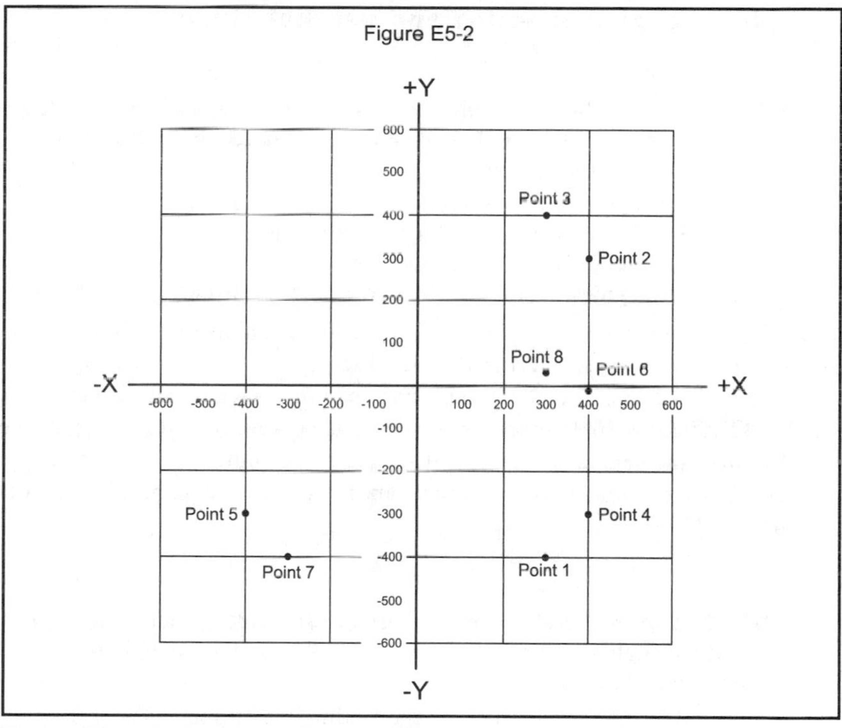


**Figure E5-2—Refer to question E5C12.**

**E5C13 What are the curved lines on a Smith chart?**

A. Portions of current circles
B. Portions of voltage circles
C. Portions of resistance circles
D. Portions of reactance circles

**D** When extended beyond the bounds of the Smith chart, the curved lines form reactance circles.

**E5C14 How are the wavelength scales on a Smith chart calibrated?**

A. In portions of transmission line electrical frequency
B. In portions of transmission line electrical wavelength
C. In portions of antenna electrical wavelength
D. In portions of antenna electrical frequency

**B** As you should remember, the Smith chart was developed for the purpose of graphically calculating impedance along a transmission line. For that reason, the scale is calibrated in terms of wavelength in a transmission line.

## E5D Phase angle between voltage and current; impedances and phase angles of series and parallel circuits

**E5D01 What is the phase angle between the voltage across and the current through a series R-L-C circuit if XC is 25 ohms, R is 100 ohms, and XL is 100 ohms?**

A. 36.9 degrees with the voltage leading the current
B. 53.1 degrees with the voltage lagging the current
C. 36.9 degrees with the voltage lagging the current
D. 53.1 degrees with the voltage leading the current

**A** Now you come to a series of problems based on the same circuit analysis principle that was used earlier. The total reactance in this series configuration is 100 Ω – 25 Ω. The phase angle between the voltage and the current is $\tan^{-1}[75\ \Omega/100\ \Omega] = 36.9°$. Because the angle is positive, the voltage leads the current. Since the net reactance is positive, the phase angle is positive. Because the net reactance is smaller than the resistance, the phase angle needs to be less than 45°.

**E5D02 What is the phase angle between the voltage across and the current through a series R-L-C circuit if XC is 500 ohms, R is 1 kilohm, and XL is 250 ohms?**

A. 68.2 degrees with the voltage leading the current
B. 14.0 degrees with the voltage leading the current
C. 14.0 degrees with the voltage lagging the current
D. 68.2 degrees with the voltage lagging the current

**C** This is the next example of this type of analysis. The total reactance in this series configuration is 250 Ω – 500 Ω. The phase angle between the voltage and the current is $\tan^{-1}[-250\ \Omega/1000\ \Omega] = -14.0°$. Because the angle is negative, the voltage lags the current. Since the net reactance is negative, the phase angle needs to be negative. Because the net reactance is smaller than the resistance, the phase angle will be less than 45°.

**E5D03 What is the phase angle between the voltage across and the current through a series R-L-C circuit if XC is 50 ohms, R is 100 ohms, and XL is 25 ohms?**

A. 76 degrees with the voltage lagging the current
B. 14 degrees with the voltage leading the current
C. 76 degrees with the voltage leading the current
D. 14 degrees with the voltage lagging the current

**D** The total reactance in this series configuration is 25 Ω – 50 Ω. The phase angle between the voltage and the current is $\tan^{-1}$[–25 Ω/100 Ω] = –14.0°.

**E5D04 What is the phase angle between the voltage across and the current through a series R-L-C circuit if XC is 100 ohms, R is 100 ohms, and XL is 75 ohms?**

A. 14 degrees with the voltage lagging the current
B. 14 degrees with the voltage leading the current
C. 76 degrees with the voltage leading the current
D. 76 degrees with the voltage lagging the current

**A** Continue with this same type of analysis in this question. The total reactance in this series configuration is 75 Ω – 100 Ω. The phase angle between the voltage and the current is $\tan^{-1}$[–25 Ω/100 Ω] = –14.0°.

**E5D05 What is the phase angle between the voltage across and the current through a series R-L-C circuit if XC is 50 ohms, R is 100 ohms, and XL is 75 ohms?**

A. 76 degrees with the voltage leading the current
B. 76 degrees with the voltage lagging the current
C. 14 degrees with the voltage lagging the current
D. 14 degrees with the voltage leading the current

**D** Here you have the next example of this type of analysis. The total reactance in this series configuration is 75 Ω – 50 Ω. The phase angle between the voltage and the current is $\tan^{-1}$[25 Ω/100 Ω] = 14.0°.

**E5D06 What is the relationship between the current through and the voltage across a capacitor?**

A. Voltage and current are in phase
B. Voltage and current are 180 degrees out of phase
C. Voltage leads current by 90 degrees
D. Current leads voltage by 90 degrees

**D** The current leads voltage by 90°. You can visualize this as a vector at minus 90° on the chart you saw earlier. In the case of pure reactance the phase shift is 90°.

Have you heard of Eli the iceman? It's an easy way to remember current and voltage relationships in reactive circuits. ELI means voltage (E) leads current (I) in an inductance (L). This case is ICE—current (I) leads voltage (E) in a capacitor (C).

**E5D07 What is the relationship between the current through an inductor and the voltage across an inductor?**

A. Voltage leads current by 90 degrees
B. Current leads voltage by 90 degrees
C. Voltage and current are 180 degrees out of phase
D. Voltage and current are in phase

**A** This is the complement to the previous question. In other words, this is "ELI." That means voltage leads current. Because this is pure reactance, the phase shift is 90°.

**E5D08 What is the phase angle between the voltage across and the current through a series RLC circuit if XC is 25 ohms, R is 100 ohms, and XL is 50 ohms?**

A. 14 degrees with the voltage lagging the current
B. 14 degrees with the voltage leading the current
C. 76 degrees with the voltage lagging the current
D. 76 degrees with the voltage leading the current

**B** The total reactance in this series configuration is 50 Ω – 25 Ω. The phase angle between the voltage and the current is $\tan^{-1}[25\ \Omega/100\ \Omega] = 14°$. The positive angle means that voltage leads current.

To review our rules of thumb: since the net reactance is positive, the phase angle needs to be positive; because the net reactance is smaller than the resistance, the phase angle needs to be less than 45°.

**E5D09 What is the phase angle between the voltage across and the current through a series RLC circuit if XC is 75 ohms, R is 100 ohms, and XL is 100 ohms?**

A. 76 degrees with the voltage leading the current
B. 14 degrees with the voltage leading the current
C. 14 degrees with the voltage lagging the current
D. 76 degrees with the voltage lagging the current

**B** Here you have the next example of this type of analysis. The total reactance in this series configuration is 100 Ω – 75 Ω. The phase angle between the voltage and the current is $\tan^{-1}[25\ \Omega/100\ \Omega] = 14.0°$.

**E5D10 What is the phase angle between the voltage across and the current through a series RLC circuit if XC is 75 ohms, R is 100 ohms, and XL is 50 ohms?**

A. 76 degrees with the voltage lagging the current
B. 14 degrees with the voltage leading the current
C. 14 degrees with the voltage lagging the current
D. 76 degrees with the voltage leading the current

**C** Here you have another example of this type of problem. The total reactance in this series configuration is 50 Ω – 75 Ω. The phase angle between the voltage and the current is $\tan^{-1}[-25\ \Omega/100\ \Omega] = -14.0°$.

**E5D11 What is the phase angle between the voltage across and the current through a series RLC circuit if XC is 250 ohms, R is 1 kilohm, and XL is 500 ohms?**

A. 81.47 degrees with the voltage lagging the current
B. 81.47 degrees with the voltage leading the current
C. 14.04 degrees with the voltage lagging the current
D. 14.04 degrees with the voltage leading the current

**D** The total reactance in this series configuration is 500 Ω – 250 Ω. The phase angle between the voltage and the current is $\tan^{-1}[250\ \Omega/1000\ \Omega] = 14.04°$.

## E5E Algebraic operations using complex numbers: rectangular coordinates (real and imaginary parts); polar coordinates (magnitude and angle)

**E5E01 In polar coordinates, what is the impedance of a network comprised of a 100-ohm-reactance inductor in series with a 100-ohm resistor?**

A. 121 ohms, /35 degrees
B. 141 ohms, /45 degrees
C. 161 ohms, /55 degrees
D. 181 ohms, /65 degrees

**B** In this section, you have a series of questions dealing with series resistance and rectangular-to-polar coordinate conversion. In rectangular coordinates, impedance is the sum of the resistive and reactive components. You plot impedance with resistance on the x-axis and reactance on the y-axis.

In polar coordinates, impedance is described by magnitude and the corresponding phase angle. You can calculate these from resistance (R) and reactance (X) using the following formulas

$$|Z| = \sqrt{(R)^2 + (X)^2}$$

and

$$\theta = \tan^{-1}\left(\frac{X}{R}\right)$$

Solving these equations you find

$$|Z| = \sqrt{(100)^2 + (100)^2} = 141\ \Omega$$

and

$$\theta = \tan^{-1}\left(\frac{100}{100}\right) = 45°$$

**E5E02 In polar coordinates, what is the impedance of a network comprised of a 100-ohm-reactance inductor, a 100-ohm-reactance capacitor, and a 100-ohm resistor all connected in series?**

A. 100 ohms, /90 degrees
B. 10 ohms, /0 degrees
C. 10 ohms, /100 degrees
D. 100 ohms, /0 degrees

**D** Here's a chance to review some things you studied earlier. This is a resonant circuit because the capacitive and inductive reactances are equal. That means that the reactances cancel and you have only the resistance left, which is an impedance of 100 Ω with no reactive phase shift (angle = 0°).

**E5E03 In polar coordinates, what is the impedance of a network comprised of a 300-ohm-reactance capacitor, a 600-ohm-reactance inductor, and a 400-ohm resistor, all connected in series?**

A. 500 ohms, /37 degrees
B. 400 ohms, /27 degrees
C. 300 ohms, /17 degrees
D. 200 ohms, /10 degrees

**A** Use the formulas for converting to polar coordinates and find

$$|Z| = \sqrt{(400)^2 + (600 - 300)^2} = 500\ \Omega$$

at an angle of

$$\theta = \tan^{-1}\left(\frac{600 - 300}{400}\right) = 37°$$

**E5E04 In polar coordinates, what is the impedance of a network comprised of a 400-ohm-reactance capacitor in series with a 300-ohm resistor?**

A. 240 ohms, /36.9 degrees
B. 240 ohms, /–36.9 degrees
C. 500 ohms, /53.1 degrees
D. 500 ohms, /–53.1 degrees

**D** Use the same two formulas to solve this problem.

$$|Z| = \sqrt{(300)^2 + (400)^2} = 500\ \Omega$$

$$\theta = \tan^{-1}\left(\frac{-400}{300}\right) = -53.1°$$

**E5E05 In polar coordinates, what is the impedance of a network comprised of a 400-ohm-reactance inductor in parallel with a 300-ohm resistor?**

A. 240 ohms, /36.9 degrees
B. 240 ohms, /–36.9 degrees
C. 500 ohms, /53.1 degrees
D. 500 ohms, /–53.1 degrees

**A** In this section, you also have questions dealing with parallel resistance and reactance. In parallel circuits, the formulas are

$$|Z| = \frac{1}{\frac{1}{R} + \frac{1}{X}} = \frac{R \times X}{\sqrt{R^2 + X^2}}$$

and

$$\theta = \tan^{-1}\left(\frac{R}{X}\right)$$

While the formula for the phase angle may look familiar, it is different. Look again and you'll see that R and X have swapped positions when compared to the formula for series circuits. Now, plug the numbers into the formulas and you get

$$Z = \frac{400 \times 300}{\sqrt{400^2 + 300^2}} = \frac{120000}{500} = 240\,\Omega$$

and the phase angle is

$$\theta = \tan^{-1}\left(\frac{300}{400}\right) = 36.9°$$

**E5E06 In polar coordinates, what is the impedance of a network comprised of a 100-ohm-reactance capacitor in series with a 100-ohm resistor?**

A. 121 ohms, /–25 degrees
B. 191 ohms, /–85 degrees
C. 161 ohms, /–65 degrees
D. 141 ohms, /–45 degrees

**D** This is another series circuit, so go back to the series formulas to calculate the impedance

$$|Z| = \sqrt{(R)^2 + (X)^2} = \sqrt{(100)^2 + (-100)^2} = 141\ \Omega$$

And the phase angle

$$\theta = \tan^{-1}\left(\frac{X}{R}\right) = \tan^{-1}\left(\frac{-100}{100}\right) = -45°$$

Remember that for the series case, the phase angle is the arctangent of the reactance divided by the resistance.

**E5E07 In polar coordinates, what is the impedance of a network comprised of a 100-ohm-reactance capacitor in parallel with a 100-ohm resistor?**

A. 31 ohms, /–15 degrees
B. 51 ohms, /–25 degrees
C. 71 ohms, /–45 degrees
D. 91 ohms, /–65 degrees

**C** Let's do another parallel network. The question looks a lot like the previous one, but that was for a series network. This time, you'll use the formulas for parallel circuits, which means the total impedance is

$$Z = \frac{R \times X}{\sqrt{R^2 + X^2}} = \frac{100 \times -100}{\sqrt{100^2 + (-100)^2}} = \frac{10000}{141} = 71\ \Omega$$

and the phase angle is

$$\theta = \tan^{-1}\left(\frac{R}{X}\right) = \tan^{-1}\left(\frac{100}{-100}\right) = -45°$$

**E5E08 In polar coordinates, what is the impedance of a network comprised of a 300-ohm-reactance inductor in series with a 400-ohm resistor?**

A. 400 ohms, /27 degrees
B. 500 ohms, /37 degrees
C. 500 ohms, /47 degrees
D. 700 ohms, /57 degrees

**B** Are you ready for one more series circuit? Use the formulas for series and compute the total impedance, which is

$$|Z| = \sqrt{(R)^2 + (X)^2} = \sqrt{(400)^2 + (300)^2} = 500\ \Omega$$

and the phase angle is

$$\theta = \tan^{-1}\left(\frac{X}{R}\right) = \tan^{-1}\left(\frac{300}{400}\right) = 37°$$

**E5E09 When using rectangular coordinates to graph the impedance of a circuit, what does the horizontal axis represent?**

A. The voltage or current associated with the resistive component
B. The voltage or current associated with the reactive component
C. The sum of the reactive and resistive components
D. The difference between the resistive and reactive components

**A** The horizontal axis represents the resistive component. You would plot voltage drop across or current through the resistive component on this axis.

**E5E10 When using rectangular coordinates to graph the impedance of a circuit, what does the vertical axis represent?**

A. The voltage or current associated with the resistive component
B. The voltage or current associated with the reactive component
C. The sum of the reactive and resistive components
D. The difference between the resistive and reactive components

**B** The vertical axis represents the reactive component. You would plot voltage drop across or current through the reactive component on this axis.

**E5E11 What do the two numbers represent that are used to define a point on a graph using rectangular coordinates?**

A. The horizontal and inverted axes
B. The vertical and inverted axes
C. The coordinate values along the horizontal and vertical axes
D. The phase angle with respect to its prime center

**C** The numbers given to graph a point in rectangular coordinates represent values along the horizontal and vertical axes.

**E5E12 If you plot the impedance of a circuit using the rectangular coordinate system and find the impedance point falls on the right side of the graph on the horizontal line, what do you know about the circuit?**

A. It has to be a direct current circuit
B. It contains resistance and capacitive reactance
C. It contains resistance and inductive reactance
D. It is equivalent to a pure resistance

**D** If the point is on the horizontal axis (resistance), it has no reactive (y-axis) component. That means you have a pure resistance.

**E5E13 Why would you plot the impedance of a circuit using the polar coordinate system?**

A. To display the data on an XY chart
B. To give a visual representation of the phase angle
C. To graphically represent the DC component
D. To show the reactance which is present

**B** The polar coordinate system shows impedance and phase angle at a glance.

**E5E14 What coordinate system can be used to display the resistive, inductive, and/or capacitive reactance components of an impedance?**

A. Maidenhead grid
B. National Bureau of Standards
C. Faraday
D. Rectangular

**D** In the rectangular coordinate system, resistance is plotted on the horizontal axis and reactance on the vertical axis.

**E5E15 What coordinate system can be used to display the phase angle of a circuit containing resistance, inductive and/or capacitive reactance?**

A. Maidenhead grid
B. National Bureau of Standards
C. Faraday
D. Polar

**D** This may appear similar to the previous question. However, it is the polar coordinate system that plots phase angle directly.

**E5E16 In polar coordinates, what is the impedance of a circuit of 100 –*j*100 ohms impedance?**

A. 141 ohms, /–45 degrees
B. 100 ohms, /45 degrees
C. 100 ohms, /–45 degrees
D. 141 ohms, /45 degrees

**A** Once again, you'll need to convert this to polar coordinates. Do you remember the formulas that you used for series networks? You'll use them again here to calculate impedance

$$|Z| = \sqrt{(R)^2 + (X)^2} = \sqrt{(100)^2 + (-100)^2} = 141\ \Omega$$

and phase angle

$$\theta = \tan^{-1}\left(\frac{X}{R}\right) = \tan^{-1}\left(\frac{-100}{100}\right) = -45°$$

**E5E17 In polar coordinates, what is the impedance of a circuit that has an admittance of 7.09 millisiemens at 45 degrees?**

A. $5.03 \times 10^{-5}$ ohms, /45 degrees
B. 141 ohms, /–45 degrees
C. 19,900 ohms, /–45 degrees
D. 141 ohms, /45 degrees

**B** Impedance and admittance are reciprocal quantities. That means that the magnitude is 1/0.00709 S = 141 Ω. The phase angle is –45 degrees.

**E5E18 In rectangular coordinates, what is the impedance of a circuit that has an admittance of 5 millisiemens at –30 degrees?**

A. 173 – $j$100 ohms
B. 200 + $j$100 ohms
C. 173 + $j$100 ohms
D. 200 – $j$100 ohms

**C** Now you'll have to convert polar coordinates to rectangular coordinates. However, first you'll want to convert admittance to impedance. That means you'll start by taking the reciprocal of the magnitude, which is 1/0.005 S = 200 Ω and the phase becomes +30 degrees. To convert from polar coordinates use

$R = \text{cosine}(\theta) \times Z = \text{cosine}(30°) \times 200 = 173\ \Omega$

and

$X = \text{sine}(\theta) \times Z = \text{sine}(30°) \times 200 = +j100\ \Omega$

**E5E19 In rectangular coordinates, what is the admittance of a circuit that has an impedance of 240 ohms at 36.9 degrees?**

A. $3.33 \times 10^{-3} - j2.50 \times 10^{-3}$ siemens
B. $3.33 \times 10^{-3} + j2.50 \times 10^{-3}$ siemens
C. 192 + $j$144 siemens
D. 3.33 – $j$2.50 siemens

**A** You're given impedance in polar coordinates in this question, and you need to convert this to admittance in rectangular coordinates. You should start by converting impedance to admittance in polar coordinates. You can make that conversion by taking the reciprocal of |Z| and θ. The reciprocal of 240 is 0.00417 (or $4.17 \times 10^{-3}$), and for 36.9° the reciprocal is –36.9°.

The final step is to convert the admittance (Y) from polar to rectangular coordinates. We'll be looking for conductance (G) and susceptance (B), which are respectively the reciprocals of resistance and reactance. Use these formulas, which are similar to the conversion equations used for rectangular coordinates.

$G = \text{cosine}(\theta) \times Y = \text{cosine}(-36.9°) \times 4.17 \times 10^{-3} = 3.33 \times 10^{-3}$ S

and

$B = \text{sine}(\theta) \times Y = \text{sine}(-36.9°) \times 4.17 \times 10^{-3} = -j2.50 \times 10^{-3}$

**E5E20 In polar coordinates, what is the impedance of a series circuit consisting of a resistance of 4 ohms, an inductive reactance of 4 ohms, and a capacitive reactance of 1 ohm?**

A. 6.4 ohms, /53 degrees
B. 5 ohms, /37 degrees
C. 5 ohms, /45 degrees
D. 10 ohms, /–51 degrees

**B** In this circuit, the total impedance is $Z = R + jXL - jXC = 4\ \Omega + j4\ \Omega - j1\ \Omega = 4\ \Omega + j3\ \Omega$. Use the conversion formulas

$$|Z| = \sqrt{(R)^2 + (X)^2} = \sqrt{(4)^2 + (3)^2} = 5\ \Omega$$

and

$$\theta = \tan^{-1}\left(\frac{X}{R}\right) = \tan^{-1}\left(\frac{3}{4}\right) = 37°$$

**E5E21 Which point on Figure E5-2 best represents that impedance of a series circuit consisting of a 400 ohm resistor and a 38 picofarad capacitor at 14 MHz?**

A. Point 2
B. Point 4
C. Point 5
D. Point 6

**B** In this circuit, the total impedance is

$$Z = R + X = R + \frac{1}{j2\pi fC} = 400 + \frac{1}{j2\pi \times 14 \times 10^{6} \times 36 \times 10^{-12}} = 400 - j300\ \Omega$$

To find this point, find +400 on the horizontal axis and then move vertically down to the point that corresponds to –300. In the Figure, that corresponds to Point 4.

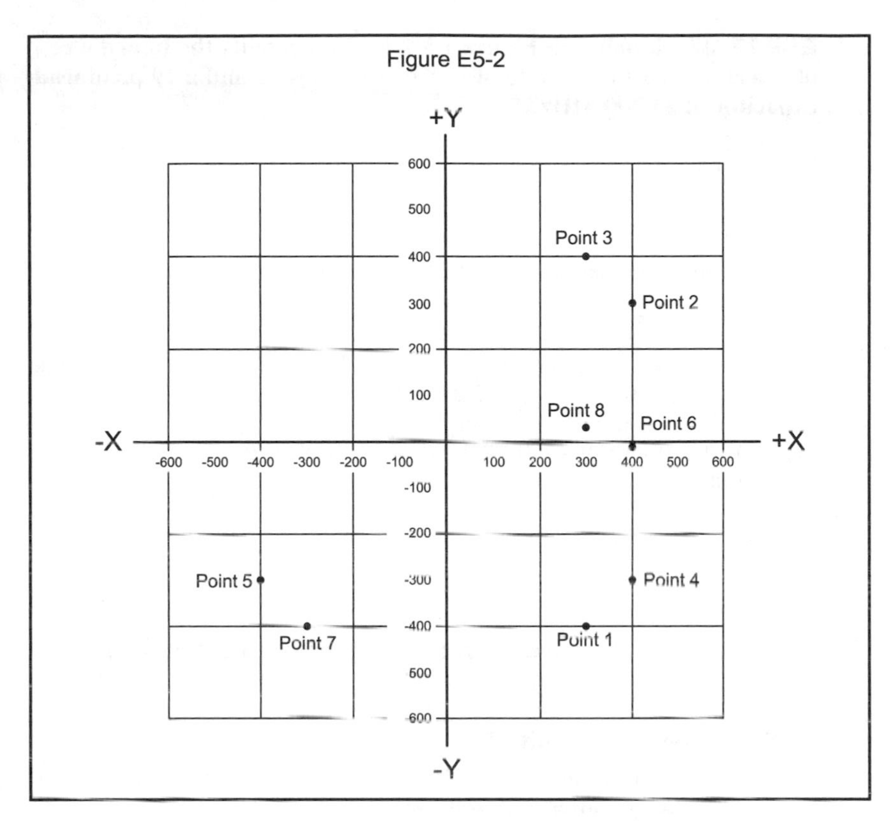


**Figure E5-2—Refer to questions E5E21 through E5E23.**

**E5E22 Which point in Figure E5-2 best represents the impedance of a series circuit consisting of a 300 ohm resistor and an 18 microhenry inductor at 3.505 MHz?**

A. Point 1
B. Point 3
C. Point 7
D. Point 8

**B** In this circuit, the total impedance is

$$Z = R + X = R + j2\pi\ f\ L = 300 + j2\pi \times 3.505 \times 10^{-6} \times 18 \times 10^{-6} = 300 + j400\Omega$$

To plot this point, find +300 on the horizontal axis, and then move up (positive direction) to +400 on the vertical axis. This corresponds to Point 3.

**E5E23 Which point on Figure E5-2 best represents the impedance of a series circuit consisting of a 300 ohm resistor and a 19 picofarad capacitor at 21.200 MHz?**

A. Point 1
B. Point 3
C. Point 7
D. Point 8

**A** Do you remember the formulas? The impedance of this circuit is

$$Z = R + X = R + \frac{1}{j2\pi f C} = 300 + \frac{1}{j2\pi \times 21.2 \times 10^{6} \times 19 \times 10^{-12}} = 300 - j400\Omega$$

The plot is horizontal to +300 then vertically (down) to –400, which corresponds to Point 1.

## E5F Skin effect; electrostatic and electromagnetic fields

**E5F01 What is the result of skin effect?**

A. As frequency increases, RF current flows in a thinner layer of the conductor, closer to the surface
B. As frequency decreases, RF current flows in a thinner layer of the conductor, closer to the surface
C. Thermal effects on the surface of the conductor increase the impedance
D. Thermal effects on the surface of the conductor decrease the impedance

**A** Skin effect happens at RF. As the frequency increases, electric and magnetic fields of the signal don't penetrate as deeply into a conductor. This results in RF current flowing in a thinner layer near the surface of the conductor as the frequency increases.

**E5F02 What effect causes most of an RF current to flow along the surface of a conductor?**

A. Layer effect
B. Seeburg effect
C. Skin effect
D. Resonance effect

**C** Based on the explanation of the previous question; you should be able to identify skin effect as the correct answer.

**E5F03 Where does almost all RF current flow in a conductor?**

A. Along the surface of the conductor
B. In the center of the conductor
C. In a magnetic field around the conductor
D. In a magnetic field in the center of the conductor

**A** After the previous two questions, you should realize that RF flows mostly along the surface of a conductor.

**E5F04 Why does most of an RF current flow near the surface of a conductor?**

A. Because a conductor has AC resistance due to self-inductance
B. Because the RF resistance of a conductor is much less than the DC resistance
C. Because of the heating of the conductor's interior
D. Because of skin effect

**D** Here you have another variation on the skin effect question. Were you able to identify the correct answer?

**E5F05 Why is the resistance of a conductor different for RF currents than for direct currents?**

A. Because the insulation conducts current at high frequencies
B. Because of the Heisenburg Effect
C. Because of skin effect
D. Because conductors are non-linear devices

**C** At RF current flows mostly along the surface, while direct currents can use the full cross section of a conductor. In other words, the conductor looks larger at dc than it does at RF.

**E5F06 What device is used to store electrical energy in an electrostatic field?**

A. A battery
B. A transformer
C. A capacitor
D. An inductor

**C** You can store energy in a capacitor by applying a dc voltage across the terminals. Current will flow into the capacitor plates creating a charge between those plates. This charge represents an electrostatic field.

**E5F07 What unit measures electrical energy stored in an electrostatic field?**

A. Coulomb
B. Joule
C. Watt
D. Volt

**B** Energy is measured in Joules, which is a measure of capacity to do work.

**E5F08 What is a magnetic field?**

A. Current through the space around a permanent magnet
B. The space through which a magnetic force acts
C. The space between the plates of a charged capacitor, through which a magnetic force acts
D. The force that drives current through a resistor

**B** A magnetic field is the space through which a magnetic force acts.

**E5F09 In what direction is the magnetic field oriented about a conductor in relation to the direction of electron flow?**

A. In the same direction as the current
B. In a direction opposite to the current
C. In all directions; omnidirectional
D. In a direction determined by the left-hand rule

**D** The direction of a magnetic field about a conductor can be determined by using the left-hand rule. With the wire going across the palm of your left hand, and with your thumb pointed in the direction of electron flow, wrap your fingers around the wire. Your fingers will be pointing in the direction of the magnetic field.

**E5F10 What determines the strength of a magnetic field around a conductor?**

A. The resistance divided by the current
B. The ratio of the current to the resistance
C. The diameter of the conductor
D. The amount of current

**D** Magnetic field strength is proportional to the current, and is stronger when the current is greater.

**E5F11 What is the term for energy that is stored in an electromagnetic or electrostatic field?**

A. Amperes-joules
B. Potential energy
C. Joules-coulombs
D. Kinetic energy

**B** Stored energy is potential energy as long as it is stored. Don't be confused. In the metric system, energy is measured in joules, but that is not a given choice.

## E5G Circuit Q; reactive power; power factor

**E5G01 What is the Q of a parallel R-L-C circuit if the resonant frequency is 14.128 MHz, L is 2.7 microhenrys and R is 18 kilohms?**

A. 75.1
B. 7.51
C. 71.5
D. 0.013

**A** The Q for parallel R-L-C circuits is calculated by dividing the resistance by the reactance. Using the component values given, you'll find

$$Q = \frac{R}{X} = \frac{R}{2\pi f L} = \frac{18 \times 10^{3}}{2\pi \times 14.128 \times 10^{6} \times 2.7 \times 10^{-6}} = 75.1$$

**E5G02 What is the Q of a parallel R-L-C circuit if the resonant frequency is 4.468 MHz, L is 47 microhenrys and R is 180 ohms?**

A. 0.00735
B. 7.35
C. 0.136
D. 13.3

**C** Use the same formula as the previous question.

$$Q = \frac{R}{X} = \frac{R}{2\pi f L} = \frac{180}{2\pi \times 4.468 \times 10^{6} \times 47 \times 10^{-6}} = 0.136$$

**E5G03** **What is the Q of a parallel R-L-C circuit if the resonant frequency is 7.125 MHz, L is 8.2 microhenrys and R is 1 kilohm?**

A. 36.8
B. 0.273
C. 0.368
D. 2.72

**D** You'll find the Q for this circuit by using the friendly formula

$$Q = \frac{R}{X} = \frac{R}{2\pi f L} = \frac{1000}{2\pi \times 7.125 \times 10^{6} \times 8.2 \times 10^{-6}} = 2.72$$

**E5G04** **What is the Q of a parallel R-L-C circuit if the resonant frequency is 7.125 MHz, L is 12.6 microhenrys and R is 22 kilohms?**

A. 22.1
B. 39
C. 25.6
D. 0.0256

**B** The Q for this circuit is

$$Q = \frac{R}{X} = \frac{R}{2\pi f L} = \frac{22 \times 10^{3}}{2\pi \times 7.125 \times 10^{6} \times 12.6 \times 10^{-6}} = 39$$

**E5G05** **What is the Q of a parallel R-L-C circuit if the resonant frequency is 3.625 MHz, L is 42 microhenrys and R is 220 ohms?**

A. 23
B. 0.00435
C. 4.35
D. 0.23

**D** Use the familiar formula to find Q

$$Q = \frac{R}{X} = \frac{R}{2\pi f L} = \frac{220}{2\pi \times 3.625 \times 10^{6} \times 42 \times 10^{-6}} = 0.23$$

**E5G06 Why is a resistor often included in a parallel resonant circuit?**

A. To increase the Q and decrease the skin effect
B. To decrease the Q and increase the resonant frequency
C. To decrease the Q and increase the bandwidth
D. To increase the Q and decrease the bandwidth

**C** The Q and the bandwidth are inversely proportional. In other words, lower Q results in greater bandwidth and vice versa.

**E5G07 What is the term for an out-of-phase, nonproductive power associated with inductors and capacitors?**

A. Effective power
B. True power
C. Peak envelope power
D. Reactive power

**D** The correct term for the out-of-phase, nonproductive power associated with inductors and capacitors is reactive power.

**E5G08 In a circuit that has both inductors and capacitors, what happens to reactive power?**

A. It is dissipated as heat in the circuit
B. It goes back and forth between magnetic and electric fields, but is not dissipated
C. It is dissipated as kinetic energy in the circuit
D. It is dissipated in the formation of inductive and capacitive fields

**B** The reactive power stays in the fields, moving back and forth between the magnetic and electric fields. Only the resistive part of a circuit will dissipate power.

**E5G09 In a circuit where the AC voltage and current are out of phase, how can the true power be determined?**

A. By multiplying the apparent power times the power factor
B. By subtracting the apparent power from the power factor
C. By dividing the apparent power by the power factor
D. By multiplying the RMS voltage times the RMS current

**A** Power factor is a quantity that relates the apparent power in a circuit to the real power. You can find the real or true power by multiplying the apparent power by the power factor.

**E5G10 What is the power factor of an R-L circuit having a 60 degree phase angle between the voltage and the current?**

A. 1.414
B. 0.866
C. 0.5
D. 1.73

**C** The power factor is also the cosine of the phase angle between the voltage and the current, and the cosine of 60° is 0.5. The cosine of 0° is 1. When the voltage and current are in phase the power factor is 1 and there is no reactive power—it is all real power. When the voltage and current are shifted by 90°, the power is all reactive and the power factor is 0 (the cosine of 90°).

**E5G11 How many watts are consumed in a circuit having a power factor of 0.2 if the input is 100-V AC at 4 amperes?**

A. 400 watts
B. 80 watts
C. 2000 watts
D. 50 watts

**B** Here you apply the power factor to compute the power from

$$P = E \times I \times pF = 100\text{ V} \times 4\text{A} \times 0.2 = 80\text{ W}$$

**E5G12 Why would the power used in a circuit be less than the product of the magnitudes of the AC voltage and current?**

A. Because there is a phase angle greater than zero between the current and voltage
B. Because there are only resistances in the circuit
C. Because there are no reactances in the circuit
D. Because there is a phase angle equal to zero between the current and voltage

**A** Power used or dissipated in a circuit will be less than the product of the voltage and current if there is a phase shift between voltage and current in the circuit.

**E5G13 What is the Q of a parallel RLC circuit if the resonant frequency is 14.128 MHz, L is 4.7 microhenrys and R is 18 kilohms?**

A. 4.31
B. 43.1
C. 13.3
D. 0.023

**B** The Q for this circuit is

$$Q = \frac{R}{X} = \frac{R}{2\pi f L} = \frac{18000}{2\pi \times 14.128 \times 10^6 \times 4.7 \times 10^{-6}} = 43.1$$

**E5G14 What is the Q of a parallel RLC circuit if the resonant frequency is 14.225 MHz, L is 3.5 microhenrys and R is 10 kilohms?**

A. 7.35
B. 0.0319
C. 71.5
D. 31.9

**D** The Q for this circuit is

$$Q = \frac{R}{X} = \frac{R}{2\pi f L} = \frac{10000}{2\pi \times 14.225 \times 10^6 \times 3.5 \times 10^{-6}} = 31.9$$

**E5G15 What is the Q of a parallel RLC circuit if the resonant frequency is 7.125 MHz, L is 10.1 microhenrys and R is 100 ohms?**

A. 0.221
B. 4.52
C. 0.00452
D. 22.1

**A** The Q for this circuit is

$$Q = \frac{R}{X} = \frac{R}{2\pi f L} = \frac{100}{2\pi \times 7.125 \times 10^6 \times 10.1 \times 10^{-6}} = 0.221$$

**E5G16 What is the Q of a parallel RLC circuit if the resonant frequency is 3.625 MHz, L is 3 microhenrys and R is 2.2 kilohms?**

A. 0.031
B. 32.2
C. 31.1
D. 25.6

**B** The Q for this circuit is

$$Q = \frac{R}{X} = \frac{R}{2\pi f L} = \frac{2200}{2\pi \times 3.625 \times 10^{6} \times 3 \times 10^{-6}} = 32.2$$

## E5H Effective radiated power; system gains and losses

**E5H01 What is the effective radiated power of a repeater station with 50 watts transmitter power output, 4-dB feed line loss, 2-dB duplexer loss, 1-dB circulator loss and 6-dBd antenna gain?**

A. 199 watts
B. 39.7 watts
C. 45 watts
D. 62.9 watts

**B** This is the first of a series of questions related to dB and effective radiated power. System gains and losses are usually expressed in dB, because it makes computations easier. In this problem there is a net loss of 1 dB in the system. Put that into the formula for dB and you get

$$\text{dB} = 10 \log\left(\frac{P_2}{P_1}\right) = \left(-4 - 2 - 1 + 6\right)\text{dB} = 10 \log\left(\frac{P_2}{50\text{ W}}\right)$$

now divide each side by 10 to get

$$-0.1\text{ dB} = \log\left(\frac{P_2}{50\text{ W}}\right)$$

next take the antilog, or inverse log, of each side and get

$$\log^{-1}\left(-0.1\text{ dB}\right) = \frac{P_2}{50\text{ W}}$$

now multiply both sides by 50 W and solve for $P_2$

$$\log^{1}\left(-0.1\text{ dB}\right) \times 50\text{ W} = P_2 = 0.79 \times 50\text{ W} = 39.7\text{ W}$$

My calculator uses "$10^x$" for the $\log^{-1}$ or antilog function.

**E5H02 What is the effective radiated power of a repeater station with 50 watts transmitter power output, 5-dB feed line loss, 3-dB duplexer loss, 1-dB circulator loss and 7-dBd antenna gain?**

A. 79.2 watts
B. 315 watts
C. 31.5 watts
D. 40.5 watts

C Use the dB formula here, just as you did for the previous question. Plug in the values

$$\text{dB} = 10\log\left(\frac{P_2}{P_1}\right) = \left(-5-3-1+7\right)\text{ dB} = 10\log\left(\frac{P_2}{50\text{ W}}\right)$$

divide each side by ten and then take the antilog

$$\log^{-1}\left(-0.2\text{ dB}\right) = \frac{P_2}{50\text{ W}}$$

multiply both sides by 50 and finish solving the problem

$$\log^{-1}\left(-0.2\text{ dB}\right) \times 50\text{ W} = P_2 = 0.63 \times 50\text{ W} = 31.5\text{ W}$$

**E5H03 What is the effective radiated power of a station with 75 watts transmitter power output, 4-dB feed line loss and 10-dBd antenna gain?**

A. 600 watts
B. 75 watts
C. 150 watts
D. 299 watts

**D** You only need to plug the numbers into the formula. Just as you've been doing.

$$\text{dB} = 10 \log\left(\frac{P_2}{P_1}\right) = \left(-4 + 10\right) \text{dB} = 10 \log\left(\frac{P_2}{75 \text{ W}}\right)$$

once again you'll divide both sides by ten and take the antilog of each side

$$\log^{-1}\left(0.6 \text{ dB}\right) = \frac{P_2}{75 \text{ W}}$$

and the final step

$$\log^{-1}\left(0.6 \text{ dB}\right) \times 75 \text{ W} = P_2 = 3.98 \times 75 \text{ W} = 299 \text{ W}$$

**E5H04 What is the effective radiated power of a repeater station with 75 watts transmitter power output, 5-dB feed line loss, 3-dB duplexer loss, 1-dB circulator loss and 6-dBd antenna gain?**

A. 37.6 watts
B. 237 watts
C. 150 watts
D. 23.7 watts

**A** Now that you are familiar with the dB formula, why don't you put it in another form. You can do it this way

$$\text{dB} = 10 \log\left(\frac{P_2}{P_1}\right)$$

Don't plug in the number, just solve for $P_2$. Do that just as you did with a number and divide both sides by 10 and then take the antilog of both sides for

$$\log^{-1}\left(\frac{dB}{10}\right) = \frac{P_2}{P_1}$$

finally multiply both sides by $P_1$

$$P_2 = P_1 \times \log^{-1}\left(\frac{dB}{10}\right)$$

now plug in the values for this problem and solve

$$P_2 = 75 \times \log^{-1}\left(\frac{-5-3-1+6}{10}\right) = 75 \times 0.5 = 37.6$$

**E5H05 What is the effective radiated power of a station with 100 watts transmitter power output, 1-dB feed line loss and 6-dBd antenna gain?**

A. 350 watts
B. 500 watts
C. 20 watts
D. 316 watts

**D** Use the formula you derived for the previous question. Now plug in the problem values

$$P_2 = P_1 \times \log^{-1}\left(\frac{dB}{10}\right) = 100\ W \times \log^{-1}\left(\frac{6-1\ dB}{10}\right)$$

$$= 100\ W \times \log^{-1}(0.5\ dB) = 316\ W$$

Was that a bit easier?

**E5H06 What is the effective radiated power of a repeater station with 100 watts transmitter power output, 5-dB feed line loss, 3-dB duplexer loss, 1-dB circulator loss and 10-dBd antenna gain?**

A. 794 watts
B. 126 watts
C. 79.4 watts
D. 1260 watts

**B** Are these starting to look familiar? The effective radiated power is

$$P_2 = P_1 \times \log^{-1}\left(\frac{dB}{10}\right) = 100\ W \times \log^{-1}\left(\frac{+10 - 5 - 3 - 1\ dB}{10}\right)$$

$$= 100\ W \times \log^{-1}(0.1\ dB) = 126\ W$$

**E5H07 What is the effective radiated power of a repeater station with 120 watts transmitter power output, 5-dB feed line loss, 3-dB duplexer loss, 1-dB circulator loss and 6-dBd antenna gain?**

A. 601 watts
B. 240 watts
C. 60 watts
D. 79 watts

**C** The effective radiated power is

$$P_2 = P_1 \times \log^{-1}\left(\frac{dB}{10}\right) = 120\ W \times \log^{-1}\left(\frac{6 - 5 - 3 - 1\ dB}{10}\right)$$

$$= 130\ W \times \log^{-1}(0.3\ dB) = 60\ W$$

**E5H08 What is the effective radiated power of a repeater station with 150 watts transmitter power output, 2-dB feed line loss, 2.2-dB duplexer loss and 7-dBd antenna gain?**

A. 1977 watts
B. 78.7 watts
C. 420 watts
D. 286 watts

**D** You know the formula and the procedure. The effective radiated power is

$$P_2 = P_1 \times \log^{-1}\left(\frac{dB}{10}\right) = 150\ W \times \log^{-1}\left(\frac{7 - 2 - 2.2\ dB}{10}\right)$$

$$= 150\ W \times \log^{-1}(0.28\ dB) = 286\ W$$

**E5H09 What is the effective radiated power of a repeater station with 200 watts transmitter power output, 4-dB feed line loss, 3.2-dB duplexer loss, 0.8-dB circulator loss and 10-dBd antenna gain?**

A. 317 watts
B. 2000 watts
C. 126 watts
D. 300 watts

**A** The effective radiated power is

$$P_2 = P_1 \times \log^{-1}\left(\frac{dB}{10}\right) = 200\ W \times \log^{-1}\left(\frac{10 - 4 - 3.2 - 0.8\ dB}{10}\right)$$

$$= 200\ W \times \log^{-1}(0.2\ dB) = 317\ W$$

**E5H10 What is the effective radiated power of a repeater station with 200 watts transmitter power output, 2-dB feed line loss, 2.8-dB duplexer loss, 1.2-dB circulator loss and 7-dBd antenna gain?**

A. 159 watts
B. 252 watts
C. 632 watts
D. 63.2 watts

**B** The effective radiated power is

$$P_2 = P_1 \times \log^{-1}\left(\frac{dB}{10}\right) = 200\ W \times \log^{-1}\left(\frac{7 - 2 - 2.8 - 1.2\ dB}{10}\right)$$

$$= 200\ W \times \log^{-1}(0.1\ dB) = 252\ W$$

**E5H11 What term describes station output (including the transmitter, antenna and everything in between), when considering transmitter power and system gains and losses?**

A. Power factor
B. Half-power bandwidth
C. Effective radiated power
D. Apparent power

**C** Effective radiated power is the station output (including the transmitter, antenna and everything in between), considering transmitter power and system gains and losses.

**E5H12 What is reactive power?**

A. Wattless, nonproductive power
B. Power consumed in wire resistance in an inductor
C. Power lost because of capacitor leakage
D. Power consumed in circuit Q

**A** Reactive power is nonproductive, wattless power.

**E5H13 What is the power factor of an RL circuit having a 45 degree phase angle between the voltage and the current?**

A. 0.866
B. 1.0
C. 0.5
D. 0.707

**D** As you learned earlier, the power factor is cos(θ). In this case, Pf = cos(45°) = 0.707.

**E5H14 What is the power factor of an RL circuit having a 30 degree phase angle between the voltage and the current?**

A. 1.73
B. 0.5
C. 0.866
D. 0.577

**C** Do you remember that power factor is the cosine of the phase angle? In this case, Pf = cos(30°) = 0.866.

**E5H15 How many watts are consumed in a circuit having a power factor of 0.6 if the input is 200V AC at 5 amperes?**

A. 200 watts
B. 1000 watts
C. 1600 watts
D. 600 watts

**D** Here you apply the power factor to an actual computation. The power is P = V × I × Pf = (200 V) × (5 A) × (0.6) = 600 W.

**E5H16 How many watts are consumed in a circuit having a power factor of 0.71 if the apparent power is 500 watts?**

A. 704 W
B. 355 W
C. 252 W
D. 1.42 mW

**B** Once again you use the power factor in the computation. The power is P = (500 W) × (0.71) = 355 W.

## E5I Photoconductive principles and effects

**E5I01 What is photoconductivity?**

A. The conversion of photon energy to electromotive energy
B. The increased conductivity of an illuminated semiconductor junction
C. The conversion of electromotive energy to photon energy
D. The decreased conductivity of an illuminated semiconductor junction

**B** The total conductance of a crystalline semiconductor material may increase and the resistance decrease when light shines on the surface. This is called the photoconductive effect, or photoconductivity.

**E5I02 What happens to the conductivity of a photoconductive material when light shines on it?**

A. It increases
B. It decreases
C. It stays the same
D. It becomes unstable

**A** The conductance of a photoconductive material increases when light shines on it.

**E5I03 What happens to the resistance of a photoconductive material when light shines on it?**

A. It increases
B. It becomes unstable
C. It stays the same
D. It decreases

**D** Be careful when reading the question. It has changed the reference from conductance to resistance, which is the reciprocal or opposite of conductance. If the conductivity increases, and you know it does, then the resistance decreases.

**E5I04 What happens to the conductivity of a semiconductor junction when light shines on it?**

A. It stays the same
B. It becomes unstable
C. It increases
D. It decreases

**C** Since semiconductors are by nature photoconductive materials, this question is a restatement of a previous one. The conductivity increases.

**E5I05 What is an optocoupler?**

A. A resistor and a capacitor
B. A frequency modulated helium-neon laser
C. An amplitude modulated helium-neon laser
D. An LED and a phototransistor

**D** An optocoupler is an LED and a phototransistor in a common IC package. Applying current to the LED causes it to light, and the light from the LED causes the phototransistor to turn on. Because they use light instead of a direct electrical connection, these devices provide a safe means to interface circuits of widely differing voltages.

**E5I06 What is an optoisolator?**

A. An LED and a phototransistor
B. A P-N junction that develops an excess positive charge when exposed to light
C. An LED and a capacitor
D. An LED and a solar cell

**A** An optoisolator or optocoupler is an LED and a phototransistor in a common IC package. That means that optoisolators and optocouplers are basically the same type of device. In addition to the coupling through the LED and phototransistor, there is a very high impedance between the input and the output of these devices. This means there is no current between the input and output.

**E5I07 What is an optical shaft encoder?**

A. An array of neon or LED indicators whose light transmission path is controlled by a rotating wheel
B. An array of optocouplers whose light transmission path is controlled by a rotating wheel
C. An array of neon or LED indicators mounted on a rotating wheel in a coded pattern
D. An array of optocouplers mounted on a rotating wheel in a coded pattern

**B** An optical shaft encoder usually consists of two pair of emitters and detectors. A plastic disc with alternating clear and black radial bands rotates through a gap between the emitters and detectors. By using two emitters and two detectors, a microprocessor can detect the rotation direction and speed of the wheel. Modern transceivers use a system like this to control the frequency of a synthesized VFO.

**E5I08 What characteristic of a crystalline solid will photoconductivity change?**

A. The capacitance
B. The inductance
C. The specific gravity
D. The resistance

**D** You might expect to find conductance among the choices, but it's not there. The correct answer is resistance, which is the reciprocal of conductance. In other words, if you change one, you change the other—but in the opposite direction.

**E5I09 Which material will exhibit the greatest photoconductive effect when visible light shines on it?**

A. Potassium nitrate
B. Lead sulfide
C. Cadmium sulfide
D. Sodium chloride

**C** Common, inexpensive photodetectors for visible light are typically made from cadmium sulfide.

**E5I10 Which material will exhibit the greatest photoconductive effect when infrared light shines on it?**

A. Potassium nitrate
B. Lead sulfide
C. Cadmium sulfide
D. Sodium chloride

**B** Lead sulfide is the best choice for sensitivity to infrared light.

**E5I11 Which material is affected the most by photoconductivity?**

A. A crystalline semiconductor
B. An ordinary metal
C. A heavy metal
D. A liquid semiconductor

**A** Crystalline semiconductors work best. Metals can be affected by photoconductivity but not as much as semiconductors. Liquid semiconductors are affected less than crystalline semiconductors.

**E5I12 What characteristic of optoisolators is often used in power supplies?**

A. They have low impedance between the light source and the phototransistor
B. They have very high impedance between the light source and the phototransistor
C. They have low impedance between the light source and the LED
D. They have very high impedance between the light source and the LED

**B** Optoisolators have a very high impedance between the light source (input) and the phototransistor (output). That characteristic makes these devices particularly useful for interfacing circuits with different voltages or ground references.

**E5I13 What characteristic of optoisolators makes them suitable for use with a triac to form the solid-state equivalent of a mechanical relay for a 120 V AC household circuit?**

A. Optoisolators provide a low impedance link between a control circuit and a power circuit

B. Optoisolators provide impedance matching between the control circuit and power circuit

C. Optoisolators provide a very high degree of electrical isolation between a control circuit and a power circuit

D. Optoisolators eliminate (isolate) the effects of reflected light in the control circuit

**C** They are called isolators because they have a very high impedance between the input and the output. This provides a high degree of electrical isolation between the controlling circuit and the controlled circuit.

Subelement **E6**

# Circuit Components

There will be five questions on your Extra class examination from the Circuit Components subelement. These five questions will be taken from the five groups of questions labeled E6A through E6E.

## E6A Semiconductor material: Germanium, Silicon, P-type, N-type; Transistor types: NPN, PNP, junction, power; field-effect transistors (FETs): enhancement mode; depletion mode; MOS; CMOS; N-channel; P-channel

**E6A01 In what application is gallium arsenide used as a semiconductor material in preference to germanium or silicon?**

A. In high current rectifier circuits
B. In high-power audio circuits
C. At microwave-frequency frequencies
D. At very low frequency RF circuits

**C** Gallium arsenide (GaAs) has performance advantages for use at microwave frequencies. For that reason, it is often used to make solid-state devices for operation on those frequencies.

**E6A02 What type of semiconductor material contains more free electrons than pure germanium or silicon crystals?**

A. N-type
B. P-type
C. Bipolar
D. Insulated gate

**A** You should remember that electrons carry a negative charge or N. A semiconductor material that contains more free electrons than pure germanium or silicon crystals electrons is called N–type material.

**E6A03 What are the majority charge carriers in P-type semiconductor material?**

A. Free neutrons
B. Free protons
C. Holes
D. Free electrons

**C** P-type material has an apparent excess positive charge. This is because the majority charge carriers in P-type material are holes. Holes are the absence of electrons (negative charge), so they act like positive charges in the material.

**E6A04 What is the name given to an impurity atom that adds holes to a semiconductor crystal structure?**

A. Insulator impurity
B. N-type impurity
C. Acceptor impurity
D. Donor impurity

**C** A hole represents a missing electron in the crystal structure. Holes easily accept free electrons to fill the empty slot created by the missing electron. For that reason the impurity atom that adds holes to a semiconductor crystal structure is called an acceptor impurity.

**E6A05 What is the alpha of a bipolar transistor?**

A. The change of collector current with respect to base current
B. The change of base current with respect to collector current
C. The change of collector current with respect to emitter current
D. The change of collector current with respect to gate current

**C** An important transistor characteristic is its alpha, which is the ratio of collector current to emitter current. The smaller the base current, the closer the collector current comes to being equal to that of the emitter, and the closer alpha comes to being 1.

**E6A06 In Figure E6-1, what is the schematic symbol for a PNP transistor?**

A. 1
B. 2
C. 4
D. 5

**A** The PNP transistor symbol is shown at **A**. Here's a memory trick. Look at the arrow and remember that to make soup, you put the **P**eas i**N** the **P**ot.

Figure E6-1 — Refer to question E6A06.

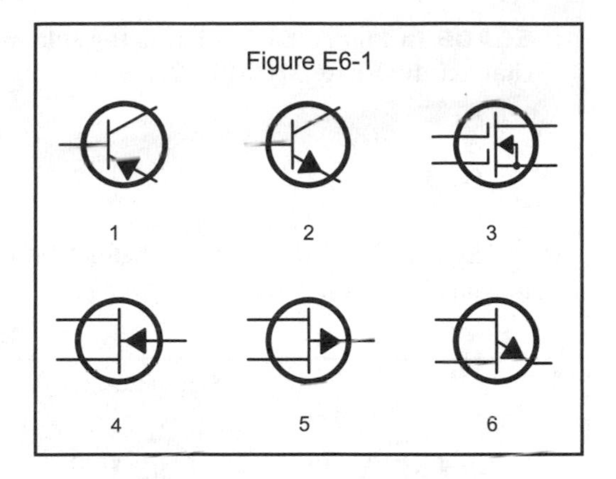


**E6A07 What term indicates the frequency at which a transistor grounded base current gain has decreased to 0.7 of the gain obtainable at 1 kHz?**

A. Corner frequency
B. Alpha rejection frequency
C. Beta cutoff frequency
D. Alpha cutoff frequency

**D** The alpha cutoff frequency of a transistor is the frequency at which a transistor grounded base current gain has decreased to 0.7 of the gain obtainable at 1 kHz.

**E6A08 What is a depletion-mode FET?**

A. An FET that has a channel with no gate voltage applied; a current flows with zero gate voltage
B. An FET that has a channel that blocks current when the gate voltage is zero
C. An FET without a channel; no current flows with zero gate voltage
D. An FET without a channel to hinder current through the gate

**A** A depletion-mode FET has a channel that passes current from the source to the drain when there is no bias voltage applied to the gate. In operation, the gate of a depletion-mode FET is reversed biased. When the reverse bias is applied to the gate, the channel is depleted of charge carriers, and current decreases.

**E6A09 In Figure E6-2, what is the schematic symbol for an N-channel dual-gate MOSFET?**

A. 2
B. 4
C. 5
D. 6

**B** Symbol 4 is a dual-gate N-channel MOSFET. The arrow points i**N** to the N-channel.

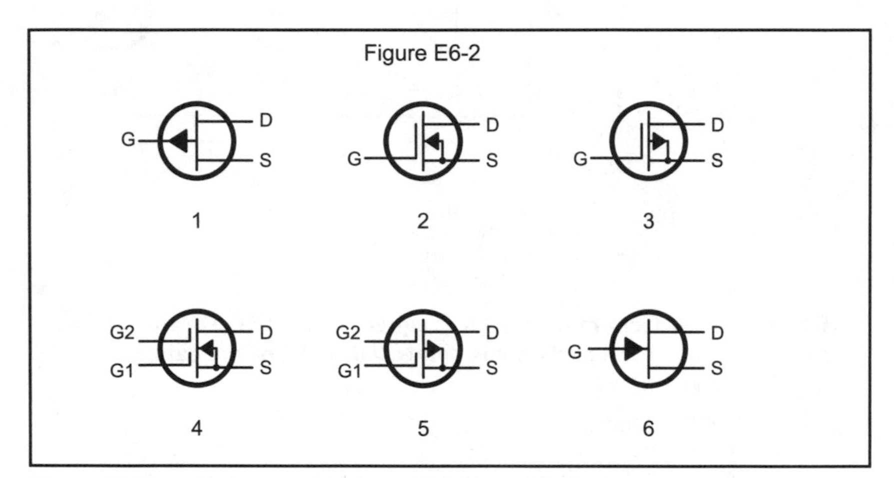


**Figure E6-2 — Refer to questions E6A09 and E6A10.**

**E6A10 In Figure E6-2, what is the schematic symbol for a P-channel junction FET?**

A. 1
B. 2
C. 3
D. 6

**A** In the figure, Symbol 1 is a P-channel junction FET. The arrow **P**oints out of the P-type channel.

**E6A11 Why do many MOSFET devices have built-in gate-protective Zener diodes?**

A. To provide a voltage reference for the correct amount of reverse-bias gate voltage
B. To protect the substrate from excessive voltages
C. To keep the gate voltage within specifications and prevent the device from overheating
D. To prevent the gate insulation from being punctured by small static charges or excessive voltages

**D** Nearly all the MOSFETs manufactured today have built-in gate-protective Zener diodes. Without this protection, the gate insulation can be perforated easily by small static charges on your hand or by the application of excessive voltages to the device.

**E6A12 What do the initials CMOS stand for?**

A. Common mode oscillating system
B. Complementary mica-oxide silicon
C. Complementary metal-oxide semiconductor
D. Complementary metal-oxide substrate

**C** Sometimes both P- and N-channel MOSFETs are placed on the same wafer. The resulting transistor arrays can be interconnected on the wafer and are designed to perform a variety of special functions. This construction is called complementary metal-oxide semiconductor (CMOS) because the P- and N-channel transistors complement each other.

**E6A13 How does DC input impedance on the gate of a field-effect transistor compare with the DC input impedance of a bipolar transistor?**

A. They cannot be compared without first knowing the supply voltage
B. An FET has low input impedance; a bipolar transistor has high input impedance
C. An FET has high input impedance; a bipolar transistor has low input impedance
D. The input impedance of FETs and bipolar transistors is the same

**C** Their modes of operation are different and so are their input impedances. The FET has a high input impedance. By contrast, the bipolar transistor has a low input impedance.

**E6A14 What two elements widely used in semiconductor devices exhibit both metallic and nonmetallic characteristics?**

A. Silicon and gold
B. Silicon and germanium
C. Galena and germanium
D. Galena and bismuth

**B** Silicon and germanium are the materials normally used to make semiconductor materials. These elements exhibit both metallic and nonmetallic characteristics, and they arrange themselves into crystals. Manufacturers add other atoms to these crystals to form the materials that are used in semiconductors.

**E6A15 What type of semiconductor material contains fewer free electrons than pure germanium or silicon crystals?**

A. N-type
B. P-type
C. Superconductor-type
D. Bipolar-type

**B** P-type material has fewer free electrons than pure crystals. This material is characterized by so called holes in the crystal structure that readily accept free electrons. The crystal atoms and the impurity atoms both have an equal number of protons and electrons, but when they combine into the crystal structure, the holes are formed.

**E6A16 What are the majority charge carriers in N-type semiconductor material?**

A. Holes
B. Free electrons
C. Free protons
D. Free neutrons

**B** N–type material has an excess of electrons (excess negative charges). The crystal atoms and the impurity atoms that comprise the material both have an equal number of protons and electrons, but when they combine into the crystal structure, there are electrons that are not bound into the crystal. These represent free electrons, which are the majority carrier in N-type material.

**E6A17 What are the three terminals of a field-effect transistor?**

A. Gate 1, gate 2, drain
B. Emitter, base, collector
C. Emitter, base 1, base 2
D. Gate, drain, source

**D** In an FET, a signal or voltage on the gate controls current flowing from the source to the drain.

## E6B Diodes: Zener, tunnel, varactor, hot-carrier, junction, point contact, PIN and light emitting; operational amplifiers (inverting amplifiers, noninverting amplifiers, voltage gain, frequency response, FET amplifier circuits, single-stage amplifier applications); phase-locked loops

**E6B01 What is the principal characteristic of a Zener diode?**

A. A constant current under conditions of varying voltage
B. A constant voltage under conditions of varying current
C. A negative resistance region
D. An internal capacitance that varies with the applied voltage

**B** Zener diodes operate with reverse bias voltage. They are specially manufactured to hold a constant voltage over a wide range of currents. They have sometimes been called a "poor man's voltage regulator" because of this ability to maintain a constant voltage.

**E6B02 What is the principal characteristic of a tunnel diode?**

A. A high forward resistance
B. A very high PIV
C. A negative resistance region
D. A high forward current rating

**C** A tunnel diode is a special type of device that has no rectifying properties. When properly biased, it possesses an unusual characteristic: negative resistance. Negative resistance means that when the voltage across the diode increases, the current decreases. This property makes the tunnel diode capable of amplification and oscillation.

**E6B03 What special type of diode is capable of both amplification and oscillation?**

A. Point contact
B. Zener
C. Tunnel
D. Junction

**C** Because of the negative resistance characteristics of tunnel diodes, they can be used to make both amplifiers and oscillators.

**E6B04 What type of semiconductor diode varies its internal capacitance as the voltage applied to its terminals varies?**

A. Varactor
B. Tunnel
C. Silicon-controlled rectifier
D. Zener

**A** Junction diodes exhibit an appreciable internal capacitance. It is possible to change the internal capacitance of a diode by varying the amount of reverse bias applied to it. Manufacturers have specially designed varactor diodes to take advantage of this property.

**E6B05 In Figure E6-3, what is the schematic symbol for a varactor diode?**

A. 8
B. 6
C. 2
D. 1

**D** In the drawing, symbol 1 is the schematic symbol for a varactor diode.

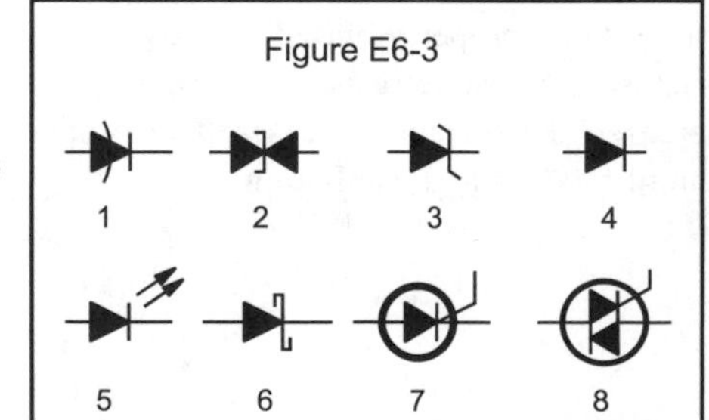


**Figure E6-3 — Refer to questions E6B05 and E6B10.**

**E6B06 What is a common use of a hot-carrier diode?**

A. As balanced mixers in FM generation
B. As a variable capacitance in an automatic frequency control circuit
C. As a constant voltage reference in a power supply
D. As VHF and UHF mixers and detectors

**D** Hot-carrier diodes have low internal capacitance and good high-frequency characteristics. They are often used in mixers and detectors at VHF and UHF.

**E6B07 What limits the maximum forward current rating in a junction diode?**

A. Peak inverse voltage
B. Junction temperature
C. Forward voltage
D. Back EMF

**B** Junction temperature limits the maximum forward current rating in a junction diode. As current flow through a junction diode increases, the junction temperature will rise. If too much current flows the junction gets too hot, and the diode is destroyed.

**E6B08 Structurally, what are the two main categories of semiconductor diodes?**

A. PN junction and metal-semiconductor junction
B. Electrolytic and PN junction
C. CMOS-field effect and metal-semiconductor junction
D. Vacuum and point contact

**A** The two main categories of semiconductor diodes are PN junction and metal-semiconductor junction.

**E6B09 What is a common use for point contact diodes?**

A. As a constant current source
B. As a constant voltage source
C. As an RF detector
D. As a high voltage rectifier

**C** Point-contact diodes have much less internal capacitance than PN-junction diodes. This means that point-contact diodes are better suited for RF applications. They are frequently used in RF detection circuits.

**E6B10** **In Figure E6-3, what is the schematic symbol for a light-emitting diode?**

A. 1
B. 5
C. 6
D. 7

**B** The schematic symbol for a light-emitting diode is shown in the drawing at number 5.

**E6B11** **What voltage gain can be expected from the circuit in Figure E6-4 when R1 is 10 ohms and RF is 470 ohms?**

A. 0.21
B. 94
C. 47
D. 24

**C** The voltage gain for the circuit in the drawing is $V_{out} / V_{in} = V_{gain} = -R_f / R1$. Plug in the resistor values, and you get $V_{gain} = -470\ \Omega / 10\ \Omega = -47$. The minus sign indicates that this is an inverting amplifier. That means that a positive input gives a negative output and vice versa. In stating gain, it is usual to ignore the inversion, and following that practice the gain is 47.

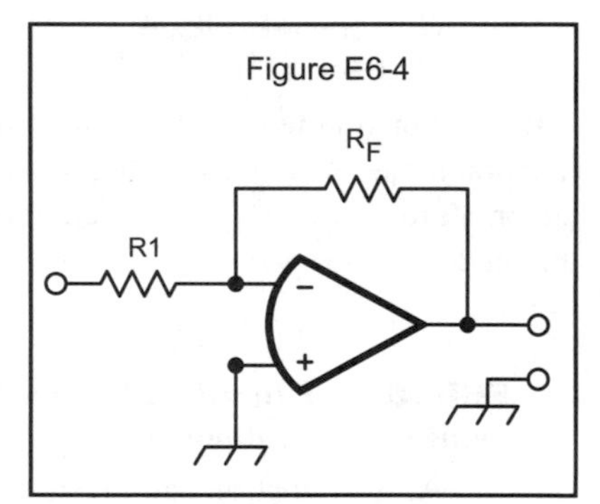


**Figure E6-4 — Refer to questions E6B11 and E6B14 through E6B16.**

**E6B12** **How does the gain of a theoretically ideal operational amplifier vary with frequency?**

A. It increases linearly with increasing frequency
B. It decreases linearly with increasing frequency
C. It decreases logarithmically with increasing frequency
D. It does not vary with frequency

**D** In an *ideal* operational amplifier, there is no change in gain as the frequency changes. In other words, the frequency response is flat.

**E6B13 What essentially determines the output impedance of a FET common-source amplifier?**

A. The drain resistor
B. The input impedance of the FET
C. The drain supply voltage
D. The gate supply voltage

**A** The output impedance of a FET common-source amplifier is approximately equal to the value of the drain load resistor.

**E6B14 What will be the voltage of the circuit shown in Figure E6-4 if R1 is 1000 ohms and RF is 10,000 ohms and 0.23 volts is applied to the input?**

A. 0.23 volts
B. 2.3 volts
C. –0.23 volts
D. –2.3 volts

**D** Use the voltage gain equation from the earlier question. The output voltage is equal to $V_{gain}$ $(-R_f/R1)$ times the input voltage. Using the numbers given here, $V_{out} = -(10000\ \Omega/1000\ \Omega) \times (0.23\ V) = -2.3\ V$.

**E6B15 What voltage gain can be expected from the circuit in Figure E6-4 when R1 is 1800 ohms and RF is 68 kilohms?**

A. 1
B. 0.03
C. 38
D. 76

**C** Use the same formula as before: $V_{gain} = V_{out}/V_{in} = -R_f/R1$. Using the resistor values given, you'll find $V_{gain} = -(68000\ \Omega/1800\ \Omega) = -38$. As before, you can ignore the minus sign when stating the circuit gain.

**E6B16 What voltage gain can be expected from the circuit in Figure E6-4 when R1 is 3300 ohms and RF is 47 kilohms?**

A. 28
B. 14
C. 7
D. 0.07

**B** Another question using the same formula: $V_{gain} = V_{out}/V_{in} = -R_f/R1$. Use the resistor values given and you'll find $V_{gain} = -(47000\ \Omega/3300\ \Omega) = -14$. Ignore the minus sign as you did before.

**E6B17** **(This question has been withdrawn)**

**E6B18** **Which of the following circuits is used to recover audio from an FM voice signal?**

A. A doubly balanced mixer
B. A phase-locked loop
C. A differential voltage amplifier
D. A variable frequency oscillator

**B** The phase-locked loop (PLL) is not only used in frequency synthesizers, it is also used as an FM demodulator. The other circuits mentioned will not recover audio from an FM voice signal.

**E6B19** **What is the capture range of a phase-locked loop circuit?**

A. The frequency range over which the circuit can lock
B. The voltage range over which the circuit can lock
C. The input impedance range over which the circuit can lock
D. The range of time it takes the circuit to lock

**A** A PLL is designed to operate over a certain frequency range. The capture range is the region in the frequency domain over which the circuit can lock.

**E6B20** **How are junction diodes rated?**

A. Maximum forward current and capacitance
B. Maximum reverse current and PIV
C. Maximum reverse current and capacitance
D. Maximum forward current and PIV

**D** Junction diodes are rated on their ability to handle reverse voltage or PIV (peak inverse voltage). They are also rated on the maximum forward current that they can handle.

**E6B21** **What is one common use for PIN diodes?**

A. As a constant current source
B. As a constant voltage source
C. As an RF switch
D. As a high voltage rectifier

**C** PIN diodes not only have areas that are doped to create P-type and N-type material, they also have an undoped, or intrinsic (I) area. These diodes are particularly useful as RF switches. If you start building RF hardware, at some point you will probably encounter a PIN diode being used as an RF switch.

**E6B22** **What type of bias is required for an LED to produce luminescence?**

A. Reverse bias
B. Forward bias
C. Zero bias
D. Inductive bias

**B** The LED glows when the junction is forward biased and current flows through it.

**E6B23** **What is an operational amplifier?**

A. A high-gain, direct-coupled differential amplifier whose characteristics are determined by components external to the amplifier
B. A high-gain, direct-coupled audio amplifier whose characteristics are determined by components external to the amplifier
C. An amplifier used to increase the average output of frequency modulated amateur signals to the legal limit
D. A program subroutine that calculates the gain of an RF amplifier

**A** The operational amplifier (op amp) is a high-gain, direct-coupled, differential amplifier that will amplify dc signals as well as ac signals. The key item to spot here is *differential amplification*.

**E6B24** **What is meant by the term op-amp input-offset voltage?**

A. The output voltage of the op-amp minus its input voltage
B. The difference between the output voltage of the op-amp and the input voltage required in the following stage
C. The potential between the amplifier input terminals of the op-amp in a closed-loop condition
D. The potential between the amplifier input terminals of the op-amp in an open-loop condition

**C** Op-amp input-offset voltage is the potential between the amplifier input terminals of the op-amp in a closed-loop condition. Offset results from imbalance between the differential input transistors in the IC.

**E6B25** **What is the input impedance of a theoretically ideal op-amp?**

A. 100 ohms
B. 1000 ohms
C. Very low
D. Very high

**D** The theoretical (perfect) op-amp has infinite input impedance. A good approximation to this is "very high."

**E6B26 What is the output impedance of a theoretically ideal op-amp?**

A. Very low
B. Very high
C. 100 ohms
D. 1000 ohms

**A** The output is the opposite of the input, and the ideal op amp has a very low output impedance.

**E6B27 What is a phase-locked loop circuit?**

A. An electronic servo loop consisting of a ratio detector, reactance modulator, and voltage-controlled oscillator
B. An electronic circuit also known as a monostable multivibrator
C. An electronic servo loop consisting of a phase detector, a low-pass filter and voltage-controlled oscillator
D. An electronic circuit consisting of a precision push-pull amplifier with a differential input

**C** The phase-locked loop is an electronic servo loop consisting of a phase detector, low-pass filter and voltage-controlled oscillator. This is illustrated in the drawing.

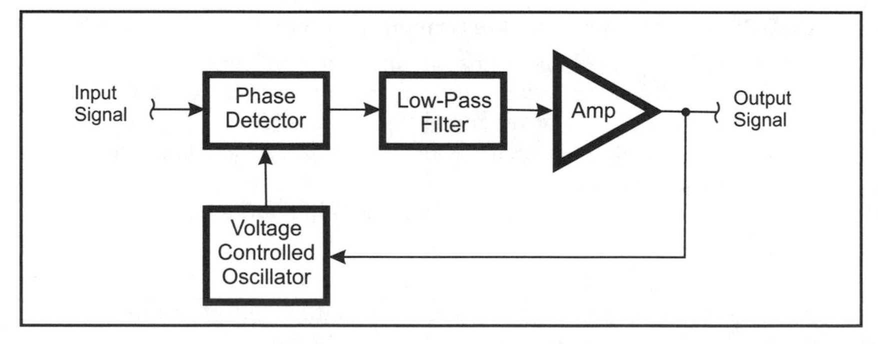


**Block diagram of a phase-locked-loop (PLL) circuit.**

**E6B28 What functions are performed by a phase-locked loop?**

A. Wide-band AF and RF power amplification
B. Comparison of two digital input signals, digital pulse counter
C. Photovoltaic conversion, optical coupling
D. Frequency synthesis, FM demodulation

**D** Phase-locked loops are used in frequency synthesis and FM demodulation applications.

## E6C TTL digital integrated circuits; CMOS digital integrated circuits; gates

**E6C01 What is the recommended power supply voltage for TTL series integrated circuits?**

A. 12 volts
B. 1.5 volts
C. 5 volts
D. 13.6 volts

**C** If you have experience with TTL, you will spot 5 V as the right answer. The supply voltage can vary between 4.7 and 5.3, but 5 V is optimum. Other logic families may use other voltages.

**E6C02 What logic state do the inputs of a TTL device assume if they are left open?**

A. A high logic state
B. A low-logic state
C. The device becomes randomized and will not provide consistent high or low- logic states
D. Open inputs on a TTL device are ignored

**A** TTL inputs that are left open, or allowed to "float," will assume a logic-one or high state. That's a result of their internal construction.

**E6C03 What level of input voltage is high in a TTL device operating with a 5-volt power supply?**

A. 2.0 to 5.5 volts
B. 1.5 to 3.0 volts
C. 1.0 to 1.5 volts
D. –5.0 to –2.0 volts

**A** TTL devices assign a logic-one to the range of voltages between 2.0 to 5.5 V.

**E6C04 What level of input voltage is low in a TTL device operating with a 5-volt power-supply?**

A. –2.0 to –5.5 volts
B. 2.0 to 5.5 volts
C. 0.0 to 0.8 volts
D. –0.8 to 0.4 volts

**C** A low TTL level is 0 to 0.8 V.

**E6C05 What is NOT a major advantage of CMOS over other devices?**

A. Small size
B. Low power consumption
C. Low cost
D. Differential output

**D** CMOS devices can be smaller, consume less power, and have a lower cost than other devices (in general). CMOS devices do NOT have a differential output.

**E6C06 Why do CMOS digital integrated circuits have high immunity to noise on the input signal or power supply?**

A. Larger bypass capacitors are used in CMOS circuit design
B. The input switching threshold is about two times the power supply voltage
C. The input switching threshold is about one-half the power supply voltage
D. Input signals are stronger

**C** CMOS levels typically are within 0.1 V of the supply levels. In other words, if you use a 9-V supply the high level will be in the range of 8.9 to 9 V. In the same circumstances a low level will be from 0 to 0.1 V. The input switching threshold is about one-half the power supply voltage, which in this case is 4.5 V. That means in this example that noise would have to be greater than about 4.4 V to upset circuit operation.

**E6C07 In Figure E6-5, what is the schematic symbol for an AND gate?**

A. 1
B. 2
C. 3
D. 4

**A** The schematic symbol for an AND gate is shown at 1.

**E6C08 In Figure E6-5, what is the schematic symbol for a NAND gate?**

A. 1
B. 2
C. 3
D. 4

**B** The schematic symbol for a NAND gate is symbol number 2 in the drawing.

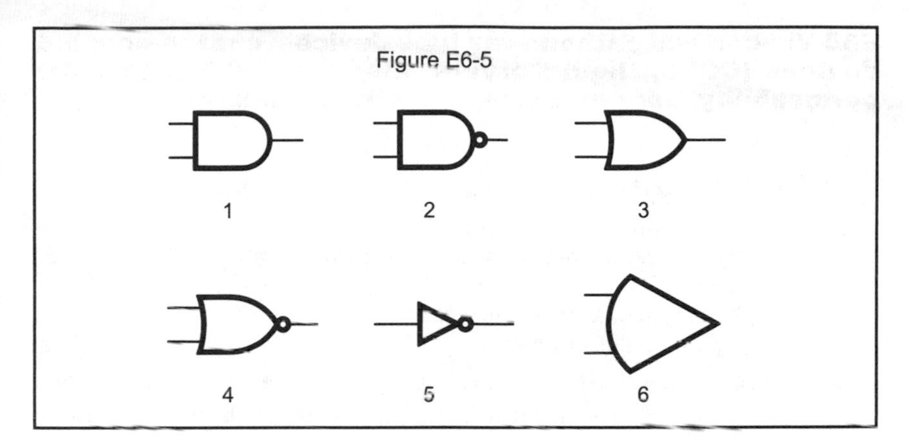


**Figure E6-5 — Refer to questions E6C07 through E6C11.**

**E6C09 In Figure E6-5, what is the schematic symbol for an OR gate?**

A. 2
B. 3
C. 4
D. 6

B The schematic symbol for an OR gate is shown in the drawing at 3.

**E6C10 In Figure E6-5, what is the schematic symbol for a NOR gate?**

A. 1
B. 2
C. 3
D. 4

D The schematic symbol for a NOR gate is shown in the drawing at 4.

**E6C11 In Figure E6-5, what is the schematic symbol for the NOT operation (inverter)?**

A. 2
B. 4
C. 5
D. 6

C The schematic symbol for the NOT operation (inverter) is shown at 5.

## E6D Vidicon and cathode-ray tube devices; charge-coupled devices (CCDs); liquid crystal displays (LCDs); toroids: permeability, core material, selecting, winding

**E6D01 How is the electron beam deflected in a vidicon?**

A. By varying the beam voltage
B. By varying the bias voltage on the beam forming grids inside the tube
C. By varying the beam current
D. By varying electromagnetic fields

**D** A vidicon tube is a relatively simple and inexpensive TV-camera pickup device. An electron beam is used to scan the picture area on the tube face. Horizontal and vertical deflection (scanning) of the electron beam in a vidicon is accomplished with fields generated by coils on the outside of the tube. Varying electromagnetic fields control the beam as it scans the tube face.

**E6D02 What is cathode ray tube (CRT) persistence?**

A. The time it takes for an image to appear after the electron beam is turned on
B. The relative brightness of the display under varying conditions of ambient light
C. The ability of the display to remain in focus under varying conditions
D. The length of time the image remains on the screen after the beam is turned off

**D** A given spot on a CRT remembers the last image on it for some period of time after the electron beam has moved away from that spot. The length of time the image remains on the CRT after the beam is turned off is called persistence.

**E6D03 If a cathode ray tube (CRT) is designed to operate with an anode voltage of 25,000 volts, what will happen if the anode voltage is increased to 35,000 volts?**

A. The image size will decrease and the tube will produce X-rays
B. The image size will increase and the tube will produce X-rays
C. The image will become larger and brighter
D. There will be no apparent change

**A** More is not always better! In this case where the anode voltage is significantly higher than the design voltage, the electrons in the scanning beam will take on a higher velocity. These higher velocity electrons will not be deflected as much, which means the image size decreases. Another effect of the higher energy electrons is that they may produce X-rays as they collide with their target.

**E6D04 Exceeding what design rating can cause a cathode ray tube (CRT) to generate X-rays?**

A. The heater voltage
B. The anode voltage
C. The operating temperature
D. The operating frequency

**B** The anode voltage controls the energy of the electrons, which can create X-rays. See the explanation to the previous question.

**E6D05 Which of the following is true of a charge-coupled device (CCD)?**

A. Its phase shift changes rapidly with frequency
B. It is a CMOS analog-to-digital converter
C. It samples an analog signal and passes it in stages from the input to the output
D. It is used in a battery charger circuit

**C** A charge-coupled device (CCD) is made from a string of metal-oxide semiconductor capacitors with a MOSFET on the input and output sides. The first capacitor stores a sample of the analog input-signal voltage. When a control pulse biases the MOSFETs to conduct, the first capacitor passes it sampled voltage on to the second capacitor, and it takes another sample. With successive control pulses, each input sample is passed to the next capacitor in the string. When the MOSFETs are biased off, each capacitor retains its stored charge. This process is sometimes described as a "bucket brigade," because the analog signal is sampled and then passed in stages through the CCD to the output.

**E6D06 What function does a charge-coupled device (CCD) serve in a modern video camera?**

A. It stores photogenerated charges as signals corresponding to pixels
B. It generates the horizontal pulses needed for electron beam scanning
C. It focuses the light used to produce a pattern of electrical charges corresponding to the image
D. It combines audio and video information to produce a composite RF signal

**A** A two-dimensional array of CCD elements using light-sensitive materials serves as the pickup in a modern video camera. The charge entering each capacitor is proportional to the amount of light striking the surface at that point. The capacitors store the charge as signals corresponding to the pixels of the array surface. The signal is shifted out of the CCD array a line at a time in a pattern that matches a vidicon scan. This CCD array forms the basis for a modern video camera.

**E6D07 What is a liquid-crystal display (LCD)?**

A. A modern replacement for a quartz crystal oscillator which displays its fundamental frequency
B. A display that uses a crystalline liquid to change the way light is refracted
C. A frequency-determining unit for a transmitter or receiver
D. A display that uses a glowing liquid to remain brightly lit in dim light

**B** When a voltage is applied across the liquid crystal material in an LCD, it changes the way light is refracted through the material. With no voltage applied, the crystal material is virtually transparent, but with voltage applied, the light is blocked, making the crystal appear black.

**E6D08 What material property determines the inductance of a toroidal inductor with a 10-turn winding?**

A. Core load current
B. Core resistance
C. Core reactivity
D. Core permeability

**D** The inductance of a toroidal inductor is determined by the number of turns of wire on the core, and on the core permeability. Permeability refers to the strength of a magnetic field in the core as compared to the strength of the field if no core were used. Cores with higher values of permeability will produce larger inductance values for the same number of turns on the coil.

**E6D09 By careful selection of core material, over what frequency range can toroidal cores produce useful inductors?**

A. From a few kHz to no more than several MHz
B. From 100 Hz to at least 1000 MHz
C. From 100 Hz to no more than 3000 kHz
D. From a few hundred MHz to at least 1000 GHz

**B** By careful selection of core material, it is possible to produce toroidal inductors that can be used from about 100 Hz to at least 1000 MHz.

**E6D10** **What is one important reason for using powdered-iron toroids rather than ferrite toroids in an inductor?**

A. Powdered-iron toroids generally have greater initial permeabilities
B. Powdered-iron toroids generally have better temperature stability
C. Powdered-iron toroids generally require fewer turns to produce a given inductance value
D. Powdered-iron toroids are easier to use with surface-mount technology

**B** The choice of core materials for a particular inductor presents a compromise of characteristics. Ferrite toroids generally have higher permeability values. Powdered-iron cores generally have better temperature stability. Since toroids can heat as current flows, temperature stability is an important consideration in some applications.

**E6D11** **What devices are commonly used as VHF and UHF parasitic suppressors at the input and output terminals of transistorized HF amplifiers?**

A. Electrolytic capacitors
B. Butterworth filters
C. Ferrite beads
D. Steel-core toroids

**C** A ferrite bead is a very small core with a hole designed to slip over a component lead. These are often used as parasitic suppressors at the input and output terminals of transistorized HF amplifiers.

**E6D12** **What is a primary advantage of using a toroidal core instead of a solenoidal core in an inductor?**

A. Toroidal cores contain most of the magnetic field within the core material
B. Toroidal cores make it easier to couple the magnetic energy into other components
C. Toroidal cores exhibit greater hysteresis
D. Toroidal cores have lower Q characteristics

**A** A primary advantage of using a toroidal core to wind an inductor rather than a linear core is that nearly all the magnetic field is contained within the core of the toroid. With a linear core, the magnetic field extends through the space surrounding the inductor.

**E6D13 How many turns will be required to produce a 1-mH inductor using a ferrite toroidal core that has an inductance index ($A_L$) value of 523 millihenrys/1000 turns?**

A. 2 turns
B. 4 turns
C. 43 turns
D. 229 turns

**C** The equation to use for ferrite cores is

$$N\left(\text{for ferrite cores}\right) = 1000\sqrt{\frac{L}{A_L}}$$

Where L = the inductance in mH.
$A_L$ = the inductance index, in mH per 1000 turns.
N = the number of turns.

Plugging the numbers into the equation gives

$$N = 1000\sqrt{\frac{L}{A_L}} = 1000\sqrt{\frac{1}{523}} = 1000 \times 0.0437 = 43.7$$

Which is approximately 43 turns.

**E6D14 How many turns will be required to produce a 5-microhenry inductor using a powdered-iron toroidal core that has an inductance index ($A_L$) value of 40 microhenrys/100 turns?**

A. 35 turns
B. 13 turns
C. 79 turns
D. 141 turns

**A** The equation to use for powdered iron cores is

$$N\left(\text{for powdered} - \text{iron cores}\right) = 100\sqrt{\frac{L}{A_L}}$$

Where L = the inductance in mH.
$A_L$ = the inductance index, in mH per 100 turns.

N = the number of turns.

Plug the numbers into the equation and you get

$$N = 100\sqrt{\frac{L}{A_L}} = 100\sqrt{\frac{5}{40}} = 100 \times 0.35 = 35$$

**E6D15 What type of CRT deflection is better when high-frequency waves are to be displayed on the screen?**

A. Electromagnetic
B. Tubular
C. Radar
D. Electrostatic

**D** While sufficient for television purposes, electromagnetic deflection is not suitable for measurement purposes. To display high-frequency signals on a lab-type oscilloscope, electrostatic deflection must be used.

**E6D16 Which is NOT true of a charge-coupled device (CCD)?**

A. It uses a combination of analog and digital circuitry
B. It can be used to make an audio delay line
C. It can be used as an analog-to-digital converter
D. It samples and stores analog signals

**C** The CCD samples the input signal voltage at times controlled by a clock signal, so this is a form of digital sampling. The actual sampled voltage is an analog value, however. The sampled voltage is not rounded to a predetermined step size, as it would be in an analog-to-digital converter. So a CCD cannot be used as an analog-to-digital converter.

**E6D17 What is the principle advantage of liquid-crystal display (LCD) devices?**

A. They consume low power
B. They can display changes instantly
C. They are visible in all light conditions
D. They can be easily interchanged with other display devices

**A** The principle advantage of LCD devices is that they consume very little power.

**E6D18 What is one important reason for using ferrite toroids rather than powdered-iron toroids in an inductor?**

A. Ferrite toroids generally have lower initial permeabilities
B. Ferrite toroids generally have better temperature stability
C. Ferrite toroids generally require fewer turns to produce a given inductance value
D. Ferrite toroids are easier to use with surface mount technology

**C** Based on the design equations and the answer to a previous question, you should be able to spot the correct answer. Ferrite material generally has a much higher permeability than that of powdered iron. For that reason, ferrite toroids generally require fewer turns to produce a given inductance value.

## E6E Quartz crystal (frequency determining properties as used in oscillators and filters); monolithic amplifiers (MMICs)

**E6E01 For single-sideband phone emissions, what would be the bandwidth of a good crystal lattice band-pass filter?**

A. 6 kHz at –6 dB
B. 2.1 kHz at –6 dB
C. 500 Hz at –6 dB
D. 15 kHz at –6 dB

**B** SSB transmissions require a bit over 2 kHz of bandwidth. A typical bandwidth is 2.1 kHz at the –6 dB points. This represents the difference between the highest and the lowest voice frequencies that will pass through the filter.

**E6E02 For double-sideband phone emissions, what would be the bandwidth of a good crystal lattice band-pass filter?**

A. 1 kHz at –6 dB
B. 500 Hz at –6 dB
C. 6 kHz at –6 dB
D. 15 kHz at –6 dB

**C** For double-sideband phone emissions, you'll need a bandwidth equal to twice the highest voice frequency that will pass through the filter. That would typically be 6 kHz at –6 dB for a good filter.

**E6E03 What is a crystal lattice filter?**

A. A power supply filter made with interlaced quartz crystals
B. An audio filter made with four quartz crystals that resonate at 1-kHz intervals
C. A filter with wide bandwidth and shallow skirts made using quartz crystals
D. A filter with narrow bandwidth and steep skirts made using quartz crystals

**D** Crystal lattice filters are made using quartz crystals. They are characterized as having a relatively narrow bandwidth and steep skirts.

**E6E04 What technique is used to construct low-cost, high-performance crystal ladder filters?**

A. Obtain a small quantity of custom-made crystals
B. Choose a crystal with the desired bandwidth and operating frequency to match a desired center frequency
C. Measure crystal bandwidth to ensure at least 20% coupling
D. Measure crystal frequencies and carefully select units with a frequency variation of less than 10% of the desired filter bandwidth

**D** If you wish to construct a low-cost, high-performance crystal ladder filter, start with a collection of crystals that have approximately the same frequency. Measure their frequencies in an oscillator circuit. Select crystals with a frequency variation of less than 10% of the desired filter bandwidth. In other words, if you want to build a 500-Hz bandwidth filter, select crystals that are all within 50 Hz of each other.

**E6E05 Which of the following factors has the greatest effect in helping determine the bandwidth and response shape of a crystal ladder filter?**

A. The relative frequencies of the individual crystals
B. The DC voltage applied to the quartz crystal
C. The gain of the RF stage preceding the filter
D. The amplitude of the signals passing through the filter

**A** The bandwidth and response shape of a crystal ladder filter mostly depends on the relative frequencies of the individual crystals.

**E6E06 What is the piezoelectric effect?**

A. Physical deformation of a crystal by the application of a voltage
B. Mechanical deformation of a crystal by the application of a magnetic field
C. The generation of electrical energy by the application of light
D. Reversed conduction states when a P-N junction is exposed to light

**A** The piezoelectric effect is the physical deformation of a crystal when a voltage is applied to it. This physical deformation results in crystal vibrations at a particular frequency and these vibrations can be used to control the operating frequency of a circuit.

**E6E07 What is the characteristic impedance of circuits in which MMICs are designed to work?**

A. 50 ohms
B. 300 ohms
C. 450 ohms
D. 10 ohms

**A** This is the first in a series of several questions about MMIC design. Since MMICs frequently interface with RF devices, they are designed with a characteristic impedance of 50 Ω for the input and the output.

**E6E08 What is the typical noise figure of a monolithic microwave integrated circuit (MMIC) amplifier?**

A. Less than 1 dB
B. Approximately 3.5 to 6 dB
C. Approximately 8 to 10 dB
D. More than 20 dB

**B** MMICs have good noise figure performance. Typical performance is in the neighborhood of 3 to 6 dB.

**E6E09 What type of amplifier device consists of a small pill sized package with an input lead, an output lead and 2 ground leads?**

A. A junction field-effect transistor (JFET)
B. An operational amplifier integrated circuit (OAIC)
C. An indium arsenide integrated circuit (IAIC)
D. A monolithic microwave integrated circuit (MMIC)

**D** The MMIC is unlike most other ICs that you may be familiar with. These ICs are quite small, often classified as "pill sized" devices, perhaps because they look like a small pill with four leads coming out of the device at 90° to each other. There is an input lead, an output lead and two ground leads on a typical MMIC.

**E6E10 What typical construction technique do amateurs use when building an amplifier for the microwave bands containing a monolithic microwave integrated circuit (MMIC)?**

A. Ground-plane "ugly" construction
B. Microstrip construction
C. Point-to-point construction
D. Wave-soldering construction

**B** MMICs are surface mount devices and MMIC construction typically uses microstrip techniques. Double-sided circuit board material is used, and one side serves to form a ground plane for the circuit. Circuit traces form sections of feed line. The line widths, along with the circuit-board thickness and dielectric constant of the insulating material determine the characteristic impedance, which is normally 50 Ω.

**E6E11 How is the operating bias voltage supplied to a monolithic microwave integrated circuit (MMIC) that uses four leads?**

A. Through a resistor and RF choke connected to the amplifier output lead
B. MMICs require no operating bias
C. Through a capacitor and RF choke connected to the amplifier input lead
D. Directly to the bias-voltage (VCC IN) lead

**A** The operating bias voltage is normally supplied to a four-lead MMIC through a resistor and RF choke connected to the amplifier output lead. This technique is illustrated in the drawing.

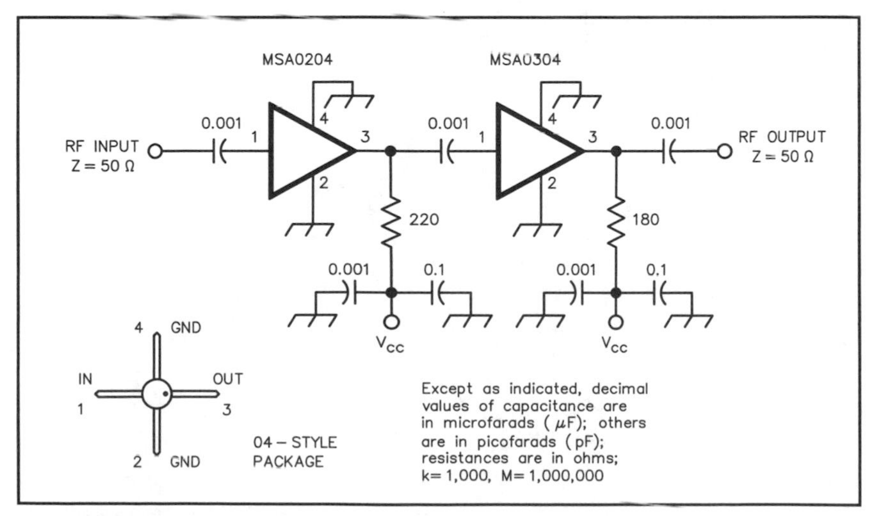


**Two MMICs in an amplifier circuit.**

**E6E12 How is the DC power from a voltage source fed to a monolithic microwave integrated circuits (MMIC)?**

A. Through a coupling capacitor
B. Through a PIN diode
C. Through a silicon-controlled rectifier
D. Through a resistor

**D** The DC power to a MMIC is normally fed through a resistor. See the drawing for an illustration of this technique.

**E6E13 What supply voltage do monolithic microwave integrated circuits (MMIC) amplifiers typically require?**

A. 1 volt DC
B. 12 volts DC
C. 20 volts DC
D. 120 volts DC

**B** MMIC amplifiers typically require 12 volts DC.

**E6E14 What is the most common package for inexpensive monolithic microwave integrated circuit (MMIC) amplifiers?**

A. Beryllium oxide packages
B. Glass packages
C. Plastic packages
D. Ceramic packages

**C** Integrated circuits typically come in plastic and ceramic packages. Of those two choices, plastic is the less expensive, and that's what they use for inexpensive MMIC amplifiers.

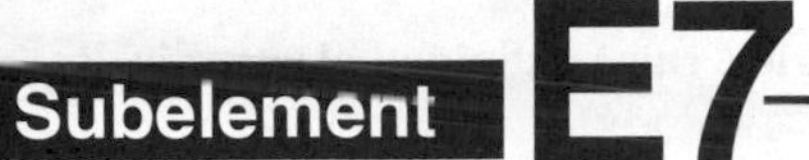

# Subelement E7

# Practical Circuits

There will be seven questions on your Extra Class examination from the Practical Circuits subelement. These seven questions will be taken from the seven groups of questions labeled E7A through E7G.

## E7A Digital logic circuits: Flip flops; Astable and monostable multivibrators; Gates (AND, NAND, OR, NOR); Positive and negative logic

**E7A01 What is a bistable multivibrator circuit?**

A. An "AND" gate
B. An "OR" gate
C. A flip-flop
D. A clock

**C** "Bistable multivibrator" is just another name for a flip-flop. It is a logic circuit that can be set to on or off. For that reason, a flip-flop can be used to store one bit of information.

**E7A02 How many output level changes are obtained for every two trigger pulses applied to the input of a "T" flip-flop circuit?**

A. None
B. One
C. Two
D. Four

**C** In the case of a toggle, or T-type, flip-flop, each pulse changes the output state. Thus, two pulses produce two output changes.

**E7A03 The frequency of an AC signal can be divided electronically by what type of digital circuit?**

A. A free-running multivibrator
B. A bistable multivibrator
C. An OR gate
D. An astable multivibrator

**B** A flip-flop, also known as a bistable multivibrator, can be used as a frequency divider. Since the output state changes for each input pulse, it takes two pulses to complete the output cycle from one binary state, to the opposite state and then back to the original state.

**E7A04 How many flip-flops are required to divide a signal frequency by 4?**

A. 1
B. 2
C. 4
D. 8

**B** Each flip-flop has the ability to divide a signal by a factor of 2, so the answer to this question is $4 \div 2 = 2$.

**E7A05 What is the characteristic function of an astable multivibrator?**

A. It alternates between two stable states
B. It alternates between a stable state and an unstable state
C. It blocks either a 0 pulse or a 1 pulse and passes the other
D. It alternates between two unstable states

**D** If you know your language, you will recognize "*a*" as meaning "*not*" so the device in question alternates between two unstable states.

**E7A06 What is the characteristic function of a monostable multivibrator?**

A. It switches momentarily to the opposite binary state and then returns after a set time to its original state
B. It is a clock that produces a continuous square wave oscillating between 1 and 0
C. It stores one bit of data in either a 0 or 1 state
D. It maintains a constant output voltage, regardless of variations in the input voltage

**A** A monostable multivibrator, sometimes called a "single shot," switches momentarily to the opposite binary state and then returns after a set time to its original state.

**E7A07 What logical operation does an AND gate perform?**

A. It produces a logic "0" at its output only if all inputs are logic "1"
B. It produces a logic "1" at its output only if all inputs are logic "1"
C. It produces a logic "1" at its output if only one input is a logic "1"
D. It produces a logic "1" at its output if all inputs are logic "0"

**B** Table 7-1 shows how logic gates work. By looking at the table, which is called a "truth table," you see that an AND gate requires a logic "1" on all inputs to produce a logic "1" at the output.

**Table 7-1**
**Output of various logic gates**

| *Input 1* | *Input 2* | *AND* | *NAND* | *OR* | *NOR* | *XOR* |
|---|---|---|---|---|---|---|
| 0 | 0 | 0 | 1 | 0 | 1 | 0 |
| 0 | 1 | 0 | 1 | 1 | 0 | 1 |
| 1 | 0 | 0 | 1 | 1 | 0 | 1 |
| 1 | 1 | 1 | 0 | 1 | 0 | 0 |

**E7A08 What logical operation does a NAND gate perform?**

A. It produces a logic "0" at its output only when all inputs are logic "0"
B. It produces a logic "1" at its output only when all inputs are logic "1"
C. It produces a logic "0" at its output if some but not all of its inputs are logic "1"
D. It produces a logic "0" at its output only when all inputs are logic "1"

**D** Look at table 7-1 where you can see that a NAND gate produces a logic "0" at its output only when all inputs are logic "1."

**E7A09 What logical operation does an OR gate perform?**

A. It produces a logic "1" at its output if any input is or all inputs are logic "1"
B. It produces a logic "0" at its output if all inputs are logic "1"
C. It only produces a logic "0" at its output when all inputs are logic "1"
D. It produces a logic "1" at its output if all inputs are logic "0"

**A** From Table 7-1, you can see that the OR gate produces a logic "1" at its output if any input is or all inputs are logic "1."

**E7A10 What logical operation does a NOR gate perform?**

A. It produces a logic "0" at its output only if all inputs are logic "0"
B. It produces a logic "1" at its output only if all inputs are logic "1"
C. It produces a logic "0" at its output if any input is or all inputs are logic "1"
D. It produces a logic "1" at its output only when none of its inputs are logic "0"

**C** Again, using Table 7-1 you can see that the NOR gate produces a logic "0" at its output if any input is or all inputs are logic "1."

**E7A11 What is a truth table?**

A. A table of logic symbols that indicate the high logic states of an op-amp
B. A diagram showing logic states when the digital device's output is true
C. A list of input combinations and their corresponding outputs that characterize the function of a digital device
D. A table of logic symbols that indicates the low logic states of an op-amp

**C** Table 7-1 is a truth table. A truth table lists input combinations and their corresponding outputs for a digital device or devices.

**E7A12 In a positive-logic circuit, what level is used to represent a logic 1?**

A. A low level
B. A positive-transition level
C. A negative-transition level
D. A high level

**D** In positive logic, a 1 is represented by a high voltage level.

**E7A13 In a negative-logic circuit, what level is used to represent a logic 1?**

A. A low level
B. A positive-transition level
C. A negative-transition level
D. A high level

**A** As you might have guessed, this is the opposite of the previous case. In a negative-logic circuit, a low level is used to represent a logic 1.

## E7B Amplifier circuits: Class A, Class AB, Class B, Class C, amplifier operating efficiency (i.e., DC input versus PEP), transmitter final amplifiers; amplifier circuits: tube, bipolar transistor, FET

**E7B01 For what portion of a signal cycle does a Class AB amplifier operate?**

A. More than 180 degrees but less than 360 degrees
B. Exactly 180 degrees
C. The entire cycle
D. Less than 180 degrees

**A** The Class AB amplifier conducts for more than 180 degrees but less than 360 degrees.

**E7B02 Which class of amplifier provides the highest efficiency?**

A. Class A
B. Class B
C. Class C
D. Class AB

**C** A Class C amplifier provides the highest efficiency of the classes listed in the question.

**E7B03 Where on the load line should a bipolar-transistor, common-emitter Class A power amplifier be operated for best efficiency and stability?**

A. Below the saturation region
B. Above the saturation region
C. At the zero bias point
D. Just below the thermal runaway point

**A** A Class A power amplifier should be operated below the saturation region for best efficiency and stability. Once an amplifier goes into saturation, it is no longer operating in Class A.

**E7B04 How can parasitic oscillations be eliminated from a power amplifier?**

A. By tuning for maximum SWR
B. By tuning for maximum power output
C. By neutralization
D. By tuning the output

**C** Neutralization is a technique that removes parasitic oscillations within a circuit.

**E7B05 How can even-order harmonics be reduced or prevented in transmitter amplifiers?**

A. By using a push-push amplifier
B. By using a push-pull amplifier
C. By operating Class C
D. By operating Class AB

**B** A push-pull amplifier reduces even-order harmonics.

**E7B06 What can occur when a nonlinear amplifier is used with a single-sideband phone transmitter?**

A. Reduced amplifier efficiency
B. Increased intelligibility
C. Sideband inversion
D. Distortion

**D** Nonlinear amplifiers cause distortion. SSB needs linear generation and recovery for proper demodulation.

**E7B07 How can a vacuum-tube power amplifier be neutralized?**

A. By increasing the grid drive
B. By feeding back an in-phase component of the output to the input
C. By feeding back an out-of-phase component of the output to the input
D. By feeding back an out-of-phase component of the input to the output

**C** A certain amount of capacitance exists between the input and output circuits in any active device. This capacitance will feedback in-phase some of the output signal to the input. This can cause instability and even oscillations. Neutralization uses a negative, or out-of-phase, feedback signal from the output to the input to offset or neutralize this in-phase feedback signal.

**E7B08** **What is the procedure for tuning a vacuum-tube power amplifier having an output pi-network?**

A. Adjust the loading capacitor to maximum capacitance and then dip the plate current with the tuning capacitor
B. Alternately increase the plate current with the tuning capacitor and dip the plate current with the loading capacitor
C. Adjust the tuning capacitor to maximum capacitance and then dip the plate current with the loading capacitor
D. Alternately increase the plate current with the loading capacitor and dip the plate current with the tuning capacitor

**D** The procedure for tuning a vacuum-tube power amplifier having an output pi-network is to alternately increase the plate current with the loading capacitor and dip the plate current with the tuning capacitor.

**E7B09** **In Figure E7-1, what is the purpose of R1 and R2?**

A. Load resistors
B. Fixed bias
C. Self bias
D. Feedback

**B** The two resistors form a voltage divider that provides a fixed bias point for the base.

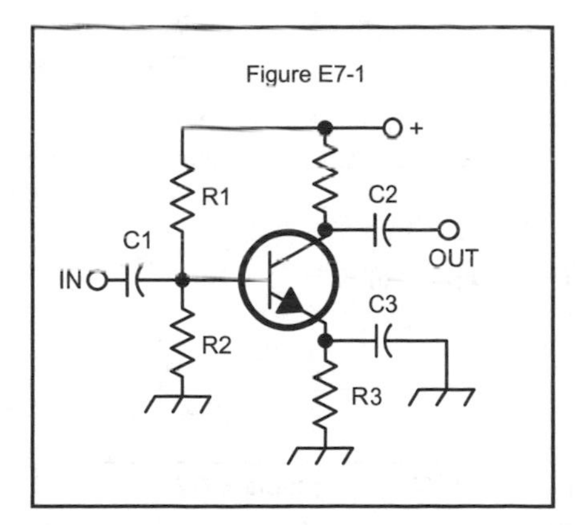


**Figure E7-1—Refer to questions E7B09 through E7B13.**

**E7B10** **In Figure E7-1, what is the purpose of C3?**

A. AC feedback
B. Input coupling
C. Power supply decoupling
D. Emitter bypass

**D** The capacitor C3 is known as an emitter bypass capacitor. It provides a low-impedance path from emitter to ground for ac signals, which allows them to bypass the emitter resistor.

**E7B11 In Figure E7-1, what is the purpose of R3?**

A. Fixed bias
B. Emitter bypass
C. Output load resistor
D. Self bias

**D** Current through R3 creates a voltage drop across the resistor, which provides a self bias.

**E7B12 What type of circuit is shown in Figure E7-1?**

A. Switching voltage regulator
B. Linear voltage regulator
C. Common emitter amplifier
D. Emitter follower amplifier

**C** This is a transistor amplifier circuit. Since the emitter is grounded and the output is taken from the collector circuit, it is called a common (or grounded) emitter amplifier.

**E7B13 In Figure E7-1, what is the purpose of C1?**

A. Decoupling
B. Output coupling
C. Self bias
D. Input coupling

**D** The capacitor is connected to the input and its job is input coupling. C1 allows the ac signal to enter the amplifier, while blocking dc currents.

**E7B14 In Figure E7-2, what is the purpose of R?**

A. Emitter load
B. Fixed bias
C. Collector load
D. Voltage regulation

**A** Since the resistor is connected to the emitter, you might guess that it is the emitter load. If so, you'd be right.

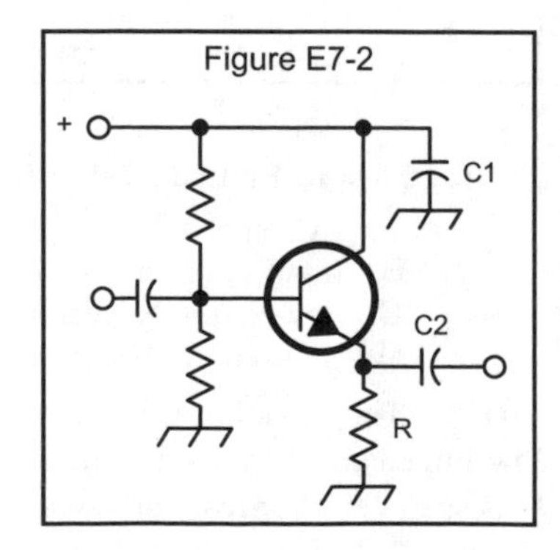


**Figure E7-2—Refer to questions E7B14 and E7B15.**

**E7B15 In Figure E7-2, what is the purpose of C2?**

A. Output coupling
B. Emitter bypass
C. Input coupling
D. Hum filtering

**A** The capacitor C2 is connected to the output terminal and its job is output coupling.

**E7B16 What is the purpose of D1 in the circuit shown in Figure E7-3?**

A. Line voltage stabilization
B. Voltage reference
C. Peak clipping
D. Hum filtering

**B** The circuit is a voltage regulator. D1 is a Zener diode and it provides a fixed reference to the base of the transistor.

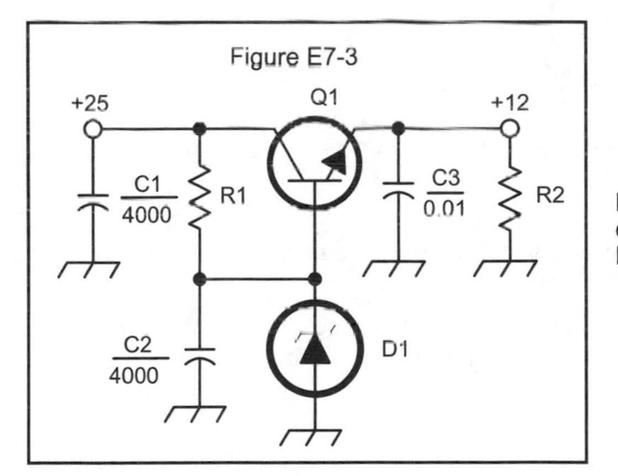


**Figure E7-3—Refer to questions E7B16 through E7B23.**

**E7B17 What is the purpose of Q1 in the circuit shown in Figure E7-3?**

A. It increases the output ripple
B. It provides a constant load for the voltage source
C. It increases the current-handling capability
D. It provides D1 with current

**C** The Zener diode will regulate voltage over a limited current range. Transistor Q1 increases that regulation range and thus increases the current-handling capability of the regulator circuit.

**E7B18** **What is the purpose of C2 in the circuit shown in Figure E7-3?**

A. It bypasses hum around D1
B. It is a brute force filter for the output
C. To self resonate at the hum frequency
D. To provide fixed DC bias for Q1

**A** The capacitor is there to bypass any AC hum to ground.

**E7B19** **What type of circuit is shown in Figure E7-3?**

A. Switching voltage regulator
B. Grounded emitter amplifier
C. Linear voltage regulator
D. Emitter follower

**C** Figure E7-3 is a linear voltage regulator.

**E7B20** **What is the purpose of C1 in the circuit shown in Figure E7-3?**

A. It resonates at the ripple frequency
B. It provides fixed bias for Q1
C. It decouples the output
D. It filters the supply voltage

**D** The purpose of C1 in the circuit is to filter the supply voltage.

**E7B21** **What is the purpose of C3 in the circuit shown in Figure E7-3?**

A. It prevents self-oscillation
B. It provides brute force filtering of the output
C. It provides fixed bias for Q1
D. It clips the peaks of the ripple

**A** C3 shunts any high-frequency ripple to ground, and by so doing prevents self-oscillation.

**E7B22** **What is the purpose of R1 in the circuit shown in Figure E7-3?**

A. It provides a constant load to the voltage source
B. It couples hum to D1
C. It supplies current to D1
D. It bypasses hum around D1

**C** R1 provides an electrical path and thus current to D1.

**E7B23** **What is the purpose of R2 in the circuit shown in Figure E7-3?**

A. It provides fixed bias for Q1
B. It provides fixed bias for D1
C. It decouples hum from D1
D. It provides a constant minimum load for Q1

**D** R2 provides a minimum load for Q1.

## E7C Impedance-matching networks: Pi, L, Pi-L; filter circuits: constant K, M-derived, band-stop, notch, crystal lattice, pi-section, T-section, L-section, Butterworth, Chebyshev, elliptical; filter applications (audio, IF, digital signal processing {DSP})

**E7C01** **How are the capacitors and inductors of a low-pass filter pi-network arranged between the network's input and output?**

A. Two inductors are in series between the input and output and a capacitor is connected between the two inductors and ground
B. Two capacitors are in series between the input and output and an inductor is connected between the two capacitors and ground
C. An inductor is in parallel with the input, another inductor is in parallel with the output, and a capacitor is in series between the two
D. A capacitor is in parallel with the input, another capacitor is in parallel with the output, and an inductor is in series between the two

**D** The correct configuration should look like the Greek letter π (pi). Since the question is looking for the low pass filter, we want the one with the inductor in the middle.

You should remember that capacitors tend to pass high frequencies and block low frequencies while inductors tend to pass low frequencies and block high frequencies. In the high-pass filter, the low frequencies are shunted to ground while the high frequencies pass through. In the low-pass filter, the high frequencies are shunted to ground while the low frequencies pass through.

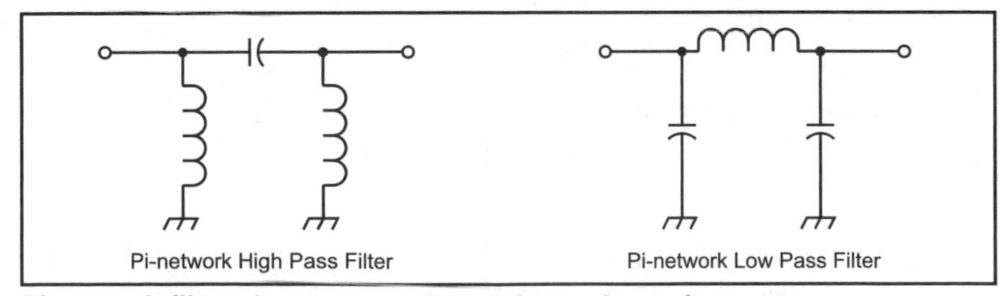


**Pi-network filters have one series and two shunt elements.**

**E7C02 What is an L-network?**

A. A network consisting entirely of four inductors
B. A network consisting of an inductor and a capacitor
C. A network used to generate a leading phase angle
D. A network used to generate a lagging phase angle

**B** An L-network is frequently used for impedance matching and is composed of an inductor and a capacitor.

**E7C03 A T-network with series capacitors and a parallel (shunt) inductor has which of the following properties?**

A. It transforms impedances and is a low-pass filter
B. It transforms reactances and is a low-pass filter
C. It transforms impedances and is a high-pass filter
D. It transforms reactances and is a narrow bandwidth notch filter

**C** The T-network described transforms impedances and is a high pass filter. It is high pass because the inductor shunts the low frequencies to ground while the capacitors allow the high frequencies to pass through.

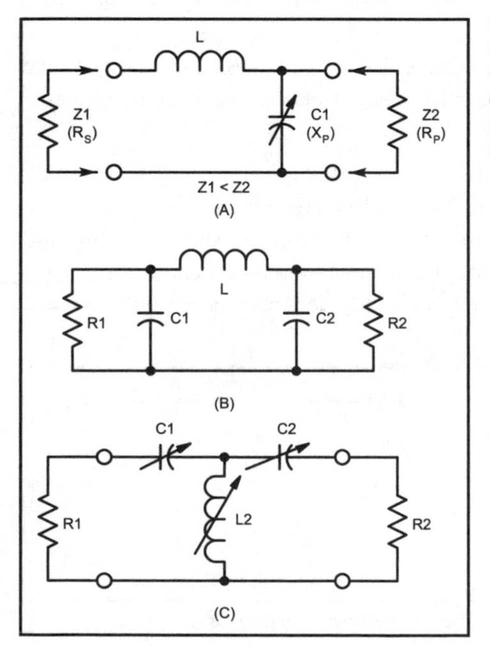


**Configurations for an L-matching network (A), a pi-network tuner (B) and a T-network tuner (C). A and B are configured for low-pass operation, but C forms a high-pass filter.**

**E7C04 What advantage does a pi-L-network have over a pi-network for impedance matching between the final amplifier of a vacuum-tube type transmitter and a multiband antenna?**

A. Greater harmonic suppression
B. Higher efficiency
C. Lower losses
D. Greater transformation range

**A** All of the suggested answers would be good goals to attain. However, only harmonic suppression is a correct response to this question.

**E7C05 How does a network transform one impedance to another?**

A. It introduces negative resistance to cancel the resistive part of an impedance
B. It introduces transconductance to cancel the reactive part of an impedance
C. It cancels the reactive part of an impedance and changes the resistive part
D. Network resistances substitute for load resistances

**C** Impedance matching networks transform one impedance to another. To accomplish this they must be able to cancel the reactive part of an impedance and change the value of the resistive part of a complex impedance.

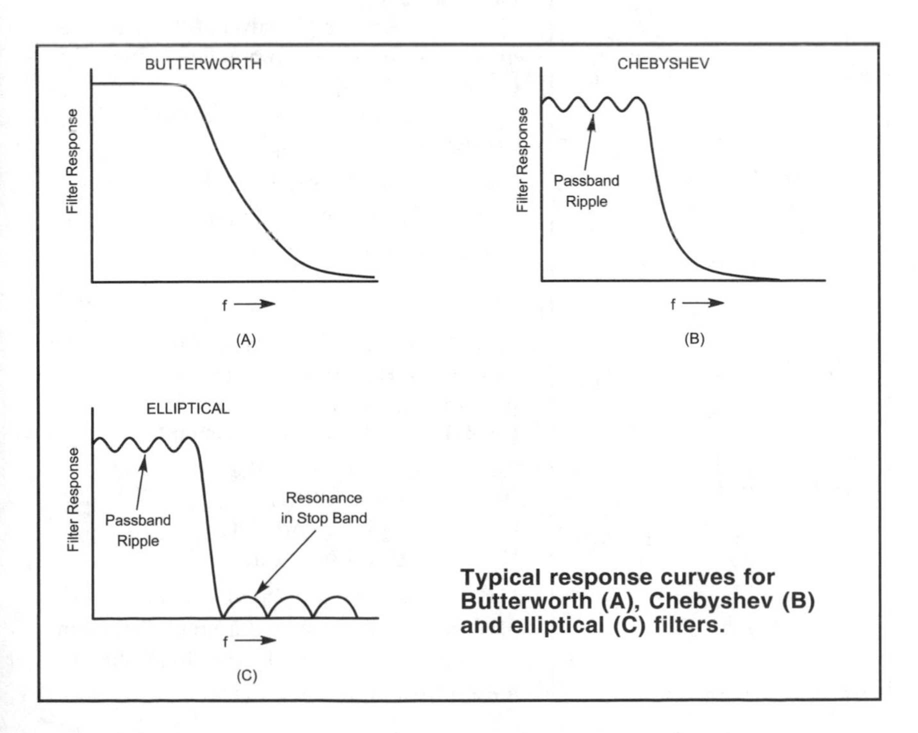


**Typical response curves for Butterworth (A), Chebyshev (B) and elliptical (C) filters.**

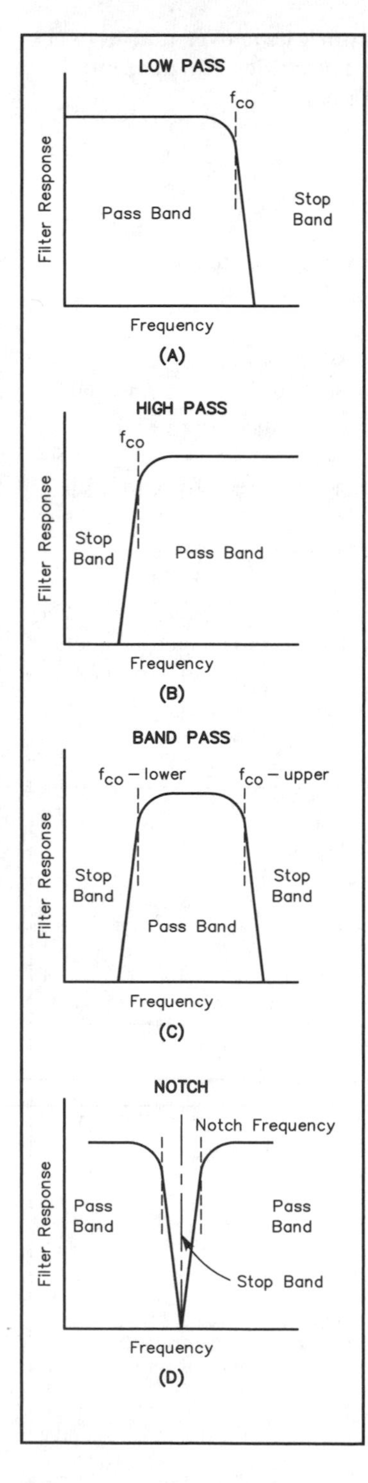


**Ideal filter-response curves for low-pass, high-pass, band-pass and notch filters.**

**E7C06 Which filter type is described as having ripple in the passband and a sharp cutoff?**

A. A Butterworth filter
B. An active LC filter
C. A passive op-amp filter
D. A Chebyshev filter

**D** A Chebyshev filter is characterized as having ripple in the passband and a sharp cutoff.

**E7C07 What are the distinguishing features of an elliptical filter?**

A. Gradual passband rolloff with minimal stop-band ripple
B. Extremely flat response over its passband, with gradually rounded stop-band corners
C. Extremely sharp cutoff, with one or more infinitely deep notches in the stop band
D. Gradual passband rolloff with extreme stop-band ripple

**C** An elliptical filter has an extremely sharp cutoff, with one or more infinitely deep notches in the stop band.

**E7C08 What kind of audio filter would you use to attenuate an interfering carrier signal while receiving an SSB transmission?**

A. A band-pass filter
B. A notch filter
C. A pi-network filter
D. An all-pass filter

**B** An unmodulated carrier is very narrow in frequency, and a notch filter can remove it with minimal reduction to the intelligibility of an SSB signal.

**E7C09 What characteristic do typical SSB receiver IF filters lack that is important to digital communications?**

A. Steep amplitude-response skirts
B. Passband ripple
C. High input impedance
D. Linear phase response

**D** Digital signals work best with linear phase response filters. Typical SSB receiver IF filters do not have linear phase response.

**E7C10 What kind of digital signal processing audio filter might be used to remove unwanted noise from a received SSB signal?**

A. An adaptive filter
B. A crystal-lattice filter
C. A Hilbert-transform filter
D. A phase-inverting filter

**A** An adaptive filter can be built using DSP. The DSP controller can be programmed to respond differently to different types of signals or conditions. This is called adaptive processing. An adaptive DSP filter can be useful for removing unwanted noise from a received SSB signal.

**E7C11 What kind of digital signal processing filter might be used in generating an SSB signal?**

A. An adaptive filter
B. A notch filter
C. A Hilbert-transform filter
D. An elliptical filter

**C** A Hilbert-transform filter introduces a 90° phase shift to all frequency components of a signal. This phase shift can be used to generate a single sideband (SSB) signal by the phasing method.

**E7C12 Which type of filter would be the best to use in a 2-meter repeater duplexer?**

A. A crystal filter
B. A cavity filter
C. A DSP filter
D. An L-C filter

**B** A duplexer is a device that allows a repeater transmitter and receiver to use the same antenna simultaneously. A cavity filter can provide the required isolation between the transmitter and receiver that is necessary. The other types listed are not suitable for the task.

**E7C13 What is a pi-network?**

A. A network consisting entirely of four inductors or four capacitors
B. A Power Incidence network
C. An antenna matching network that is isolated from ground
D. A network consisting of one inductor and two capacitors or two inductors and one capacitor

**D** The pi network takes its name from its resemblance to the Greek letter π. A pi network consists of one inductor and two capacitors or two inductors and one capacitor.

**E7C14 What is a pi-L-network?**

A. A Phase Inverter Load network
B. A network consisting of two inductors and two capacitors
C. A network with only three discrete parts
D. A matching network in which all components are isolated from ground

**B** A pi-L-network is essentially a pi-network with an additional series element. The pi-L-network consists of two inductors and two capacitors.

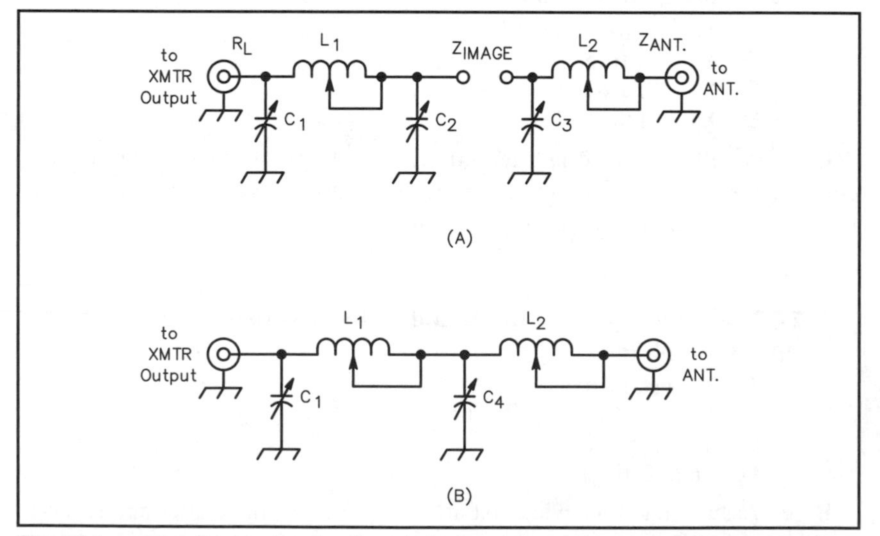


**The pi-L network uses a pi network to transform the transmitter output impedance ($R_L$) to the image impedance ($Z_{IMAGE}$). An L network transforms $Z_{IMAGE}$ to the antenna impedance, $A_{ANT}$. This is shown at A. Because $C_2$ and $C_3$ are in parallel, only a single capacitor ($C_4$) is needed. The actual configuration of the circuit is shown at B.**

**E7C15 Which type of network provides the greatest harmonic suppression?**

A. L-network
B. Pi-network
C. Pi-L-network
D. Inverse Pi network

**C** A pi-L-network provides the greatest harmonic suppression of those types listed. That's the advantage for the added complexity.

## E7D Oscillators: types, applications, stability; voltage-regulator circuits: discrete, integrated and switched mode

**E7D01 What are three major oscillator circuits often used in Amateur Radio equipment?**

A. Taft, Pierce and negative feedback
B. Colpitts, Hartley and Taft
C. Taft, Hartley and Pierce
D. Colpitts, Hartley and Pierce

**D** Colpitts, Hartley and Pierce are the "big three" oscillator types.

**E7D02 What condition must exist for a circuit to oscillate?**

A. It must have a gain of less than 1
B. It must be neutralized
C. It must have positive feedback sufficient to overcome losses
D. It must have negative feedback sufficient to cancel the input

**C** An oscillator requires positive feedback, which reinforces oscillation. You'll need enough positive feedback to overcome circuit losses in order to sustain oscillation.

**E7D03 How is the positive feedback coupled to the input in a Hartley oscillator?**

A. Through a tapped coil
B. Through a capacitive divider
C. Through link coupling
D. Through a neutralizing capacitor

**A** Hartley starts with H, and so does Henry—the basic unit of inductance. You can use that as a mnemonic to help you remember that the Hartley oscillator uses a tapped coil to provide the positive feedback needed for operation.

**E7D04 How is the positive feedback coupled to the input in a Colpitts oscillator?**

A. Through a tapped coil
B. Through link coupling
C. Through a capacitive divider
D. Through a neutralizing capacitor

**C** Colpitts starts with C, and so does capacitor. You can use that as a mnemonic to help you remember that the Colpitts oscillator uses a capacitive voltage divider to provide the positive feedback needed for operation.

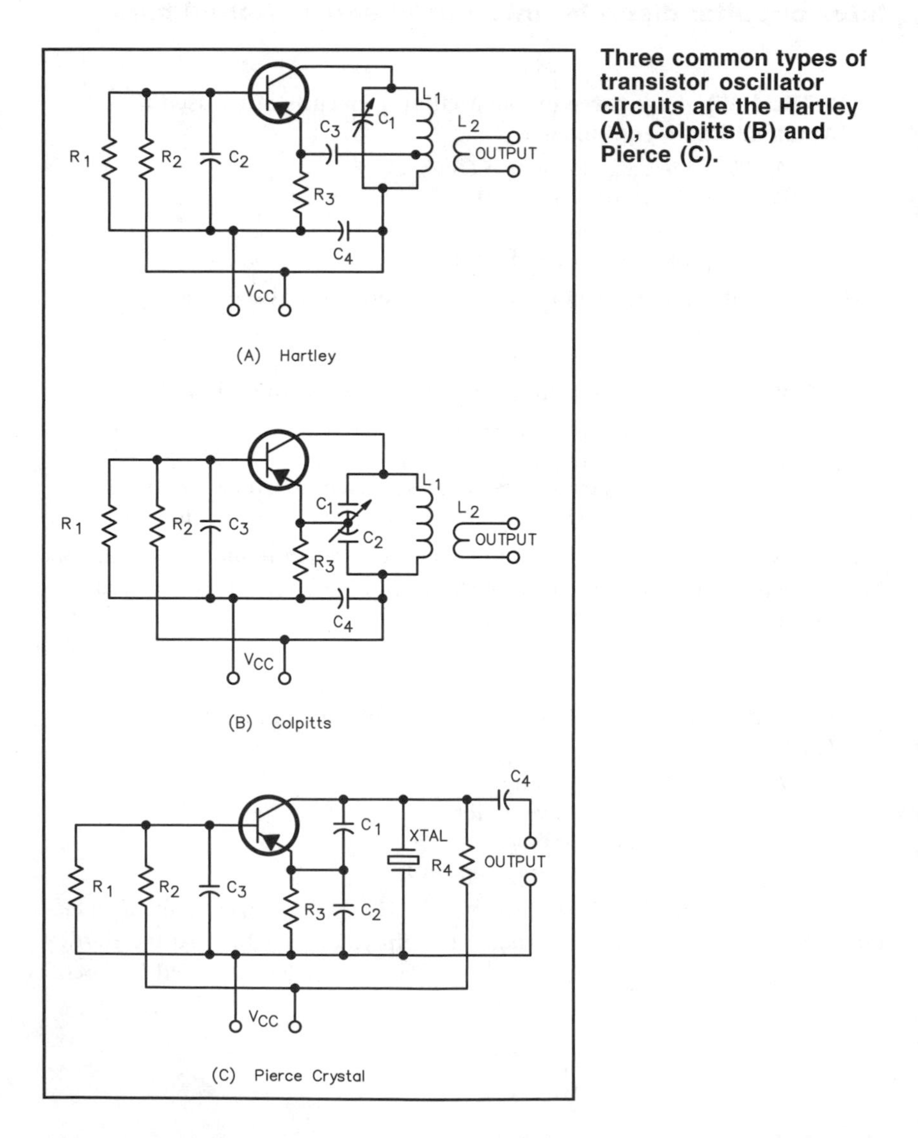


**Three common types of transistor oscillator circuits are the Hartley (A), Colpitts (B) and Pierce (C).**

**E7D05 How is the positive feedback coupled to the input in a Pierce oscillator?**

A. Through a tapped coil
B. Through link coupling
C. Through a neutralizing capacitor
D. Through a quartz crystal

**D** The Pierce oscillator provides positive feedback through a quartz crystal.

**E7D06 Which type of oscillator circuits are commonly used in a VFO?**

A. Pierce and Zener
B. Colpitts and Hartley
C. Armstrong and deForest
D. Negative feedback and Balanced feedback

**B** The right choice is Colpitts and Hartley, but you probably guessed that. The other answers are nonsense.

**E7D07 Why is very stable reference oscillator normally used as part of a phase-locked loop (PLL) frequency synthesizer?**

A. Any amplitude variations in the reference oscillator signal will prevent the loop from locking to the desired signal
B. Any phase variations in the reference oscillator signal will produce phase noise in the synthesizer output
C. Any phase variations in the reference oscillator signal will produce harmonic distortion in the modulating signal
D. Any amplitude variations in the reference oscillator signal will prevent the loop from changing frequency

**B** Phase-locked loop (PLL) frequency synthesizers derive their output from a reference oscillator. Any phase variations in this reference oscillator signal will produce phase noise in the synthesizer output. For that reason, you'll want to use a very stable oscillator for the reference.

**E7D08 What is one characteristic of a linear electronic voltage regulator?**

A. It has a ramp voltage as its output
B. The pass transistor switches from the "off" state to the "on" state
C. The control device is switched on or off, with the duty cycle proportional to the line or load conditions
D. The conduction of a control element is varied in direct proportion to the load current to maintain a constant output voltage

**D** A linear voltage regulator varies the conductance of a control element in direct proportion to the load current. This maintains a constant output voltage from the regulator. Because this is a linear circuit, the control is continual or proportional. There are no switching elements used in this type of regulator.

**E7D09 What is one characteristic of a switching electronic voltage regulator?**

A. The conduction of a control element is varied in direct proportion to the line voltage or load current
B. It provides more than one output voltage
C. The control device is switched on or off, with the duty cycle automatically adjusted to maintain a constant average output voltage
D. It gives a ramp voltage at its output

**C** A switching regulator, in contrast to a linear regulator has a switching circuit. In this type of regulator the control device is switched on and off electronically, with the duty cycle automatically adjusted to maintain a constant average output voltage. Switching frequencies of several kilohertz are normally used, to avoid the need for extensive filtering to smooth the switching frequency from the dc output.

**E7D10 What device is typically used as a stable reference voltage in a linear voltage regulator?**

A. A Zener diode
B. A tunnel diode
C. An SCR
D. A varactor diode

**A** A Zener diode can provide a stable voltage reference, and is frequently used for that purpose in linear voltage regulators.

**E7D11 What type of linear regulator is used in applications requiring efficient use of the primary power source?**

A. A constant current source
B. A series regulator
C. A shunt regulator
D. A shunt current source

**B** The series regulator draws current from the primary power source in proportion to the load. In other words, it only draws power from the primary source when that power is needed.

**E7D12 What type of linear voltage regulator is used in applications requiring a constant load on the unregulated voltage source?**

A. A constant current source
B. A series regulator
C. A shunt current source
D. A shunt regulator

**D** The shunt regulator regulates output voltage by providing a constant load to the unregulated (primary) voltage source. When more power is needed in the load, less power is diverted through the shunt regulator. When less power is needed in the load, more power is sent to the shunt element of the regulator.

**E7D13 Which of the following Zener diodes voltages will result in the best temperature stability for a voltage reference?**

A. 2.4 volts
B. 3.0 volts
C. 5.6 volts
D. 12.0 volts

**C** The breakdown voltage of Zener diodes varies with temperature. Those rated for operation between 5 and 6 V have the smallest variation with temperature changes, and so are most often used as a voltage reference.

**E7D14 What are the important characteristics of a three-terminal regulator?**

A. Maximum and minimum input voltage, minimum output current and voltage
B. Maximum and minimum input voltage, maximum and minimum output current and maximum output voltage
C. Maximum and minimum input voltage, minimum output current and maximum output voltage
D. Maximum and minimum input voltage, minimum output voltage and Maximum input and output current

**B** To design a three-terminal regulator circuit, you will need to know the input voltage range, the output current range and the maximum output voltage.

**E7D15 What type of voltage regulator limits the voltage drop across its junction when a specified current passes through it in the reverse-breakdown direction?**

A. A Zener diode
B. A three-terminal regulator
C. A bipolar regulator
D. A pass-transistor regulator

**A** This is a technically correct way to describe the action of a Zener diode.

## E7E Modulators: reactance, phase, balanced; detectors; mixer stages; frequency synthesizers

**E7E01 How is an F3E FM-phone emission produced?**

A. With a balanced modulator on the audio amplifier
B. With a reactance modulator on the oscillator
C. With a reactance modulator on the final amplifier
D. With a balanced modulator on the oscillator

**B** A reactance modulator is a simple and satisfactory device for producing FM in an amateur transmitter. The only way to produce a true emission F3E signal is with a reactance modulator on the transmitter oscillator.

**E7E02 How does a reactance modulator work?**

A. It acts as a variable resistance or capacitance to produce FM signals
B. It acts as a variable resistance or capacitance to produce AM signals
C. It acts as a variable inductance or capacitance to produce FM signals
D. It acts as a variable inductance or capacitance to produce AM signals

**C** A reactance modulator is typically a transistor connected to the RF tank circuit of an oscillator so that it acts as a variable inductance or capacitance. Think of FM when you hear reactance modulator. Also, remember that reactance deals with inductors and capacitors not resistors.

**E7E03 How does a phase modulator work?**

A. It varies the tuning of a microphone preamplifier to produce PM signals
B. It varies the tuning of an amplifier tank circuit to produce AM signals
C. It varies the tuning of an amplifier tank circuit to produce PM signals
D. It varies the tuning of a microphone preamplifier to produce AM signals

**C** A phase modulator varies the tuning of an RF amplifier tank circuit to produce PM signals.

**E7E04 How can a single-sideband phone signal be generated?**

A. By using a balanced modulator followed by a filter
B. By using a reactance modulator followed by a mixer
C. By using a loop modulator followed by a mixer
D. By driving a product detector with a DSB signal

**A** You can generate a single-sideband phone signal by using a balanced modulator followed by a filter. The balanced modulator produces a double-sideband suppressed-carrier signal. The filter removes the unwanted sideband.

**E7E05 What audio shaping network is added at a transmitter to proportionally attenuate the lower audio frequencies, giving an even spread to the energy in the audio band?**

A. A de-emphasis network
B. A heterodyne suppressor
C. An audio prescaler
D. A pre-emphasis network

**D** A pre-emphasis circuit is used in a transmitter to proportionally attenuate the lower audio frequencies, giving an even spread to the energy in the audio band.

**E7E06 What audio shaping network is added at a receiver to restore proportionally attenuated lower audio frequencies?**

A. A de-emphasis network
B. A heterodyne suppressor
C. An audio prescaler
D. A pre-emphasis network

**A** In a receiver, a de-emphasis circuit restores the proportionally attenuated lower audio frequencies. You can remember the order from pre-emphasis applied before (or pre) transmission.

**E7E07 What is the mixing process?**

A. The elimination of noise in a wideband receiver by phase comparison
B. The elimination of noise in a wideband receiver by phase differentiation
C. The recovery of the intelligence from a modulated RF signal
D. The combination of two signals to produce sum and difference frequencies

**D** In the mixing process, two signals are combined to produce their sum and difference frequencies.

**E7E08 What are the principal frequencies that appear at the output of a mixer circuit?**

A. Two and four times the original frequency
B. The sum, difference and square root of the input frequencies
C. The original frequencies and the sum and difference frequencies
D. 1.414 and 0.707 times the input frequency

**C** In the mixing process, two signals are combined to produce their sum and difference frequencies. However, the original frequencies do not disappear.

**E7E09 What occurs in a receiver when an excessive amount of signal energy reaches the mixer circuit?**

A. Spurious mixer products are generated
B. Mixer blanking occurs
C. Automatic limiting occurs
D. A beat frequency is generated

**A** Spurious mixer products will be produced if an excessive amount of input-signal energy reaches the mixer circuit. The level of these spurious mixer products may be increased to the point that they appear in the output. One result of these effects is that the receiver may be useless in the presence of extremely strong signals.

**E7E10 What type of frequency synthesizer circuit uses a stable voltage-controlled oscillator, programmable divider, phase detector, loop filter and a reference frequency source?**

A. A direct digital synthesizer
B. A hybrid synthesizer
C. A phase-locked loop synthesizer
D. A diode-switching matrix synthesizer

**C** A phase-locked loop synthesizer uses a stable voltage-controlled oscillator, programmable divider, phase detector, loop filter and a reference frequency source. See the block diagram.

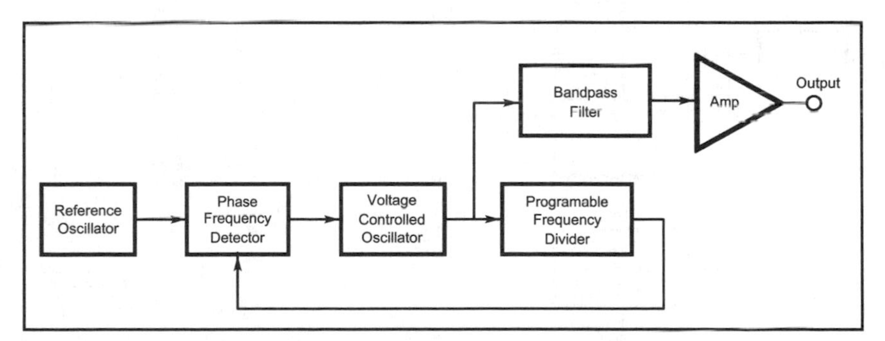


**Block diagram of a phase-locked loop frequency synthesizer.**

**E7E11 What type of frequency synthesizer circuit uses a phase accumulator, lookup table, digital to analog converter and a low-pass antialias filter?**

A. A direct digital synthesizer
B. A hybrid synthesizer
C. A phase-locked loop synthesizer
D. A diode-switching matrix synthesizer

**A** A direct digital synthesizer uses a phase accumulator, lookup table, digital to analog converter and a low-pass antialias filter. See the block diagram.

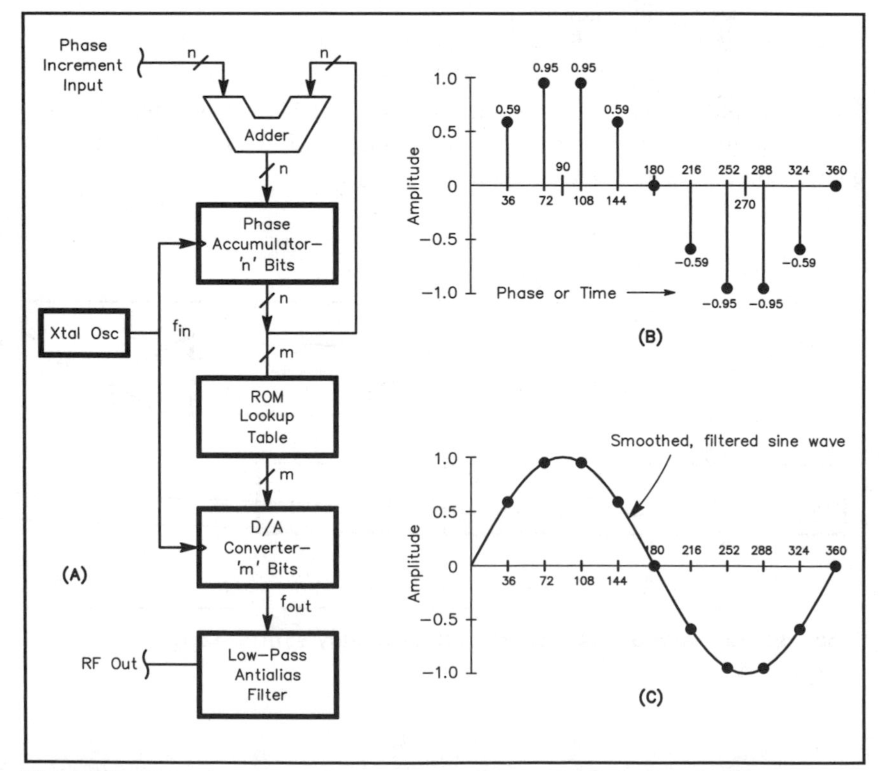


**Block diagram of a direct digital synthesizer at A. At B, the amplitude values found in the ROM lookup table for a particular sine wave being generated by the synthesizer. The smoothed output signal from the synthesizer after it goes through the low-pass antialias filter is shown at C.**

**E7E12 What are the main blocks of a direct digital frequency synthesizer?**

A. A variable-frequency crystal oscillator, phase accumulator, digital to analog converter and a loop filter
B. A stable voltage-controlled oscillator, programmable divider, phase detector, loop filter and a digital to analog converter
C. A variable-frequency oscillator, programmable divider, phase detector and a low-pass antialias filter
D. A phase accumulator, lookup table, digital to analog converter and a low-pass antialias filter

**D** The main blocks of a direct digital frequency synthesizer are a phase accumulator, a lookup table, a digital to analog converter and a low-pass antialias filter.

**E7E13 What information is contained in the lookup table of a direct digital frequency synthesizer?**

A. The phase relationship between a reference oscillator and the output waveform
B. The amplitude values that represent a sine-wave output
C. The phase relationship between a voltage-controlled oscillator and the output waveform
D. The synthesizer frequency limits and frequency values stored in the radio memories

**B** The look-up table of a direct digital frequency synthesizer is a list of sine-wave values at various angles.

**E7E14 What are the major spectral impurity components of direct digital synthesizers?**

A. Broadband noise
B. Digital conversion noise
C. Spurs at discrete frequencies
D. Nyquist limit noise

**C** The major spectral impurity components produced by a direct digital synthesizer are spurious (unwanted) signals, or spurs, at specific discrete frequencies.

**E7E15 What are the major spectral impurity components of phase-locked loop synthesizers?**

A. Broadband noise
B. Digital conversion noise
C. Spurs at discrete frequencies
D. Nyquist limit noise

**A** A phase-locked loop synthesizer is constantly "correcting" the output signal frequency. This results in slight phase shifts from one cycle to the next. This in turn results in phase noise, which is a broadband noise around the desired output frequency and which is the major spectral impurity component of a PLL synthesizer.

**E7E16 What is the process of detection?**

A. The masking of the intelligence on a received carrier
B. The recovery of the intelligence from a modulated RF signal
C. The modulation of a carrier
D. The mixing of noise with a received signal

**B** A detector is used to recover the information or intelligence that has been superimposed through modulation on an RF signal at a transmitter.

**E7E17 What is the principle of detection in a diode detector?**

A. Rectification and filtering of RF
B. Breakdown of the Zener voltage
C. Mixing with noise in the transition region of the diode
D. The change of reactance in the diode with respect to frequency

**A** The diode detector operates by rectification and filtering of the received RF signal.

**E7E18 What does a product detector do?**

A. It provides local oscillations for input to a mixer
B. It amplifies and narrows bandpass frequencies
C. It mixes an incoming signal with a locally generated carrier
D. It detects cross-modulation products

**C** A product detector mixes an incoming signal with a local signal or beat-frequency oscillator (BFO).

**E7E19 How are FM-phone signals detected?**

A. With a balanced modulator
B. With a frequency discriminator
C. With a product detector
D. With a phase splitter

**B** FM signals are typically detected with a frequency discriminator.

**E7E20 What is a frequency discriminator?**

A. An FM generator
B. A circuit for filtering two closely adjacent signals
C. An automatic band-switching circuit
D. A circuit for detecting FM signals

**D** A frequency discriminator is found in an FM receiver, where it functions as a detector.

**E7E21 How can an FM-phone signal be produced?**

A. By modulating the supply voltage to a Class-B amplifier
B. By modulating the supply voltage to a Class-C amplifier
C. By using a reactance modulator on an oscillator
D. By using a balanced modulator on an oscillator

**C** You can produce an FM-phone signal by using a reactance modulator on an oscillator.

## E7F Digital frequency divider circuits; frequency marker generators; frequency counters

**E7F01 What is the purpose of a prescaler circuit?**

A. It converts the output of a JK flip-flop to that of an RS flip-flop
B. It multiplies an HF signal so a low-frequency counter can display the operating frequency
C. It prevents oscillation in a low-frequency counter circuit
D. It divides an HF signal so a low-frequency counter can display the operating frequency

**D** A prescaler is basically a frequency divider that allows a slower device to measure a high-frequency signal.

**E7F02 How many states does a decade counter digital IC have?**

A. 2
B. 10
C. 20
D. 100

**B** Internally, a decade counter IC has 10 distinct states. Each input pulse toggles the counter to the next state.

**E7F03 What is the function of a decade counter digital IC?**

A. It produces one output pulse for every ten input pulses
B. It decodes a decimal number for display on a seven-segment LED display
C. It produces ten output pulses for every input pulse
D. It adds two decimal numbers

**A** A decade counter produces one output pulse for every ten input pulses. Counter circuits are also called dividers.

**E7F04 What additional circuitry is required in a 100-kHz crystal-controlled marker generator to provide markers at 50 and 25 kHz?**

A. An emitter-follower
B. Two frequency multipliers
C. Two flip-flops
D. A voltage divider

**C** You'll need to divide the frequency by both two and four. This will require two flip-flops. The first will divide the 100-kHz signal by two, giving you markers at 50-kHz intervals. The second flip-flop also divides the 50-kHz signal by two giving you markers at 25-kHz intervals.

**E7F05 If a 1-MHz oscillator is used with a divide-by-ten circuit to make a marker generator, what will the output be?**

A. A 1-MHz sinusoidal signal with harmonics every 100 kHz
B. A 100-kHz signal with harmonics every 100 kHz
C. A 1-MHz square wave with harmonics every 1 MHz
D. A 100-kHz signal modulated by a 10-kHz signal

**B** If the 1 MHz signal is divided by 10 then the output signal will be 100 kHz. This output signal is a square wave, so it will have harmonics every 100 kHz.

**E7F06 What is a crystal-controlled marker generator?**

A. A low-stability oscillator that sweeps through a band of frequencies
B. An oscillator often used in aircraft to determine the craft's location relative to the inner and outer markers at airports
C. A high-stability oscillator whose output frequency and amplitude can be varied over a wide range
D. A high-stability oscillator that generates a series of reference signals at known frequency intervals

**D** A crystal-controlled marker generator is a high-stability oscillator that generates a series of reference signals at known frequency intervals.

**E7F07 What type of circuit does NOT make a good marker generator?**

A. A sinusoidal crystal oscillator
B. A crystal oscillator followed by a class C amplifier
C. A TTL device wired as a crystal oscillator
D. A crystal oscillator and a frequency divider

**A** A sinusoidal crystal oscillator generates a single frequency (no harmonics), so it is not a good marker generator.

**E7F08 What is the purpose of a marker generator?**

A. To add audio markers to an oscilloscope
B. To provide a frequency reference for a phase locked loop
C. To provide a means of calibrating a receiver's frequency settings
D. To add time signals to a transmitted signal

**C** A marker generator is used to calibrate receiver frequency settings.

**E7F09 What does the accuracy of a frequency counter depend on?**

A. The internal crystal reference
B. A voltage-regulated power supply with an unvarying output
C. Accuracy of the AC input frequency to the power supply
D. Proper balancing of the power-supply diodes

**A** The accuracy of a frequency counter depends on its internal crystal reference.

**E7F10** **How does a frequency counter determine the frequency of a signal?**

A. It counts the total number of pulses in a circuit
B. It monitors a WWV reference signal for comparison with the measured signal
C. It counts the number of input pulses in a specific period of time
D. It converts the phase of the measured signal to a voltage which is proportional to the frequency

**C** A frequency counter determines the frequency of a signal by counting the number of input pulses in a specific period of time.

**E7F11** **What is the purpose of a frequency counter?**

A. To indicate the frequency of the strongest input signal which is within the counter's frequency range
B. To generate a series of reference signals at known frequency intervals
C. To display all frequency components of a transmitted signal
D. To compare the difference between the input and a voltage-controlled oscillator and produce an error voltage

**A** The purpose of a frequency counter is to indicate the frequency of the strongest input signal which is within the counter's frequency range.

## E7G Active audio filters: characteristics; basic circuit design; preselector applications

**E7G01** **What determines the gain and frequency characteristics of an op-amp RC active filter?**

A. The values of capacitances and resistances built into the op-amp
B. The values of capacitances and resistances external to the op-amp
C. The input voltage and frequency of the op-amp's DC power supply
D. The output voltage and smoothness of the op-amp's DC power supply

**B** The gain and frequency characteristics of an op-amp RC active filter are determined by values of capacitances and resistances external to the op-amp.

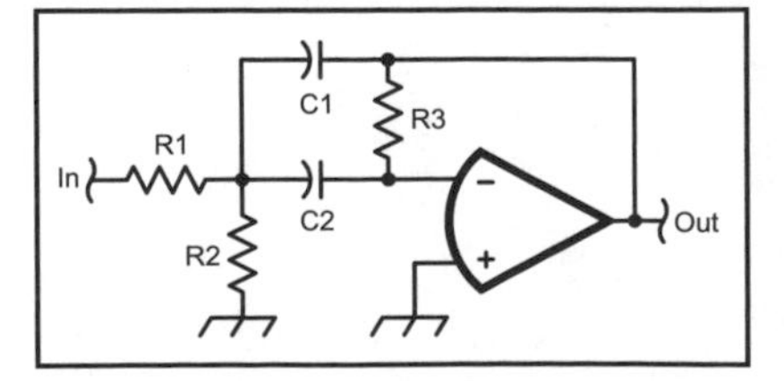


**Circuit diagram of a basic RC active band-pass filter.**

**E7G02 What causes ringing in a filter?**

A. The slew rate of the filter
B. The bandwidth of the filter
C. The filter shape, as measured in the frequency domain
D. The gain of the filter

**C** The filter response measured in the frequency domain will show if it has characteristics that lead to ringing. Filter ringing occurs when the filter shape is too narrow for the signal being received.

**E7G03 What are the advantages of using an op-amp instead of LC elements in an audio filter?**

A. Op-amps are more rugged and can withstand more abuse than can LC elements
B. Op-amps are fixed at one frequency
C. Op-amps are available in more varieties than are LC elements
D. Op-amps exhibit gain rather than insertion loss

**D** One of the advantages of using an op-amp instead of LC elements in an audio filter is that op-amp filters exhibit gain rather than insertion loss.

**E7G04 What type of capacitors should be used in a high-stability op-amp RC active filter circuit?**

A. Electrolytic
B. Disc ceramic
C. Polystyrene
D. Paper dielectric

**C** Capacitors that you use in a high-stability op-amp RC active filter circuit should be high Q and temperature stable. Polystyrene units are excellent for such use.

**E7G05 How can unwanted ringing and audio instability be prevented in a multisection op-amp RC audio filter circuit?**

A. Restrict both gain and Q
B. Restrict gain, but increase Q
C. Restrict Q, but increase gain
D. Increase both gain and Q

**A** To avoid unwanted ringing and audio instability in a multisection op-amp RC audio filter circuit, you should limit (restrict) both the gain and the Q of the circuit.

**E7G06** **What parameter must be selected when selecting the resistor and capacitor values for an RC active filter using an op-amp?**

A. Filter bandwidth
B. Desired current gain
C. Temperature coefficient
D. Output-offset overshoot

**A** The design process for the circuit requires one to select the filter bandwidth. The other parameters are not determined in the design process.

**E7G07** **The design of a preselector involves a trade-off between bandwidth and what other factor?**

A. The amount of ringing
B. Insertion loss
C. The number of parts
D. The choice of capacitors or inductors

**B** The design of a preselector involves a trade-off between bandwidth and insertion loss.

**E7G08** **When designing an op-amp RC active filter for a given frequency range and Q, what steps are typically followed when selecting the external components?**

A. Standard capacitor values are chosen first, the resistances are calculated, then resistors of the nearest standard value are used
B. Standard resistor values are chosen first, the capacitances are calculated, then capacitors of the nearest standard value are used
C. Standard resistor and capacitor values are used, the circuit is tested, then additional resistors are added to make any adjustments
D. Standard resistor and capacitor values are used, the circuit is tested, then additional capacitors are added to make any adjustments

**A** When designing an op-amp RC active filter for a given frequency range and Q, first choose standard capacitor values. Then calculate resistances and use the nearest standard value.

**E7G09 When designing an op-amp RC active filter for a given frequency range and Q, why are the external capacitance values usually chosen first, then the external resistance values calculated?**

A. An op-amp will perform as an active filter using only standard external capacitance values
B. The calculations are easier to make with known capacitance values rather than with known resistance values
C. Capacitors with unusual capacitance values are not widely available, so standard values are used to begin the calculations
D. The equations for the calculations can only be used with known capacitance values

**C** Usually, the range of capacitors available is much smaller (more limited) than the range of resistors so it is better to select the capacitor values and then determine the resistors.

**E7G10 What are the principal uses of an op-amp RC active filter in amateur circuitry?**

A. High-pass filters used to block RFI at the input to receivers
B. Low-pass filters used between transmitters and transmission lines
C. Filters used for smoothing power-supply output
D. Audio filters used for receivers

**D** Op-amp RC active filters are well suited for audio-frequency applications.

**E7G11 Where should an op-amp RC active audio filter be placed in an amateur receiver?**

A. In the IF strip, immediately before the detector
B. In the audio circuitry immediately before the speaker or phone jack
C. Between the balanced modulator and frequency multiplier
D. In the low-level audio stages

**D** Because of the levels involved, it is best to place op-amp RC active audio filters in the low-level audio stages of an amateur receiver.

# Signals and Emissions

There will be four questions on your Extra class examination from the Signals and Emissions subelement. These four questions will be taken from the four groups of questions labeled E8A through E8D.

## E8A AC waveforms: sine wave, square wave, sawtooth wave; AC measurements: peak, peak-to-peak and root-mean-square (RMS) value, peak-envelope-power (PEP) relative to average

**E8A01** **Starting at a positive peak, how many times does a sine wave cross the zero axis in one complete cycle?**

A. 180 times
B. 4 times
C. 2 times
D. 360 times

**C** As can be seen in the graph, the sinusoid wave has two zero crossings as it completes a full cycle from one positive peak to the next.

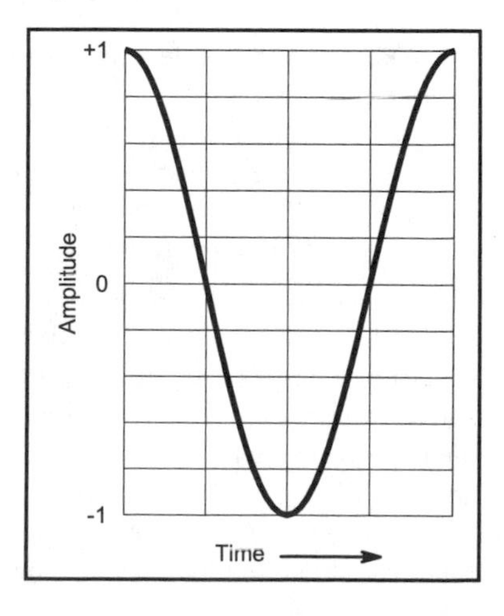


**A full cycle of a sine wave starting at a positive peak.**

**E8A02** **What is a wave called that abruptly changes back and forth between two voltage levels and remains an equal time at each level?**

A. A sine wave
B. A cosine wave
C. A square wave
D. A sawtooth wave

**C** A square wave abruptly changes back and forth between two voltage levels and remains an equal time at each level. (If the wave spends an unequal time at each level, it is known as a rectangular wave.)

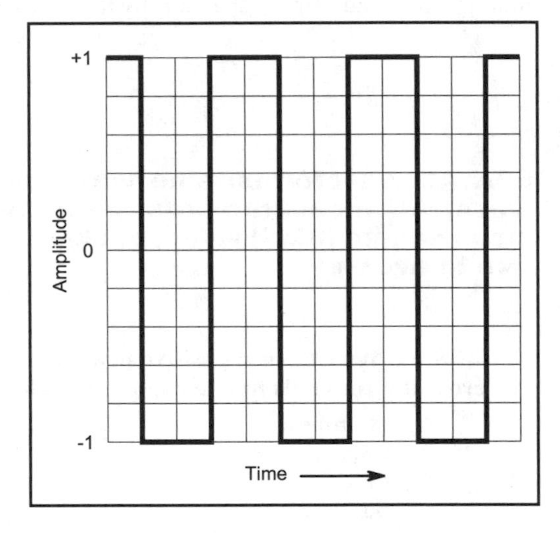


**A square wave abruptly changes back and forth between two voltage levels and remains an equal time at each level.**

**E8A03** **What sine waves added to a fundamental frequency make up a square wave?**

A. A sine wave 0.707 times the fundamental frequency
B. All odd and even harmonics
C. All even harmonics
D. All odd harmonics

**D** A square wave comprises the fundamental frequency and all odd harmonics. It may help you remember if you know how the waveforms look on a spectrum analyzer. The drawing on the next page compares a sine wave and a square wave in the frequency domain. In other words, how they would appear on a spectrum analyzer. In the display for the square wave, you can see components at 10, 30, 50, 70 Hz, and on out to infinity. Since these are odd multiples of the fundamental frequency, the square wave is said to be made up of the fundamental and all odd harmonics.

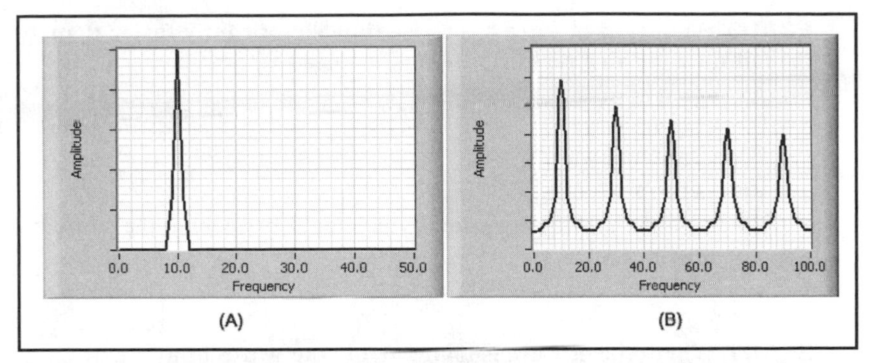


**Spectrum analyzer display of a 10-Hz sine wave at A. The display of a 10-Hz square wave is shown at B. The sine wave contains only the fundamental frequency (10 Hz). By contrast, in the square wave you see components at 10 Hz, 30 Hz, 50 Hz, 70 Hz, etc.**

**E8A04 What type of wave is made up of a sine wave of a fundamental frequency and all its odd harmonics?**

A. A square wave
B. A sine wave
C. A cosine wave
D. A tangent wave

**A** This is a variation of the previous question, so you should be able to spot the correct answer. A square wave is made up of a fundamental frequency and all its odd harmonics.

**E8A06 What is a sawtooth wave?**

A. A wave that alternates between two values and spends an equal time at each level
B. A wave with a straight line rise time faster than the fall time (or vice versa)
C. A wave that produces a phase angle tangent to the unit circle
D. A wave whose amplitude at any given instant can be represented by a point on a wheel rotating at a uniform speed

**B** A sawtooth wave appears on an oscilloscope as a straight-line wave form that has a rise time faster than the fall time (or vice versa). You can see a sawtooth wave in the drawing.

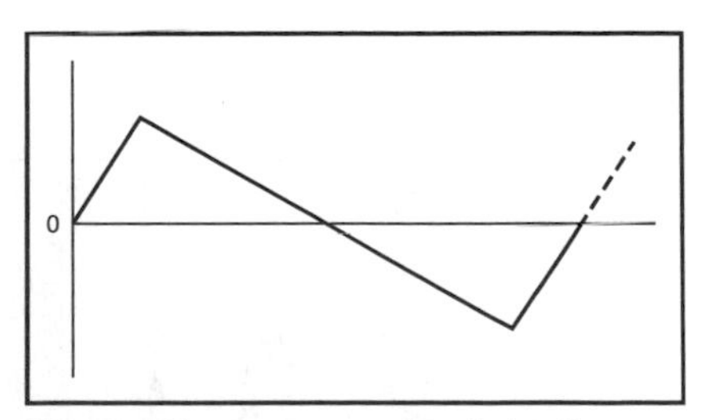


**Sawtooth waves are straight-line waveforms, which have unequal rise and fall times. Sawtooth waves consist of both odd and even harmonics as well as the fundamental.**

**E8A06 What type of wave has a rise time significantly faster than the fall time (or vice versa)?**

A. A cosine wave
B. A square wave
C. A sawtooth wave
D. A sine wave

**C** Based on the previous question, you should be picking the sawtooth wave, as the right choice.

**E8A07 What type of wave is made up of sine waves of a fundamental frequency and all harmonics?**

A. A sawtooth wave
B. A square wave
C. A sine wave
D. A cosine wave

**A** A sawtooth wave is made up of sine waves of a fundamental frequency and all harmonics. Look at the drawing to see how the waveform will look on a spectrum analyzer. The setup is the same as used with the square wave but this time with a sawtooth wave to the input of a spectrum analyzer. Here, you see components at 10 Hz, 20 Hz, 30 Hz, 40 Hz, 50 Hz, 60 Hz, 70 Hz, and on out to infinity. Since these are both the even and the odd multiples of the fundamental frequency (10 Hz), the sawtooth wave is said to be made up of the fundamental frequency and all harmonics.

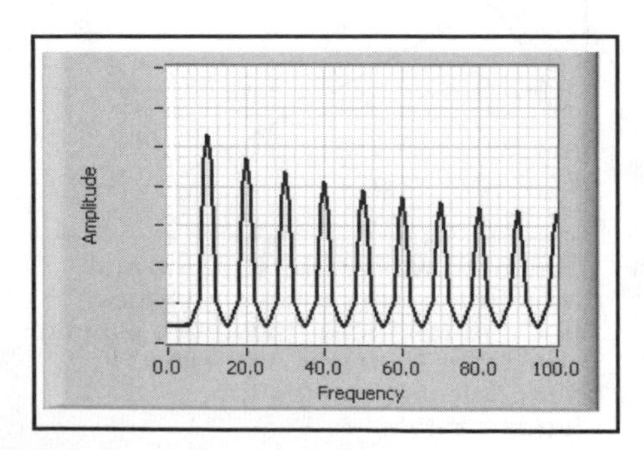


**Spectrum analyzer display of a 10-Hz sawtooth wave. You can see components at 10 Hz, 20 Hz, 30 Hz, 40 Hz, 50 Hz, 60 Hz, 70 Hz, etc. This shows that the sawtooth wave is made up of the fundamental and all harmonics.**

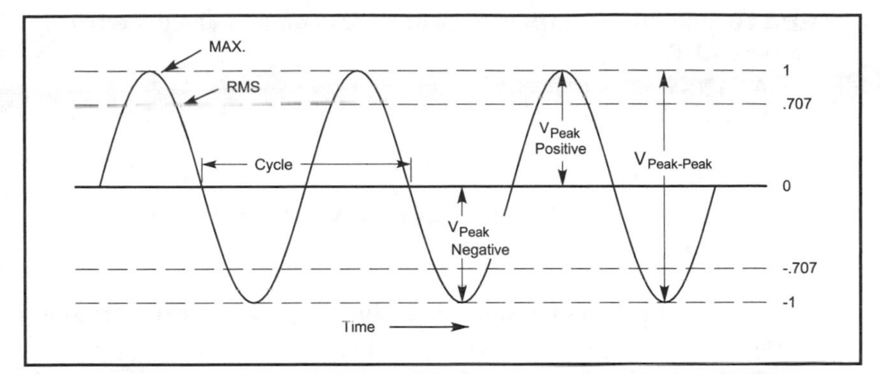

**This diagram shows the relationship of peak, peak-to-peak and RMS voltage in a sinusoidal waveform.**

**E8A08 What is the peak voltage at a common household electrical outlet?**

A. 240 volts
B. 170 volts
C. 120 volts
D. 340 volts

**B** The common household voltage is 120 V, but this is the RMS value. The question is asking for the peak voltage. To convert this to a peak measurement, use this formula

$$V_{Peak} = V_{RMS} \times \sqrt{2} = 120 \times 1.414 = 170\ V$$

The relationships among RMS, peak and peak-to-peak are shown in the drawing above.

**E8A09 What is the peak-to-peak voltage at a common household electrical outlet?**

A. 240 volts
B. 120 volts
C. 340 volts
D. 170 volts

**C** You'll remember that the normal household RMS voltage is 120 V. To convert this to a peak-to-peak measurement, use this formula

$$V_{P-P} = V_{Peak} \times 2 = V_{RMS} \times 2 \times \sqrt{2} = 120 \times 2 \times \sqrt{2} = 340\ V$$

**E8A10 What is the RMS voltage at a common household electrical power outlet?**

A. 120-V AC
B. 340-V AC
C. 85-V AC
D. 170-V AC

**A** By now you should be able to spot 120 V AC as the correct answer.

**E8A11 What is the RMS value of a 340-volt peak-to-peak pure sine wave?**

A. 120-V AC
B. 170-V AC
C. 240-V AC
D. 300-V AC

**A** This question requires you to solve a previous problem in reverse. To compute RMS from the peak-to-peak value of a sinusoid, you can start with the formula that you used earlier

$$V_{P-P} = V_{RMS} \times 2 \times \sqrt{2}$$

Now, rearrange the formula and solve the problem.

$$V_{RMS} = \frac{V_{P-P}}{2 \times \sqrt{2}} = \frac{340}{2.828} = 120 \text{ V AC}$$

**E8A12 What is the equivalent to the root-mean-square value of an AC voltage?**

A. The AC voltage found by taking the square of the average value of the peak AC voltage
B. The DC voltage causing the same heating in a given resistor as the peak AC voltage
C. The DC voltage causing the same heating in a given resistor as the RMS AC voltage of the same value
D. The AC voltage found by taking the square root of the average AC value

**C** When an AC voltage is applied to a resistor, the resistor will dissipate energy in the form of heat, just as if the voltage were DC. The DC voltage that would cause identical heating in the AC-excited resistor is called the root-mean-square (RMS) or effective value of the AC voltage.

**E8A13 What would be the most accurate way of measuring the RMS voltage of a complex waveform?**

A. By using a grid dip meter
B. By measuring the voltage with a D'Arsonval meter
C. By using an absorption wavemeter
D. By measuring the heating effect in a known resistor

**D** This is a variation of the previous question. You should have no trouble identifying the heating effect in a known resistor as the most accurate way of measuring the RMS voltage of a complex waveform. Earlier, you saw how to compute this for sine waves.

**E8A14 For many types of voices, what is the approximate ratio of PEP to average power during a modulation peak in a single-sideband phone signal?**

A. 2.5 to 1
B. 25 to 1
C. 1 to 1
D. 100 to 1

**A** PEP (peak envelope power) is the average power during one cycle at a modulation peak. These envelope peaks occur sporadically during voice transmission. In the drawing, you can see a couple of examples of PEP to average power in SSB signals. The ratio of peak-to-average amplitude varies widely with voices of different characteristics. The PEP of an SSB signal may be about 2 to 3 times greater than the average power output.

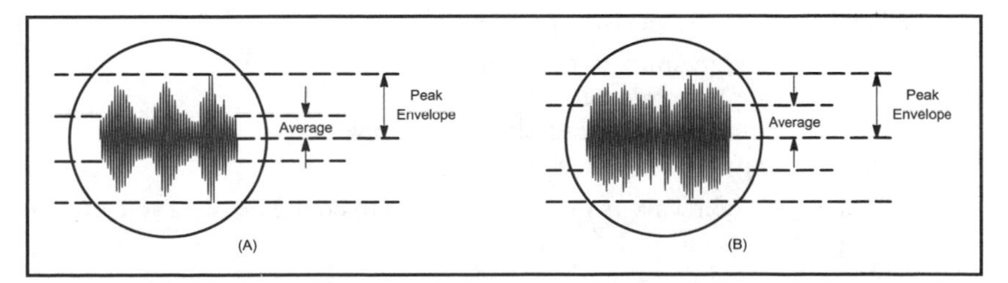


**Two RF envelope patterns that show the difference between average and peak levels. In each case, the RF amplitude is plotted as a function of time. In B, the average level is greater, which raises the average output power compared to the peak value.**

**E8A15 In a single-sideband phone signal, what determines the PEP-to-average power ratio?**

A. The frequency of the modulating signal
B. The speech characteristics
C. The degree of carrier suppression
D. The amplifier power

**B** The PEP to average power ratio is determined by the shape of the voice waveform. In other words, the ratio is determined by the modulating speech characteristics.

**E8A16 What is the approximate DC input power to a Class B RF power amplifier stage in an FM-phone transmitter when the PEP output power is 1500 watts?**

A. 900 watts
B. 1765 watts
C. 2500 watts
D. 4500 watts

**C** A Class-B amplifier has approximately 60% efficiency. If the output is 1500 W, then the input is 1500 W ÷ 0.6 = 2500 W.

**E8A17 What is the approximate DC input power to a Class AB RF power amplifier stage in an unmodulated carrier transmitter when the PEP output power is 500 watts?**

A. 250 watts
B. 600 watts
C. 1000 watts
D. 1500 watts

**C** A Class-AB amplifier has approximately 50% efficiency. If the output is 500 W then the input is 500 W ÷ 0.5 = 1000 W.

**E8A18 What is the period of a wave?**

A. The time required to complete one cycle
B. The number of degrees in one cycle
C. The number of zero crossings in one cycle
D. The amplitude of the wave

**A** The period of a wave is the time required to complete one cycle of that wave (regardless of its shape).

## E8B FCC emission designators versus emission types; modulation symbols and transmission characteristics; modulation methods; modulation index; deviation ratio; pulse modulation: width; position

**E8B01** What is emission A3C?

A. Facsimile
B. RTTY
C. ATV
D. Slow Scan TV

**A** The designator *A3C* means: *A* - amplitude modulation, *3* - single analog channel, and *C* - facsimile. Check the table for a list of emissions designators.

**Table 8-1**
**Partial List of Emissions Designators**

*(1) First Symbol — Modulation Type*

| | |
|---|---|
| Unmodulated carrier | N |
| Double sideband full carrier | A |
| Single sideband reduced carrier | R |
| Single sideband suppressed carrier | J |
| Vestigial sidebands | C |
| Frequency modulation | F |
| Phase modulation | G |
| Various forms of pulse modulation | P, K, L, M, Q, V, W, X |

*(2) Second Symbol — Nature of Modulating Signals*

| | |
|---|---|
| No modulating signal | 0 |
| A single channel containing quantized or digital information without the use of a modulating subcarrier | 1 |
| A single channel containing quantized or digital information with the use of a modulating subcarrier | 2 |
| A single channel containing analog information | 3 |
| Two or more channels containing quantized or digital information | 7 |
| Two or more channels containing analog information | 8 |

*(3) Third Symbol — Type of Transmitted Information*

| | |
|---|---|
| No information transmitted | N |
| Telegraphy — for aural reception | A |
| Telegraphy — for automatic reception | B |
| Facsimile | C |
| Data transmission, telemetry, telecommand | D |
| Telephony | E |
| Television | F |

**E8B02 What type of emission is produced when an AM transmitter is modulated by a facsimile signal?**

A. A3F
B. A3C
C. F3F
D. F3C

**B** Based on the previous question and the table, you should be able to spot A3C as the correct answer. Did you?

**E8B03 What does a facsimile transmission produce?**

A. Tone-modulated telegraphy
B. A pattern of printed characters designed to form a picture
C. Printed pictures by electrical means
D. Moving pictures by electrical means

**C** Facsimile is the transmission of fixed images or pictures by electronic means, with the intent to reproduce the images in a permanent (printed) form.

**E8B04 What is emission F3F?**

A. Modulated CW
B. Facsimile
C. RTTY
D. Television

**D** The designator *F3F* means: *F* - frequency modulation, *3* - single analog channel, and *F* - Television. Putting it all together means that you have television.

**E8B05 What type of emission is produced when an SSB transmitter is modulated by a slow-scan television signal?**

A. J3A
B. F3F
C. A3F
D. J3F

**D** J3F, means SSB, single channel, TV and this is the correct designator. See the table.

**E8B06 If the first symbol of an ITU emission designator is J, representing a single-sideband, suppressed-carrier signal, what information about the emission is described?**

A. The nature of any signal multiplexing
B. The type of modulation of the main carrier
C. The maximum permissible bandwidth
D. The maximum signal level, in decibels

**B** The first letter in an ITU emission designator describes the main carrier modulation type or technique.

**E8B07 If the second symbol of an ITU emission designator is 1, representing a single channel containing quantized, or digital information, what information about the emission is described?**

A. The maximum transmission rate, in bauds
B. The maximum permissible deviation
C. The nature of signals modulating the main carrier
D. The type of information to be transmitted

**C** The second symbol of an ITU emission designator describes the nature of the modulating signals.

**E8B08 If the third symbol of an ITU emission designator is D, representing data transmission, telemetry or telecommand, what information about the emission is described?**

A. The maximum transmission rate, in bauds
B. The maximum permissible deviation
C. The nature of signals modulating the main carrier
D. The type of information to be transmitted

**D** The third symbol of an ITU emission designator describes the type of transmitted information.

**E8B09 (There is no question in the pool with this number.)**

**E8B10 How does the modulation index of a phase-modulated emission vary with RF carrier frequency (the modulated frequency)?**

A. It increases as the RF carrier frequency increases
B. It decreases as the RF carrier frequency increases
C. It varies with the square root of the RF carrier frequency
D. It does not depend on the RF carrier frequency

**D** The modulation index is not dependent on the carrier frequency. It is the ratio of the maximum carrier-frequency deviation to the (instantaneous) modulating frequency. You'll see more about this in following questions.

**E8B11 In an FM-phone signal having a maximum frequency deviation of 3000 Hz either side of the carrier frequency, what is the modulation index when the modulating frequency is 1000 Hz?**

A. 3
B. 0.3
C. 3000
D. 1000

**A** For FM systems being modulated by a tone, the modulation index is given by $\beta = \Delta f / f_m$.

where:

$\Delta f$ = peak deviation in hertz.
$f_m$ = modulating frequency in hertz at any given instant.

Using the values given in the question gives $\beta$ = 3000 Hz/1000 Hz = 3.

**E8B12 What is the modulation index of an FM-phone transmitter producing a maximum carrier deviation of 6 kHz when modulated with a 2-kHz modulating frequency?**

A. 6000
B. 3
C. 2000
D. 1/3

**B** Use the same formula that you did for the previous question. The modulation index is given by $\beta = \Delta f / f_m$. Using the parameters given in the question gives $\beta$ = 6000 Hz/2000 Hz = 3.

**E8B13 What is the deviation ratio of an FM-phone signal having a maximum frequency swing of plus or minus 5 kHz and accepting a maximum modulation rate of 3 kHz?**

A. 60
B. 0.167
C. 0.6
D. 1.67

**D** The formula for deviation ratio is similar to the one for the modulation index. However, you have to replace the instantaneous modulating frequency with the maximum frequency in the modulating signal. For FM systems, the deviation ratio is given by $D = \Delta f / f_{Max}$.

where:

$\Delta f$ = peak deviation in hertz.

$f_{Max}$ = maximum modulating frequency in hertz.

Using the parameters given in the question gives $D$ = 5000 Hz/3000 Hz = 1.67.

**E8B14 In a pulse width-modulation system, why is the transmitter's peak power much greater than its average power?**

A. The signal duty cycle is less than 100%
B. The signal reaches peak amplitude only when voice modulated
C. The signal reaches peak amplitude only when voltage spikes are generated within the modulator
D. The signal reaches peak amplitude only when the pulses are also amplitude modulated

**A** In a pulse width-modulation system the width (duration) of pulses varies according with the applied modulation. The transmitted pulses are all of the same amplitude. In most cases, the duty cycle of the transmission is very low. A pulse of relatively short duration is transmitted, with a relatively long period of time separating each pulse. This causes the peak power of a pulse-modulated signal to be much greater than its average power. See the drawing on the next page.

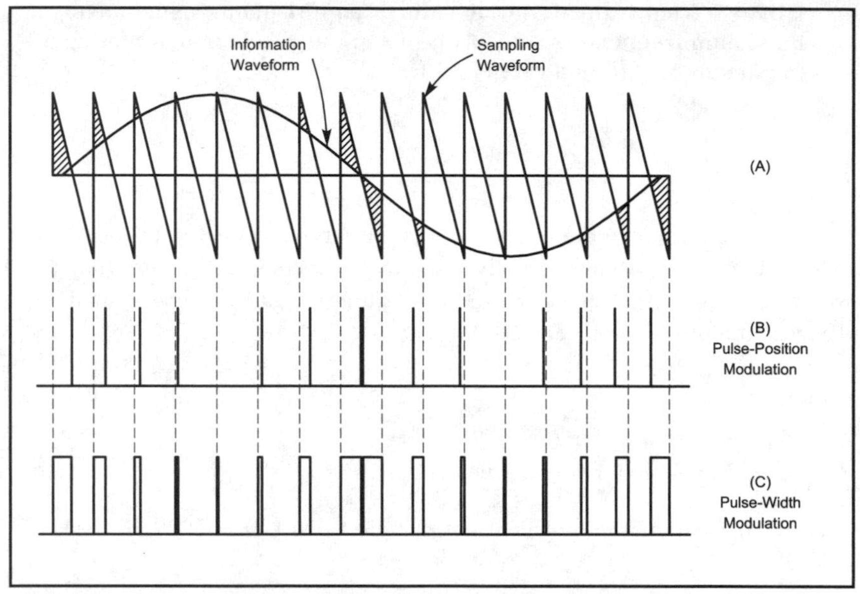


**An information signal and a sampling waveform are shown at A. B shows how the sampled information signal can produce pulse-position modulation, and C shows how it can produce pulse-width modulation.**

**E8B15 What is one way that voice is transmitted in a pulse-width modulation system?**

A. A standard pulse is varied in amplitude by an amount depending on the voice waveform at that instant
B. The position of a standard pulse is varied by an amount depending on the voice waveform at that instant
C. A standard pulse is varied in duration by an amount depending on the voice waveform at that instant
D. The number of standard pulses per second varies depending on the voice waveform at that instant

**C** In a pulse-width modulation system, a standard pulse is varied in duration (width) by an amount depending on the voice waveform at that instant. You might want to go back and check the drawing again to see how this works.

**E8B16 (There is no question in the pool with this number.)**

**E8B17 Which of the following describe the three most-used symbols of an ITU emission designator?**

A. Type of modulation, transmitted bandwidth and modulation code designator
B. Bandwidth of the modulating signal, nature of the modulating signal and transmission rate of signals
C. Type of modulation, nature of the modulating signal and type of information to be transmitted
D. Power of signal being transmitted, nature of multiplexing and transmission speed

**C** The three most-used symbols of an ITU emission designator are a letter, a number and another letter. These respectively stand for the type of modulation, nature of the modulating signal and type of information to be transmitted. For example, F3E is the designator for frequency-modulated telephony. You can go back and review these in Table 8-1.

**E8B18 If the first symbol of an ITU emission designator is G, representing a phase-modulated signal, what information about the emission is described?**

A. The nature of any signal multiplexing
B. The maximum permissible deviation
C. The nature of signals modulating the main carrier
D. The type of modulation of the main carrier

**D** Do you remember that the first letter of the emission designator tells the type of modulation?

**E8B19 In a pulse-position modulation system, what parameter does the modulating signal vary?**

A. The number of pulses per second
B. Both the frequency and amplitude of the pulses
C. The duration of the pulses
D. The time at which each pulse occurs

**D** Pulse-position modulation varies the pulse position (or the time at which each pulse occurs) according with the modulating signal.

**E8B20 In a pulse-width modulation system, what parameter does the modulating signal vary?**

A. Pulse frequency
B. Pulse duration
C. Pulse amplitude
D. Pulse intensity

**B** It should be obvious that pulse-width modulation would vary the pulse width or duration.

**E8B21 How are the pulses of a pulse-modulated signal usually transmitted?**

A. A pulse of relatively short duration is sent; a relatively long period of time separates each pulse
B. A pulse of relatively long duration is sent; a relatively short period of time separates each pulse
C. A group of short pulses are sent in a relatively short period of time; a relatively long period of time separates each group
D. A group of short pulses are sent in a relatively long period of time; a relatively short period of time separates each group

**A** A typical pulse modulated system transmits pulses of relatively short duration. A relatively long period of time separates each pulse.

**E8B22 In an FM-phone signal, what is the term for the ratio between the deviation of the frequency modulated signal and the modulating frequency?**

A. FM compressibility
B. Quieting index
C. Percentage of modulation
D. Modulation index

**D** Do you remember the formula, $\beta = \Delta f/f_m$? That formula tells you that modulation index is the ratio between the deviation of the frequency-modulated signal and the modulating frequency.

**E8B23** **What is meant by deviation ratio?**

A. The ratio of the audio modulating frequency to the center carrier frequency
B. The ratio of the maximum carrier frequency deviation to the highest audio modulating frequency
C. The ratio of the carrier center frequency to the audio modulating frequency
D. The ratio of the highest audio modulating frequency to the average audio modulating frequency

**B** For this one you'll need to go back to the formula, $D = \Delta f/f_{Max}$. It tells you that deviation ratio is the ratio of the maximum carrier frequency deviation to the highest audio modulating frequency.

**E8B24** **What is the deviation ratio of an FM-phone signal having a maximum frequency swing of plus or minus 7.5 kHz and accepting a maximum modulation rate of 3.5 kHz?**

A. 2.14
B. 0.214
C. 0.47
D. 47

**A** Use the formula given in the previous question to compute the deviation ratio, $D$ = 7.5 kHz/3.5 kHz = 2.14.

## E8C Digital signals: including CW; digital signal information rate vs bandwidth; spread-spectrum communications

**E8C01** **What digital code consists of elements having unequal length?**

A. ASCII
B. AX.25
C. Baudot
D. Morse code

**D** Morse code dits and dahs are of different (unequal) length. ASCII, AX.25 (packet) and Baudot code elements are of uniform length.

**E8C02 What are some of the differences between the Baudot digital code and ASCII?**

A. Baudot uses four data bits per character, ASCII uses seven; Baudot uses one character as a shift code, ASCII has no shift code
B. Baudot uses five data bits per character, ASCII uses seven; Baudot uses two characters as shift codes, ASCII has no shift code
C. Baudot uses six data bits per character, ASCII uses seven; Baudot has no shift code, ASCII uses two characters as shift codes
D. Baudot uses seven data bits per character, ASCII uses eight; Baudot has no shift code, ASCII uses two characters as shift codes

**B** It will help if you can remember Baudot 5 and ASCII 7. The 5 data bits in the Baudot (ITA2) code can be arranged into 32 different combinations. (That's not enough to cover all the letters and the digits 0 through 9.) Fortunately, some of these combinations can be used twice, that's done by using the letters and figures shift characters to shift between those combinations. With 7 data bits, ASCII code has 128 distinctive patterns, and for that reason doesn't need shift codes.

**E8C03 What is one advantage of using the ASCII code for data communications?**

A. It includes built-in error-correction features
B. It contains fewer information bits per character than any other code
C. It is possible to transmit both upper and lower case text
D. It uses one character as a shift code to send numeric and special characters

**C** With 7 data bits, ASCII code has 128 distinctive patterns. That makes it possible to transmit both upper and lower case text and still have patterns left for numbers, punctuation and special purpose characters.

**E8C04 What digital communications system is well suited for meteor-scatter communications at times other than during meteor showers?**

A. ACSSB
B. Computerized high speed CW (HSCW)
C. AMTOR
D. Spread spectrum

**B** HSCW is useful for meteor-scatter communications at times other than during meteor showers. Even at these low periods, the ionized tails of tiny meteors constantly bombarding the Earth's atmosphere lend themselves to the brief contact, high-speed nature of HSCW. None of the other choices are designed as high-speed data formats.

**E8C05 What type of error control system does Mode A AMTOR use?**

A. Each character is sent twice
B. The receiving station checks the calculated frame check sequence (FCS) against the transmitted FCS
C. The receiving station checks the calculated frame parity against the transmitted parity
D. The receiving station automatically requests repeats when needed

**D** AMTOR Mode A uses an error-control system in which the receiving station automatically requests repeats when needed. Mode A is also known as ARQ, which stands for *A*utomatic *R*epeat re*Q*uest.

**E8C06 What type of error control system does Mode B AMTOR use?**

A. Each character is sent twice
B. The receiving station checks the calculated frame check sequence (FCS) against the transmitted FCS
C. The receiving station checks the calculated frame parity against the computer-sequencing clock
D. The receiving station automatically requests repeats when needed

**A** Mode B AMTOR uses a simple error-control technique of sending each character twice. This system is called *F*orward *E*rror *C*orrection, or FEC.

**E8C07 What is the necessary bandwidth of a 13-WPM international Morse code emission A1A transmission?**

A. Approximately 13 Hz
B. Approximately 26 Hz
C. Approximately 52 Hz
D. Approximately 104 Hz

**C** You can calculate the necessary bandwidth of a CW signal with this formula

$$Bw = B \times K$$

where:

Bw = the necessary bandwidth of the signal in Hz.

B = the speed of the transmission in bauds.

K = a factor relating to shape of the keying envelope

Divide WPM by 1.2 to convert to bauds. K is typically between 3 (soft keying) and 5 (hard keying). A typical value for K is 4.8. The necessary bandwidth for a CW signal then becomes

$$Bw = B \times K = \frac{WPM}{1.2} \times K = \frac{13}{1.2} \times 4.8 = 52 \text{ Hz}$$

If you look at the formula you can see that with a K of 4.8, the necessary bandwidth of a CW signal in Hz is the speed in WPM times 4.

**E8C08 What is the necessary bandwidth for a 170-hertz shift, 300-baud ASCII emission J2D transmission?**

A. 0 Hz
B. 0.3 kHz
C. 0.5 kHz
D. 1.0 kHz

**C** A J2D emission is generated by injecting two audio tones, separated by the correct shift into the microphone input of an SSB transmitter. The necessary bandwidth for this type of data transmission is

$$Bw = (K \times \text{Shift}) + B$$

where:

Bw = the necessary bandwidth in hertz.

K = a constant that for amateur radio you can assume to be 1.2.

Shift = frequency shift in hertz

B = data rate in bauds

Plug the numbers into the formula and you get

Bw = (K × Shift) + B = (1.2 × 170) + 300 = 504 Hz

This is approximately 0.5 kHz.

**E8C09 What is the necessary bandwidth of a 1000-Hz shift, 1200-baud ASCII emission F1D transmission?**

A. 1000 Hz
B. 1200 Hz
C. 440 Hz
D. 2400 Hz

**D** F1D is data sent by frequency-shift keying (FSK). A receiver can't tell the difference between F1D and J2D emissions. The necessary bandwidth formula is the same for both.

Bw = (K × Shift) + B = (1.2 × 1000) + 1200 = 2400 Hz

**E8C10 What is the necessary bandwidth of a 4800-Hz frequency shift, 9600-baud ASCII emission F1D transmission?**

A. 15.36 kHz
B. 9.6 kHz
C. 4.8 kHz
D. 5.76 kHz

**A** Use the same formula here. Plug in the numbers and you get

Bw = (K × Shift) + B = (1.2 × 4800) + 9600 = 15.36 kHz

**E8C11 What term describes a wide-bandwidth communications system in which the RF carrier varies according to some predetermined sequence?**

A. Amplitude compandored single sideband
B. AMTOR
C. Time-domain frequency modulation
D. Spread-spectrum communication

**D** The keys here are the phrases "wide band" and "predetermined sequence." This describes spread spectrum (SS) communication, and that is the right answer.

**E8C12 What spread-spectrum communications technique alters the center frequency of a conventional carrier many times per second in accordance with a pseudo-random list of channels?**

A. Frequency hopping
B. Direct sequence
C. Time-domain frequency modulation
D. Frequency compandored spread-spectrum

**A** Frequency hopping spread spectrum alters the center frequency of a conventional carrier many times per second in accordance with a pseudo-random list of channels.

**E8C13 What spread-spectrum communications technique uses a very fast binary bit stream to shift the phase of an RF carrier?**

A. Frequency hopping
B. Direct sequence
C. Binary phase-shift keying
D. Phase compandored spread-spectrum

**B** Direct sequence spread spectrum uses a very fast binary bit stream to shift the phase of an RF carrier.

**E8C14 What controls the spreading sequence of an amateur spread-spectrum transmission?**

A. A frequency-agile linear amplifier
B. A crystal-controlled filter linked to a high-speed crystal switching mechanism
C. A binary linear-feedback shift register
D. A binary code which varies if propagation changes

**C** The spreading sequence is a "random appearing" (pseudo random) series of high-speed digital bits that are used to "spread" the output of a spread-spectrum transmitter. This sequence is, in fact, not random. It follows a well defined pattern, because the receiver has to use exactly the same pattern to "despread" the transmission for reception. The spreading sequence is generated in a binary linear-feedback shift register. In any particular system the number of stages in the register and the number and position of feedback taps must be clearly defined.

**E8C15** **What makes spread-spectrum communications resistant to interference?**

A. Interfering signals are removed by a frequency-agile crystal filter
B. Spread-spectrum transmitters use much higher power than conventional carrier-frequency transmitters
C. Spread-spectrum transmitters can hunt for the best carrier frequency to use within a given RF spectrum
D. Only signals using the correct spreading sequence are received

**D** One of the major advantages to spread-spectrum communications is that only signals using the correct spreading sequence are received. That makes this mode highly resistant to interference.

**E8C16** **What reduces interference from spread-spectrum transmitters to conventional communications in the same band?**

A. A spread-spectrum transmitter avoids channels within the band which are in use by conventional transmitters
B. Spread-spectrum signals appear only as low-level noise in conventional receivers
C. Spread-spectrum signals change too rapidly to be detected by conventional receivers
D. Special crystal filters are needed in conventional receivers to detect spread-spectrum signals

**B** The energy from a spread-spectrum transmitter is distributed or spread over a wide frequency range. In the presence of a spread spectrum signal, a conventional communications receiver will only detect a low-level increase in noise. That is unless the transmitter is very close to the receiver.

## E8D Peak amplitude (positive and negative); peak-to-peak values: measurements; Electromagnetic radiation; wave polarization; signal-to-noise (S/N) ratio

**E8D01** **What is the term for the amplitude of the maximum positive excursion of a signal as viewed on an oscilloscope?**

A. Peak-to-peak voltage
B. Inverse peak negative voltage
C. RMS voltage
D. Peak positive voltage

**D** The amplitude of the maximum positive excursion of a signal as viewed on an oscilloscope is called the peak positive voltage. In the drawing, you can see the terminology that's used and the relationships among values in wave-forms.

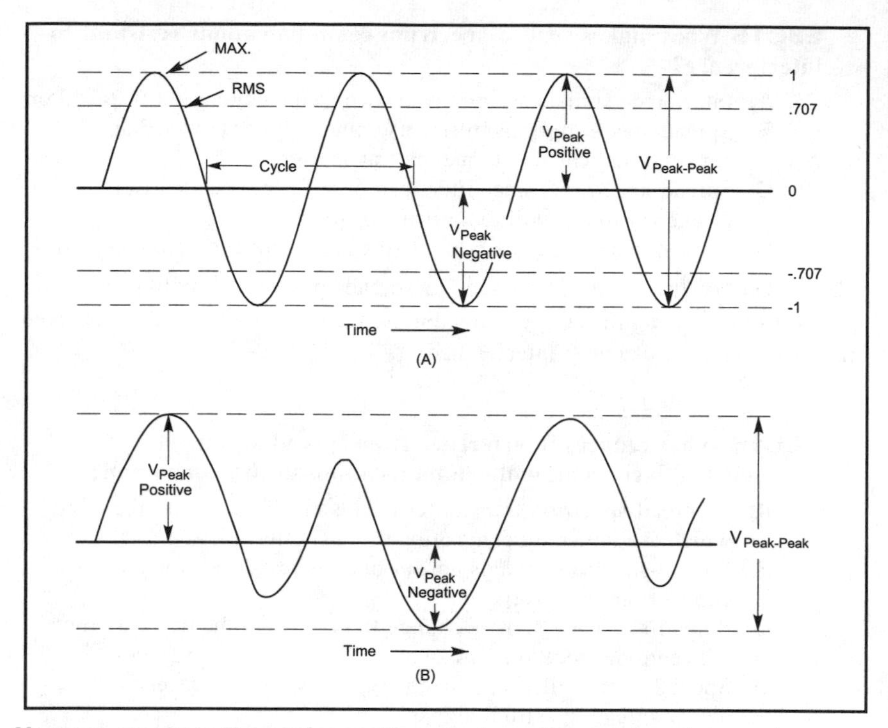


**You can measure the peak negative, peak positive and peak-to-peak values of a waveform on an oscilloscope display. A shows a sine waveform and B shows a complex waveform.**

**E8D02 What is the easiest voltage amplitude dimension to measure by viewing a pure sine wave signal on an oscilloscope?**

A. Peak-to-peak voltage
B. RMS voltage
C. Average voltage
D. DC voltage

**A** Of the choices given, the peak-to-peak voltage, or the full span of the wave, is the easiest to measure on an oscilloscope. There is no need for calculations after you've taken the measurement.

**E8D03 What is the relationship between the peak-to-peak voltage and the peak voltage amplitude in a symmetrical waveform?**

A. 1:1
B. 2:1
C. 3:1
D. 4:1

**B** In a symmetrical waveform the positive peak voltage and the negative peak are equal amplitude, but in opposite directions. In other words, peak positive voltage equals peak negative voltage times –1. That means that peak-to-peak voltage is twice the peak voltage. The two are related by a 2:1 ratio. You can see this relationship in the last drawing.

**E8D04 What input-amplitude parameter is valuable in evaluating the signal-handling capability of a Class A amplifier?**

A. Peak voltage
B. RMS voltage
C. An average reading power output meter
D. Resting voltage

**A** Since class A amplifiers are linear, the output is an amplified, but undistorted, representation of the input. You can evaluate a Class A amplifier by determining the greatest peak voltage that the amplifier can handle without distortion.

**E8D05 What is the PEP output of a transmitter that has a maximum peak of 30 volts to a 50-ohm load as observed on an oscilloscope?**

A. 4.5 watts
B. 9 watts
C. 16 watts
D. 18 watts

**B** The formula for power is the square of the RMS voltage divided by the impedance. You are given the peak voltage, so you'll have to convert that to RMS and then calculate the power at the peak, which is the peak envelope power (PEP). Use the peak to RMS formula from earlier in the chapter .

$$V_{RMS} = \frac{V_{Peak}}{\sqrt{2}}$$

Now use this conversion in the power formula, and you find

$$PEP = \frac{\left(\frac{V_{Peak}}{\sqrt{2}}\right)^2}{Z} = \frac{V_{Peak}^{\ 2}}{2 \times Z} = \frac{30^2}{2 \times 50} = \frac{900}{100} = 9\ W$$

**E8D06 If an RMS reading AC voltmeter reads 65 volts on a sinusoidal waveform, what is the peak-to-peak voltage?**

A. 46 volts
B. 92 volts
C. 130 volts
D. 184 volts

**D** The peak voltage is computed by 1.414 (square root of 2) times the RMS voltage and the peak-to-peak is twice that value. Plugging in the numbers, $V_{P\text{-}P} = 2 \times 1.414 \times 65\ V = 184\ V$.

**E8D07 What is the advantage of using a peak-reading voltmeter to monitor the output of a single-sideband transmitter?**

A. It would be easy to calculate the PEP output of the transmitter
B. It would be easy to calculate the RMS output power of the transmitter
C. It would be easy to calculate the SWR on the transmission line
D. It would be easy to observe the output amplitude variations

**A** Since the PEP can easily be computed from the peak voltage, that is the right choice. You should know that RMS power is never used—the product of RMS voltage and RMS current is average power.

**E8D08 What is an electromagnetic wave?**

A. Alternating currents in the core of an electromagnet
B. A wave consisting of two electric fields at right angles to each other
C. A wave consisting of an electric field and a magnetic field at right angles to each other
D. A wave consisting of two magnetic fields at right angles to each other

**C** An electromagnetic wave derives its name from the fact that it has both an electric and a magnetic field component. The fields exist at right angles to one another. Which means, for example, when one is horizontal the other is vertical and vice versa.

**E8D09 Which of the following best describes electromagnetic waves traveling in free space?**

A. Electric and magnetic fields become aligned as they travel
B. The energy propagates through a medium with a high refractive index
C. The waves are reflected by the ionosphere and return to their source
D. Changing electric and magnetic fields propagate the energy across a vacuum

**D** The electromagnetic wave comprises electric and magnetic fields that are at right angles to each other. It is the changing electric and magnetic fields that propagate electromagnetic energy across the vacuum of free space. These fields never align as the wave travels along its path.

**E8D10 What is meant by circularly polarized electromagnetic waves?**

A. Waves with an electric field bent into a circular shape
B. Waves with a rotating electric field
C. Waves that circle the Earth
D. Waves produced by a loop antenna

**B** It is possible to generate waves with rotating field lines. This condition, where the electric field lines are continuously rotating through horizontal and vertical orientations, is called circular polarization. It is particularly helpful to use circular polarization in satellite communication, where polarization tends to shift.

**E8D11 What is the polarization of an electromagnetic wave if its magnetic field is parallel to the surface of the Earth?**

A. Circular
B. Horizontal
C. Elliptical
D. Vertical

**D** Polarization is defined in terms of the electric field and the two fields are perpendicular to each other. If the magnetic field is parallel to the surface then the electric field is perpendicular to the surface and the polarization is vertical.

**E8D12 What is the polarization of an electromagnetic wave if its magnetic field is perpendicular to the surface of the Earth?**

A. Horizontal
B. Circular
C. Elliptical
D. Vertical

**A** Again, polarization is defined in terms of the electric field and the two fields are perpendicular to each other. If the magnetic field is perpendicular to the surface then the electric field is horizontal and the polarization is horizontal.

**E8D13 What is the primary source of noise that can be heard in an HF-band receiver with an antenna connected?**

A. Detector noise
B. Induction motor noise
C. Receiver front-end noise
D. Atmospheric noise

**D** The troposphere is always active with thunderstorms somewhere on the face of the planet. For that reason, the primary source of noise heard on an HF receiver with an antenna connected is atmospheric noise.

**E8D14 At approximately what speed do electromagnetic waves travel in free space?**

A. 300 million meters per second
B. 468 million meters per second
C. 186, 300 feet per second
D. 300 million miles per second

**A** The speed of light is approximately 300,000,000 meters per second. In English customary units this is about 186,300 miles (not feet) per second. Be careful when you come to this question.

**E8D15 To ensure you do not exceed the maximum allowable power, what kind of meter would you use to monitor the output signal of a properly adjusted single- sideband transmitter?**

A. An SWR meter reading in the forward direction
B. A modulation meter
C. An average reading wattmeter
D. A peak-reading wattmeter

**D** If you wish to avoid violating the power rules, then you'll need to monitor your peak power (PEP) output. You can do that with a peak-reading wattmeter.

**E8D16 What is the average power dissipated by a 50-ohm resistive load during one complete RF cycle having a peak voltage of 35 volts?**

A. 12.2 watts
B. 9.9 watts
C. 24.5 watts
D. 16 watts

**A** You can calculate the correct answer plugging the appropriate values into the formula for average power. Remember that you'll have to convert peak voltage to RMS.

$$P = \frac{\left(\frac{V_{Peak}}{\sqrt{2}}\right)^2}{R} = \frac{{V_{Peak}}^2}{2 \times R} = \frac{35^2}{2 \times 50} = \frac{1225}{100} \approx 12.2 \text{ W}$$

**E8D17 If an RMS reading voltmeter reads 34 volts on a sinusoidal waveform, what is the peak voltage?**

A. 123 volts
B. 96 volts
C. 55 volts
D. 48 volts

**D** For a sinusoidal waveform, you multiply the RMS voltage by 1.414 (square root of 2) to get the peak voltage. When you multiply 34 $V_{RMS}$ by 1.414 you get 48 $V_{Peak}$.

## Subelement E9

# Antennas

There will be five questions on your Extra Class examination from the Antennas subelement. These five questions will be taken from the five groups of questions labeled E9A through E9E.

### E9A Isotropic radiators: definition; used as a standard for comparison; radiation pattern; basic antenna parameters: radiation resistance and reactance (including wire dipole, folded dipole), gain, beamwidth, efficiency

**E9A01 Which of the following describes an isotropic radiator?**

A. A grounded radiator used to measure earth conductivity
B. A horizontal radiator used to compare Yagi antennas
C. A theoretical radiator used to compare other antennas
D. A spacecraft radiator used to direct signals toward the earth

**C** You'll never see one, because an isotropic radiator is a theoretical (mathematical) concept that is useful for comparing antenna performance. It is a point-source radiator located in space that exhibits no directivity in any direction. In other words, it radiates equally in all directions.

**E9A02 When is it useful to refer to an isotropic radiator?**

A. When comparing the gains of directional antennas
B. When testing a transmission line for standing-wave ratio
C. When directing a transmission toward the tropical latitudes
D. When using a dummy load to tune a transmitter

**A** An isotropic radiator is particularly useful as a standard reference for gauging or comparing the gains of real-world antennas.

**E9A03 How much gain does a 1/2-wavelength dipole have over an isotropic radiator?**

A. About 1.5 dB
B. About 2.1 dB
C. About 3.0 dB
D. About 6.0 dB

**B** A 1/2-wavelength dipole has directivity. That means that there is more radiation in some directions than there is in others. Apart from the influence of the earth or other objects, a dipole has a bit over 2-dB gain when compared to an isotropic radiator.

**E9A04 Which of the following antennas has no gain in any direction?**

A. Quarter-wave vertical
B. Yagi
C. Half-wave dipole
D. Isotropic radiator

**D** By definition, an isotropic radiator transmits uniformly in all directions. Gain is a measure of departure from this uniform pattern.

**E9A05 Which of the following describes the radiation pattern of an isotropic radiator?**

A. A teardrop in the vertical plane
B. A circle in the horizontal plane
C. A sphere with the antenna in the center
D. Crossed polarized with a spiral shape

**C** Since the antenna pattern for an isotropic antenna is uniform in all directions; it is often described as a spherical pattern. A circle describes the pattern in two dimensions, but you must consider three dimensions. For that reason, only the sphere correctly describes the radiation pattern.

**E9A06 Why would one need to know the feed point impedance of an antenna?**

A. To match impedances for maximum power transfer
B. To measure the near-field radiation density from a transmitting antenna
C. To calculate the front-to-side ratio of the antenna
D. To calculate the front-to-back ratio of the antenna

**A** You would normally desire to have as much of the available RF energy radiated as possible. This is accomplished, in part, by matching the antenna impedance to the feed line.

**E9A07 What factors determine the radiation resistance of an antenna?**

A. Transmission-line length and antenna height
B. Antenna location with respect to nearby objects and the conductors' length/diameter ratio
C. It is a physical constant and is the same for all antennas
D. Sunspot activity and time of day

**B** An antenna's location with respect to nearby objects—especially the earth—helps determine the radiation resistance. So does the conductors' length/diameter ratio.

**E9A08 What is the term for the ratio of the radiation resistance of an antenna to the total resistance of the system?**

A. Effective radiated power
B. Radiation conversion loss
C. Antenna efficiency
D. Beamwidth

**C** Radiation resistance is an assumed resistance, which, if actually present, would dissipate the power actually radiated from the antenna. Real, or ohmic, resistance in the system dissipates energy as heat. Total resistance is the sum of radiation resistance plus ohmic resistance. The ratio of the radiation resistance of an antenna to the total resistance of the system represents the antenna's efficiency.

**E9A09 What is included in the total resistance of an antenna system?**

A. Radiation resistance plus space impedance
B. Radiation resistance plus transmission resistance
C. Transmission-line resistance plus radiation resistance
D. Radiation resistance plus ohmic resistance

**D** If you read the explanation to the previous question, you already know the answer. The total resistance of an antenna system is the sum of the radiation resistance plus ohmic resistance.

**E9A10 What is a folded dipole antenna?**

A. A dipole one-quarter wavelength long
B. A type of ground-plane antenna
C. A dipole whose ends are connected by a one-half wavelength piece of wire
D. A hypothetical antenna used in theoretical discussions to replace the radiation resistance

**C** A folded dipole antenna is a wire antenna consisting of two (or more) parallel wires that are closely spaced and connected at their ends. One of the wires is fed at its center. Another way of describing it is a dipole whose ends are connected by a one-half wavelength piece of wire. See the drawing.

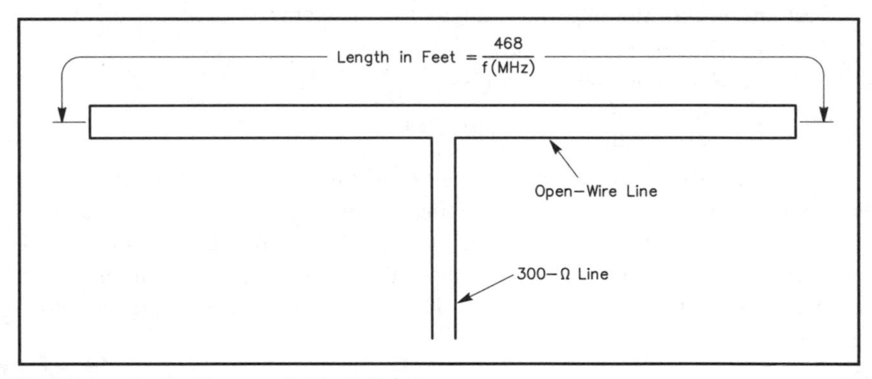


**Drawing of a half-wave folded dipole.**

**E9A11 What is meant by antenna gain?**

A. The numerical ratio relating the radiated signal strength of an antenna to that of another antenna
B. The numerical ratio of the signal in the forward direction to the signal in the back direction
C. The numerical ratio of the amount of power radiated by an antenna compared to the transmitter output power
D. The final amplifier gain minus the transmission-line losses (including any phasing lines present)

**A** Gain is a ratio involving an antenna's radiation performance compared to that of another antenna.

**E9A12 What is meant by antenna bandwidth?**

A. Antenna length divided by the number of elements
B. The frequency range over which an antenna can be expected to perform well
C. The angle between the half-power radiation points
D. The angle formed between two imaginary lines drawn through the ends of the elements

**B** Bandwidth is a frequency domain measurement. That means you're looking for the frequency range over which an antenna can be expected to perform well. This is frequently taken to mean the range over which the antenna exhibits an SWR of, say, 2:1 or less.

**E9A13 How can the approximate beamwidth of a beam antenna be determined?**

A. Note the two points where the signal strength of the antenna is down 3 dB from the maximum signal point and compute the angular difference
B. Measure the ratio of the signal strengths of the radiated power lobes from the front and rear of the antenna
C. Draw two imaginary lines through the ends of the elements and measure the angle between the lines
D. Measure the ratio of the signal strengths of the radiated power lobes from the front and side of the antenna

**A** The beamwidth is typically defined in terms of the half-power points. These are the points on either side and closest to the main lobe where the pattern is down 3 dB from the peak gain. The beamwidth is the angular difference between these two points.

**E9A14 How is antenna efficiency calculated?**

A. (radiation resistance / transmission resistance) × 100%
B. (radiation resistance / total resistance) × 100%
C. (total resistance / radiation resistance) × 100%
D. (effective radiated power / transmitter output) × 100%

**B** You can calculate the efficiency of an antenna by dividing the radiation resistance by the total resistance. Multiply by 100 to get the answer in percent. Total resistance is radiation resistance plus ohmic resistance.

**E9A15 How can the efficiency of an HF grounded vertical antenna be made comparable to that of a half-wave dipole antenna?**

A. By installing a good ground radial system
B. By isolating the coax shield from ground
C. By shortening the vertical
D. By lengthening the vertical

**A** To significantly improve antenna efficiency, you'll need to lower ohmic resistance. Do you remember the formula? In the case of a typical HF grounded vertical antenna, the ground system is the chief source of ohmic resistance. Installing a good ground radial system can lower this resistance.

**E9A16 What theoretical reference antenna provides a comparison for antenna measurements?**

A. Quarter-wave vertical
B. Yagi
C. Bobtail curtain
D. Isotropic radiator

**D** Antennas are usually compared with the isotropic radiation pattern. The isotropic radiator provides a theoretical reference.

**E9A17 How much gain does an antenna have over a 1/2-wavelength dipole when it has 6 dB gain over an isotropic radiator?**

A. About 3.9 dB
B. About 6.0 dB
C. About 8.1 dB
D. About 10.0 dB

**A** A ½-wave dipole has a gain of 2.1 dB relative to an isotropic antenna. The gain relative to the dipole would then be 6 dB – 2.1 dB = 3.9 dB.

**E9A18 How much gain does an antenna have over a 1/2-wavelength dipole when it has 12 dB gain over an isotropic radiator?**

A. About 6.1 dB
B. About 9.9 dB
C. About 12.0 dB
D. About 14.1 dB

**B** Again, the ½-wave dipole has a gain of 2.1 dB relative to an isotropic antenna. The gain relative to the dipole would then be 12 dB – 2.1 dB = 9.9 dB.

**E9A19 Which of the following describes the directivity of an isotropic radiator?**

A. Directivity in the E plane
B. Directivity in the H plane
C. Directivity in the Z plane
D. No directivity at all

**D** Since an isotropic antenna radiates in all directions, it has no preferred direction. This is another way of saying that it has no directivity at all.

**E9A20 What is meant by the radiation resistance of an antenna?**

A. The combined losses of the antenna elements and feed line
B. The specific impedance of the antenna
C. The equivalent resistance that would dissipate the same amount of power as that radiated from an antenna
D. The resistance in the atmosphere that an antenna must overcome to be able to radiate a signal

**C** Radiation resistance is the equivalent resistance that would dissipate the same amount of power as that radiated from an antenna.

## E9B Free-space antenna patterns: E and H plane patterns (i.e., azimuth and elevation in free-space); gain as a function of pattern; antenna design (computer modeling of antennas)

**E9B01 What determines the free-space polarization of an antenna?**

A. The orientation of its magnetic field (H Field)
B. The orientation of its free-space characteristic impedance
C. The orientation of its electric field (E Field)
D. Its elevation pattern

**C** The polarization of an antenna is determined by the orientation of the electric field. For example, if the electric field is horizontally oriented relative to the earth, we say that the polarization of the antenna is horizontal.

**E9B02 In the free-space H-Field radiation pattern shown in Figure E9-1, what is the 3-dB beamwidth?**

A. 75 degrees
B. 50 degrees
C. 25 degrees
D. 30 degrees

**B** By looking at the figure, the pattern drops 3 dB at about ± 25 degrees from the peak of the main lobe. That makes the beamwidth about 50 degrees.

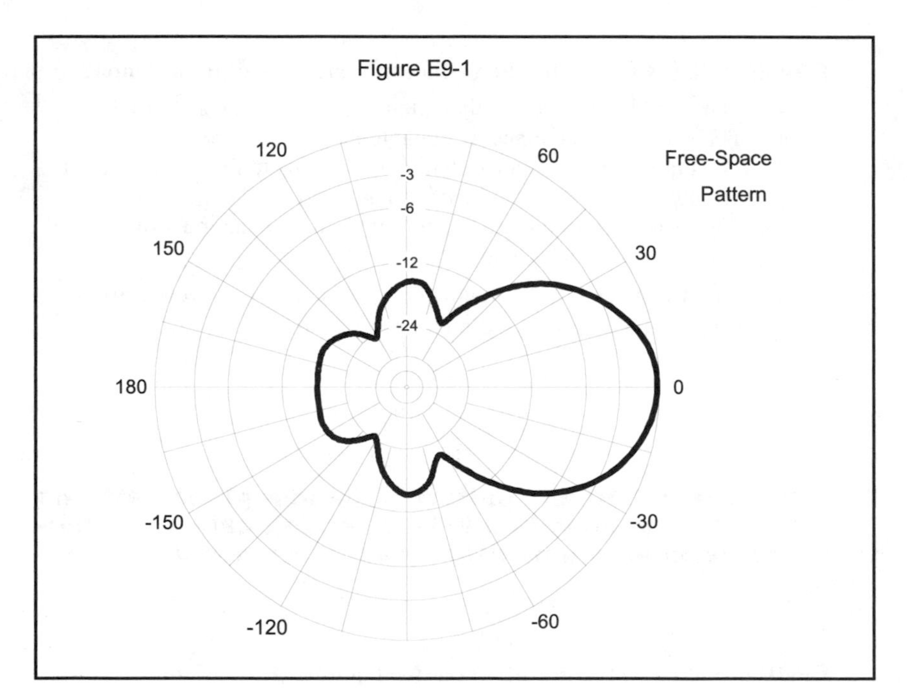


**Figure E9-1 — Refer to questions E9B02 through E9B04.**

**E9B03 In the free-space H-Field pattern shown in Figure E9-1, what is the front-to-back ratio?**

A. 36 dB
B. 18 dB
C. 24 dB
D. 14 dB

**B** The antenna gain at 0 degrees is 0 dB while the gain at 180 degrees is about halfway between –12 and –24 dB on this scale. You should read this as 18 dB.

**E9B04 In the free-space H-field pattern shown in Figure E9-1, what is the front-to-side ratio?**

A. 12 dB
B. 14 dB
C. 18 dB
D. 24 dB

**B** The antenna gain at 0 degrees is 0 dB while the gain at 90 degrees or 270 degrees is a bit more than –12 dB. This corresponds to 14 dB.

**E9B05 What information is needed to accurately evaluate the gain of an antenna?**

A. Radiation resistance
B. E-Field and H-Field patterns
C. Loss resistance
D. All of these choices

**D** Radiation and loss resistance values are needed to calculate efficiency. E-Field and H-Field patterns determine directivity. To perform a full evaluation, each of these items is required.

**E9B06 Which is NOT an important reason to evaluate a gain antenna across the whole frequency band for which it was designed?**

A. The gain may fall off rapidly over the whole frequency band
B. The feed-point impedance may change radically with frequency
C. The rearward pattern lobes may vary excessively with frequency
D. The dielectric constant may vary significantly

**D** The dielectric constant is not frequency dependent. For that reason it is not a factor if antenna performance varies across the frequency band for which it was designed.

**E9B07 What usually occurs if a Yagi antenna is designed solely for maximum forward gain?**

A. The front-to-back ratio increases
B. The feed-point impedance becomes very low
C. The frequency response is widened over the whole frequency band
D. The SWR is reduced

**B** You can design a Yagi antenna for maximum forward gain, but in that case the feedpoint impedance usually becomes very low.

**E9B08 If the boom of a Yagi antenna is lengthened and the elements are properly retuned, what usually occurs?**

A. The gain increases
B. The SWR decreases
C. The front-to-back ratio increases
D. The gain bandwidth decreases rapidly

**A** As a rule, the gain of a Yagi antenna is directly proportional to the length of its boom. This requires that the number, spacing and lengths of the elements be properly adjusted. In other words, the gain of a Yagi increases as the boom is lengthened if the elements are properly retuned.

**E9B09 What type of computer program is commonly used for modeling antennas?**

A. Graphical analysis
B. Method of Moments
C. Mutual impedance analysis
D. Calculus differentiation with respect to physical properties

**B** Antenna modeling software uses the Method of Moments to analyze antenna performance. This analysis technique divides an antenna into segments, computes the current in each segment, and vector sums the radiation resulting from the currents in all segments.

**E9B10 What is the principle of a Method of Moments analysis?**

A. A wire is modeled as a series of segments, each having a distinct value of current
B. A wire is modeled as a single sine-wave current generator
C. A wire is modeled as a series of points, each having a distinct location in space
D. A wire is modeled as a series of segments, each having a distinct value of voltage across it

**A** The Method of Moments analysis technique divides wires into segments and assigns an appropriate current value to each segment.

## E9C Phased vertical antennas; radiation patterns; beverage antennas; rhombic antennas: resonant; terminated; radiation pattern; antenna patterns: elevation above real ground, ground effects as related to polarization, take-off angles as a function of height above ground

**E9C01 What is the radiation pattern of two 1/4-wavelength vertical antennas spaced 1/2-wavelength apart and fed 180 degrees out of phase?**

A. Unidirectional cardioid
B. Omnidirectional
C. Figure-8 broadside to the antennas
D. Figure-8 end-fire in line with the antennas

**D** The radiation pattern of two 1/4-wavelength vertical antennas spaced 1/2-wavelength apart and fed 180 degrees out of phase is a figure-8 end-fire in line with the antennas. See the illustration on the next page.

**E9C02 What is the radiation pattern of two 1/4-wavelength vertical antennas spaced 1/4-wavelength apart and fed 90 degrees out of phase?**

A. Unidirectional cardioid
B. Figure-8 end-fire
C. Figure-8 broadside
D. Omnidirectional

**A** In this case, the pattern is a cardioid, as you can see in the illustration.

**E9C03 What is the radiation pattern of two 1/4-wavelength vertical antennas spaced 1/2-wavelength apart and fed in phase?**

A. Omnidirectional
B. Cardioid unidirectional
C. Figure-8 broadside to the antennas
D. Figure-8 end-fire in line with the antennas

**C** Refer to the illustration, and you'll find that the pattern is a figure-8 broadside to the antennas.

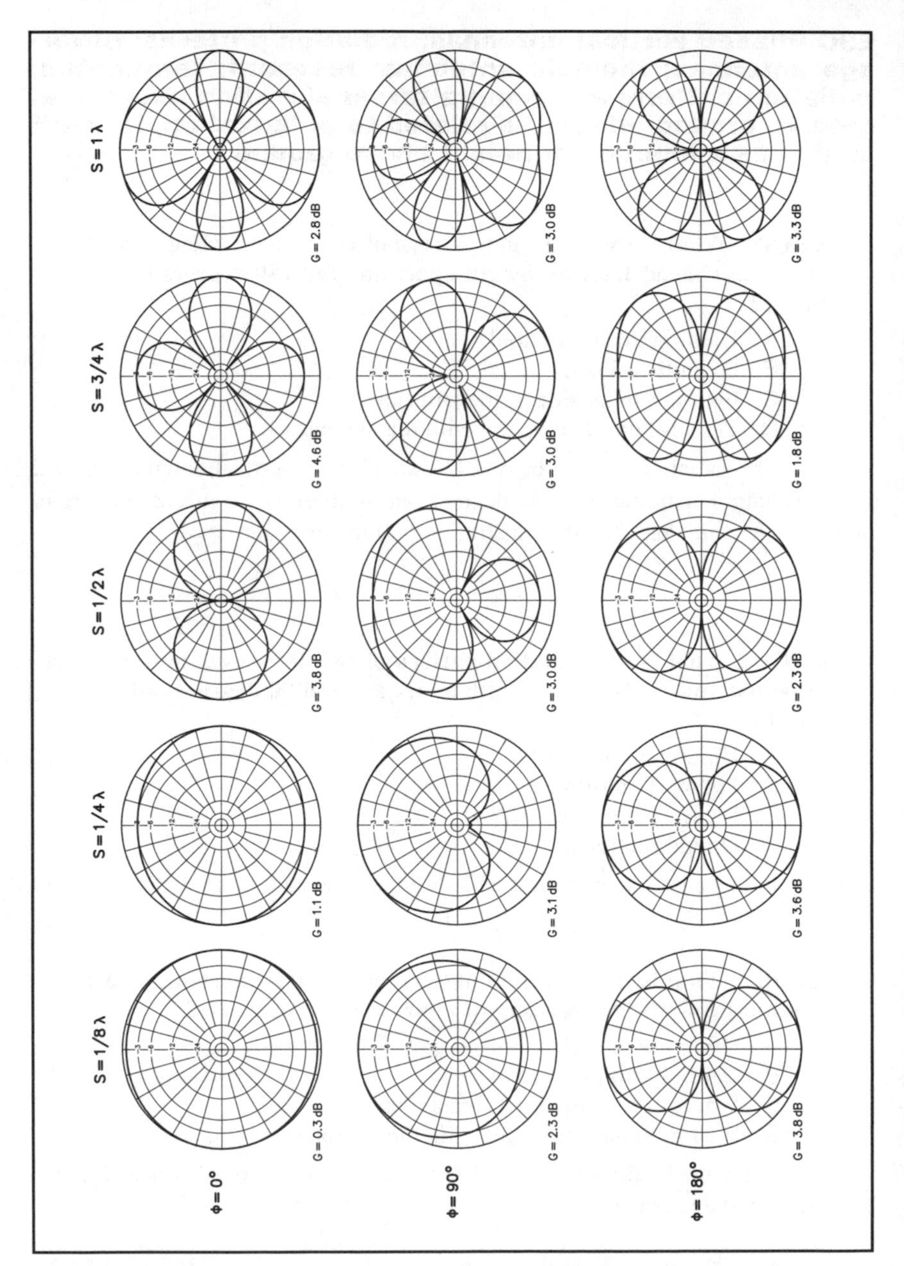


**Horizontal directive patterns of two phased verticals, spaced and phased as indicated. In these plots, the elements are aligned with the vertical axis, and the uppermost element is the one of lagging phase at angles other than zero degrees. The two elements are assumed to be the same length, with exactly equal currents. The gain values associated with each pattern indicate the gain of the two vertical antennas over a single vertical.**

**E9C04 What is the radiation pattern of two 1/4-wavelength vertical antennas spaced 1/4-wavelength apart and fed 180 degrees out of phase?**

A. Omnidirectional
B. Cardioid unidirectional
C. Figure-8 broadside to the antennas
D. Figure-8 end-fire in line with the antennas

**D** The illustration shows that the pattern is a figure-8 end-fire.

**E9C05 What is the radiation pattern for two 1/4-wavelength vertical antennas spaced 1/8-wavelength apart and fed 180 degrees out of phase?**

A. Omnidirectional
B. Cardioid unidirectional
C. Figure-8 broadside to the antennas
D. Figure-8 end-fire in line with the antennas

**D** According to the illustration, the figure-8 end-fire is the right choice.

**E9C06 What is the radiation pattern for two 1/4-wavelength vertical antennas spaced 1/4-wavelength apart and fed in phase?**

A. Substantially unidirectional
B. Elliptical
C. Cardioid unidirectional
D. Figure-8 end-fire in line with the antennas

**B** Check the illustration. In this case, the pattern is elliptical.

**E9C07 Which of the following is the best description of a resonant rhombic antenna?**

A. Unidirectional; four-sided, each side a half-wavelength long; terminated in a resistance equal to its characteristic impedance
B. Bidirectional; four-sided, each side approximately one wavelength long; open at the end opposite the transmission line connection
C. Four-sided; an LC network at each vertex except for the transmission connection; tuned to resonate at the operating frequency
D. Four-sided, each side of a different physical length; traps at each vertex for changing resonance according to band usage

**B** There are two major types of rhombic antennas: resonant and nonresonant (or terminated). You'll need to know the differences between the two and the advantages and disadvantages of each. Both are diamond shaped (four-sided) and each side is approximately one wavelength long.

The resonant rhombic antenna is open at the end opposite the feedpoint. It has a bidirectional pattern. See the drawing.

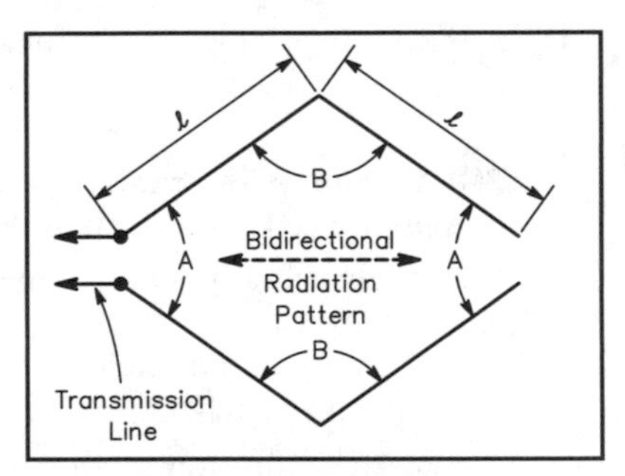


**The resonant rhombic is a diamond-shaped antenna. All legs are the same length, and opposite angles of the diamond are equal.**

**E9C08 What are the advantages of a terminated rhombic antenna?**

A. Wide frequency range, high gain and high front-to-back ratio
B. High front-to-back ratio, compact size and high gain
C. Unidirectional radiation pattern, high gain and compact size
D. Bidirectional radiation pattern, high gain and wide frequency range

**A** A terminated rhombic differs from a resonant rhombic most obviously by the end opposite the feedpoint being terminated with a resistor. That termination changes the pattern from bidirectional to unidirectional and gives the antenna a wide frequency range (bandwidth). This is not a compact antenna.

**The terminated (or nonresonant) rhombic antenna has a terminating resistor added at the end opposite the feedpoint. The main effect of this resistor is to change the pattern from one that is primarily bidirectional to one that is primarily unidirectional.**

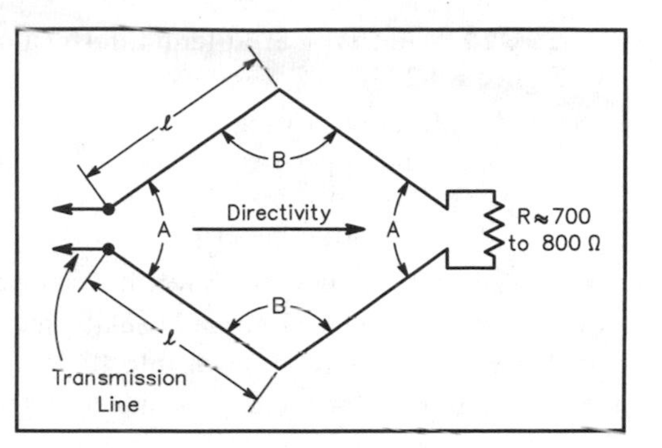


**E9C09 What are the disadvantages of a terminated rhombic antenna for the HF bands?**

A. A large area for proper installation and a narrow bandwidth
B. A large area for proper installation and a low front-to-back ratio
C. A large area and four sturdy supports for proper installation
D. A large amount of aluminum tubing and a low front-to back ratio

**C** It takes a large area to properly install an HF rhombic antenna. You'll also need four sturdy supports to hold up its four corners.

**E9C10 What is the effect of a terminating resistor on a rhombic antenna?**

A. It reflects the standing waves on the antenna elements back to the transmitter
B. It changes the radiation pattern from essentially bidirectional to essentially unidirectional
C. It changes the radiation pattern from horizontal to vertical polarization
D. It decreases the ground loss

**B** The main effect of a terminating resistor on a rhombic antenna is to change the radiation pattern from essentially bidirectional to essentially unidirectional.

**E9C11** **What type of antenna pattern over real ground is shown in Figure E9-2?**

A. Elevation pattern
B. Azimuth pattern
C. E-Plane pattern
D. Polarization pattern

**A** The antenna pattern shown in Figure E9-2 is an elevation pattern. An elevation pattern over real ground usually shows only half a circle. Any radiation that would have gone down into the ground is reflected back into space above the Earth, and that energy is added to the pattern above the antenna.

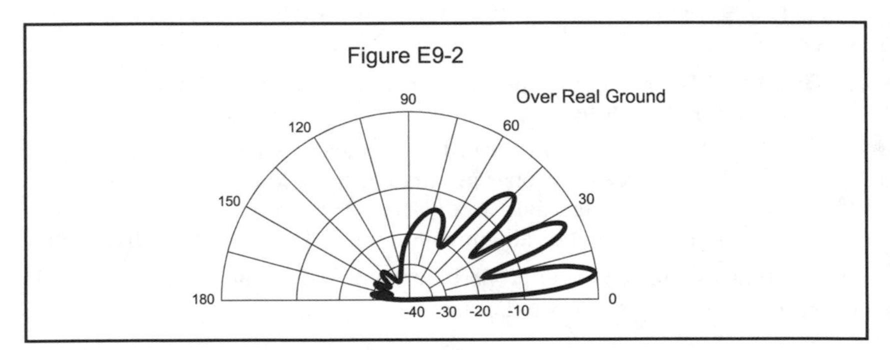


**Figure E9-2 — Refer to questions E9C11 through E9C14.**

**E9C12** **In the H field antenna radiation pattern shown in Figure E9-2, what is the elevation angle of the peak response?**

A. 45 degrees
B. 75 degrees
C. 7.5 degrees
D. 25 degrees

**C** By looking at the pattern plot, you can see the largest lobe is centered at 7.5 degrees. This is the peak response.

**E9C13** **In the H field antenna radiation pattern shown in Figure E9-2, what is the front-to-back ratio?**

A. 15 dB
B. 28 dB
C. 3 dB
D. 24 dB

**B** The back lobes rise to just above the -30 dB line and the maximum is at the 0-dB line. This means you have a front-to-back ratio of about 28 dB.

**E9C14 In the H field antenna radiation pattern shown in Figure E9-2, how many elevation lobes appear in the forward direction?**

A. 4
B. 3
C. 1
D. 7

**A** The forward direction would be those lobes between 0 degrees and 90 degrees. The count is four.

**E9C15 How is the far-field elevation pattern of a vertically polarized antenna affected by being mounted over seawater versus rocky ground?**

A. The low-angle radiation decreases
B. The high-angle radiation increases
C. Both the high- and low-angle radiation decrease
D. The low-angle radiation increases

**D** Seawater has excellent conductivity and rocky ground is a poor conductor. If you mount a vertically polarized antenna over seawater, it will have the effect of increasing the low-angle radiation as compared to a similar antenna over rocky ground.

**E9C16 If only a modest on-ground radial system can be used with an eighth-wavelength-high, inductively loaded vertical antenna, what would be the best compromise to minimize near-field losses?**

A. 4 radial wires, 1 wavelength long
B. 8 radial wires, a half-wavelength long
C. A wire-mesh screen at the antenna base, an eighth-wavelength square
D. 4 radial wires, 2 wavelengths long

**C** This type of antenna system needs a good ground system. More wires are better and longer wires (half-wavelength and longer) don't help much with this short antenna. A wire mesh would be the best choice among those given.

**E9C17 What is one characteristic of a Beverage antenna?**

A. For best performance it must not exceed 1/4 wavelength in length at the desired frequency
B. For best performance it must be mounted more than 1 wavelength above ground at the desired frequency
C. For best performance it should be configured as a four-sided loop
D. For best performance it should be longer than one wavelength

**D** The correct characteristic for the Beverage antenna is greater than one wavelength in length.

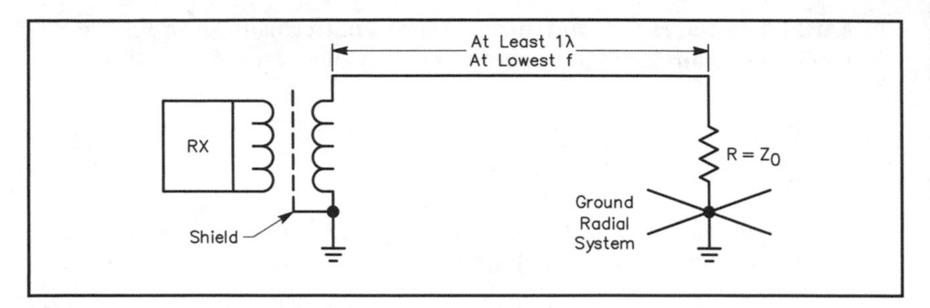


**A simple Beverage antenna with terminating resistor and matching transformer for the receiver.**

**E9C18 How would the electric field be oriented for a Yagi with three elements mounted parallel to the ground?**

A. Vertically
B. Horizontally
C. Right-hand elliptically
D. Left-hand elliptically

**B** This configuration, with the elements in a horizontal position, produces horizontal polarization. That is to say, the electric field is aligned horizontally.

**E9C19 What strongly affects the shape of the far-field, low-angle elevation pattern of a vertically polarized antenna?**

A. The conductivity and dielectric constant of the soil
B. The radiation resistance of the antenna
C. The SWR on the transmission line
D. The transmitter output power

**A** The radiation pattern of an antenna over real ground is always affected by the electrical conductivity and dielectric constant of the soil. This is especially true of the low-elevation-angle far-field pattern of a vertically polarized antenna. The low-angle radiation pattern from a vertically polarized antenna mounted over seawater will be much stronger than for a similar antenna mounted over rocky soil, for example.

**E9C20** **Why are elevated-radial counterpoises popular with vertically polarized antennas?**

A. They reduce the far-field ground losses
B. They reduce the near-field ground losses, compared to on-ground radial systems using more radials
C. They reduce the radiation angle
D. None of these choices is correct

**B** Some amateurs raise their vertical antennas above ground and use elevated-radial counterpoise systems. The counterpoise takes the place of a direct connection to the ground. An elevated counterpoise under a vertically polarized antenna can reduce the near-field ground losses, as compared to on-ground radial systems that are much more extensive.

**E9C21** **What is a terminated rhombic antenna?**

A. An antenna resonant at approximately double the frequency of the intended band of operation
B. An open-ended bidirectional antenna
C. A unidirectional antenna terminated in a resistance equal to its characteristic impedance
D. A horizontal triangular antenna consisting of two adjacent sides and the long diagonal of a resonant rhombic antenna

**C** If you remember the earlier questions, you will remember that the terminated rhombic antenna produces a unidirectional pattern. This antenna is terminated in a resistance equal to its characteristic impedance.

## E9D Space and satellite communications antennas: gain; beamwidth; tracking; losses in real antennas and matching: resistivity losses, losses in resonating elements (loading coils, matching networks, etc. {i.e., mobile, trap}); SWR bandwidth; efficiency

**E9D01 What factors determine the receiving antenna gain required at an amateur satellite station in earth operation?**

A. Height, transmitter power and antennas of satellite
B. Length of transmission line and impedance match between receiver and transmission line
C. Preamplifier location on transmission line and presence or absence of RF amplifier stages
D. Height of earth antenna and satellite orbit

**A** If you want to determine how much receiving antenna gain is required, you'll need to know the strength of the arriving signal from a given satellite. The power and antennas of a satellite determine its ERP (effective radiated power). The satellite height above ground determines the path length, and that means the path loss. These are the major factors in determining the required receiving antenna gain.

**E9D02 What factors determine the EIRP required by an amateur satellite station in earth operation?**

A. Satellite antennas and height, satellite receiver sensitivity
B. Path loss, earth antenna gain, signal-to-noise ratio
C. Satellite transmitter power and orientation of ground receiving antenna
D. Elevation of satellite above horizon, signal-to-noise ratio, satellite transmitter power

**A** Effective isotropic radiated power (EIRP) is the standard measure of power radiation for space communications. It takes into account transmitter power, antenna gain and system losses. In other words, it a measure of transmitted signal strength. How much strength (EIRP) your earth-based station needs depends on the path loss, which is determined by the distance to (height of) the satellite. It also depends on the satellite antenna gain and receiver sensitivity.

**E9D03 What is the approximate beamwidth of a symmetrical pattern antenna with a gain of 20 dB as compared to an isotropic radiator?**

A. 10 degrees
B. 20 degrees
C. 45 degrees
D. 60 degrees

**B** The beamwidth of a symmetrical pattern antenna can be estimated by the formula

$$\theta = \frac{203}{\sqrt{\text{Gain Ratio}}}$$

A gain of 20 dB is a gain of 100. Plug the numbers into the equation and you get

$$\theta = \frac{203}{\sqrt{\text{Gain Ratio}}} = \frac{203}{\sqrt{100}} = 20.3$$

Which is approximately 20 degrees.

**E9D04 How does the gain of a parabolic dish antenna change when the operating frequency is doubled?**

A. Gain does not change
B. Gain is multiplied by 0.707
C. Gain increases 6 dB
D. Gain increases 3 dB

**C** For a parabolic dish, the gain is proportional to the square of the frequency so if you double the frequency, you will raise the gain by a factor of four. In dB units, a factor of 4 is a gain of 6 dB.

**E9D05 How is circular polarization produced using linearly polarized antennas?**

A. Stack two Yagis, fed 90 degrees out of phase, to form an array with the respective elements in parallel planes
B. Stack two Yagis, fed in phase, to form an array with the respective elements in parallel planes
C. Arrange two Yagis perpendicular to each other, with the driven elements in the same plane, fed 90 degrees out of phase
D. Arrange two Yagis perpendicular to each other, with the driven elements in the same plane, fed in phase

**C** Two Yagi antennas built on the same boom, with elements placed perpendicular to each form the basis of a circularly polarized antenna. The driven elements are located at the same position along the boom, so they lie on the same plane, which is perpendicular to the boom. The driven elements are then fed 90 degrees out of phase. You can see how this works in the drawing.

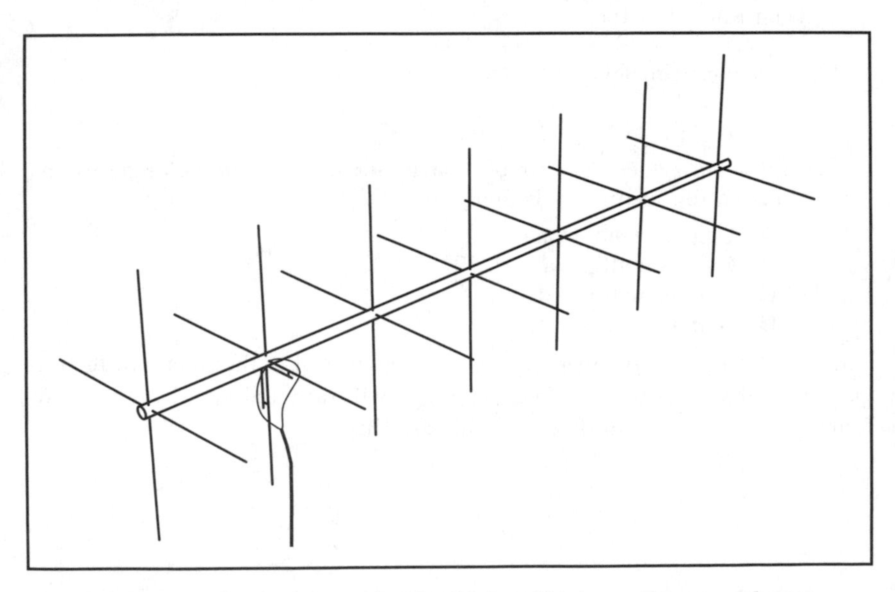

**A circularly polarized antenna built with two Yagis on the same boom. See text.**

**E9D06 How does the beamwidth of an antenna vary as the gain is increased?**

A. It increases geometrically
B. It increases arithmetically
C. It is essentially unaffected
D. It decreases

**D** The higher the gain, the more directive the antenna pattern. In other words, the beamwidth will decrease as gain increases.

**E9D07 Why does a satellite communications antenna system for earth operation need to have rotators for both azimuth and elevation control?**

A. In order to track the satellite as it orbits the earth
B. Because the antennas are large and heavy
C. In order to point the antenna above the horizon to avoid terrestrial interference
D. To rotate antenna polarization along the azimuth and elevate the system towards the satellite

**A** For terrestrial communications, you would mount a beam antenna parallel to the earth. A single rotator turns your antenna to any desired compass heading, or azimuth. As a satellite passes your location, however, it may be high above the horizon for a significant part of the time. You'll need a second rotator to change the antenna elevation angle to track the satellite across the sky.

**E9D08 For a shortened vertical antenna, where should a loading coil be placed to minimize losses and produce the most effective performance?**

A. Near the center of the vertical radiator
B. As low as possible on the vertical radiator
C. As close to the transmitter as possible
D. At a voltage node

**A** As you move a loading coil higher on the vertical, it requires more inductance. More inductance means more ohmic losses. However, as the coil moves up, the radiation resistance goes up, which results in higher efficiency. You'll find that a loading coil placed near the center of the vertical provides the most effective performance from your mobile antenna.

**E9D09 Why should an HF mobile antenna loading coil have a high ratio of reactance to resistance?**

A. To swamp out harmonics
B. To maximize losses
C. To minimize losses
D. To minimize the Q

**C** Higher resistance means lower efficiency. In other words as the resistance goes up so do the ohmic and system losses. You want to use a loading coil with a high ratio of reactance to resistance, because it minimizes losses.

**E9D10 What is a disadvantage of using a trap antenna?**

A. It will radiate harmonics
B. It can only be used for single-band operation
C. It is too sharply directional at lower frequencies
D. It must be neutralized

**A** Because the trap antenna is a multiband antenna, it can do a good job of radiating harmonics.

**E9D11 How must the driven element in a 3-element Yagi be tuned to use a hairpin matching system?**

A. The driven element reactance is capacitive
B. The driven element reactance is inductive
C. The driven element resonance is lower than the operating frequency
D. The driven element radiation resistance is higher than the characteristic impedance of the transmission line

**A** The hairpin adds some inductive reactance. For that reason, the Yagi driven element must be tuned so it has capacitive reactance.

**E9D12 What is the equivalent lumped-constant network for a hairpin matching system on a 3-element Yagi?**

A. Pi network
B. Pi-L network
C. L network
D. Parallel-resonant tank

**C** The hairpin match is an inductive network and the feed point is capacitive. Together they form the equivalent of an L network. This is illustrated in the drawing on the next page.

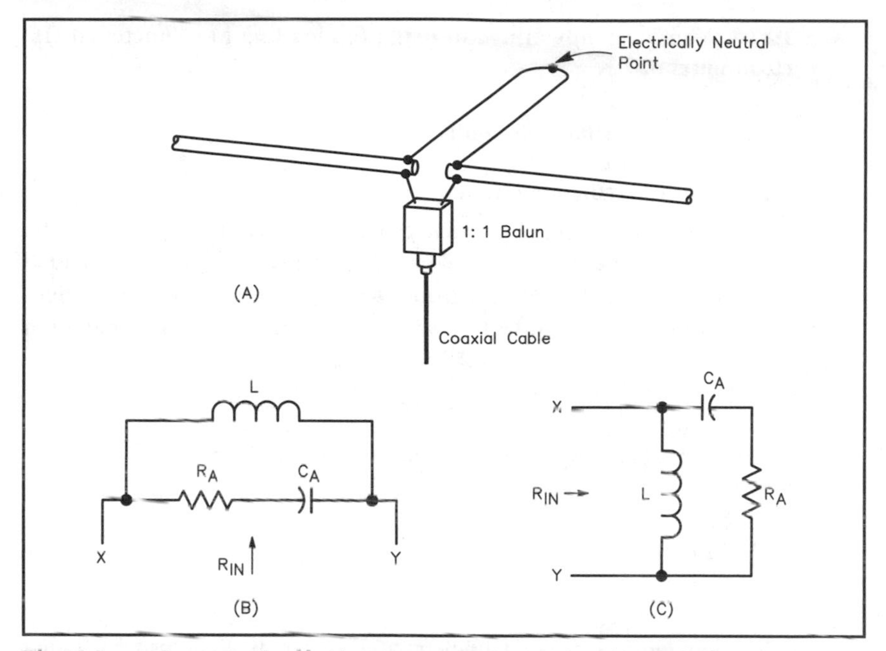


**The driven element of a Yagi antenna can be fed with a hairpin matching system, as shown at A. At B, the lumped constant equivalent circuit, where $R_A$ and $C_A$ represent the antenna feed-point impedance, and L represents the parallel inductance of the hairpin. Points X and Y represent the feed-line connection. When the equivalent circuit is redrawn as shown at C, you can see that L and $C_A$ form an L network to match the feed line to the antenna resistance $R_A$.**

**E9D13 What happens to the bandwidth of an antenna as it is shortened through the use of loading coils?**

A. It is increased
B. It is decreased
C. No change occurs
D. It becomes flat

**B** The bandwidth will decrease if loading coils are used to shorten an antenna.

**E9D14 What is an advantage of using top loading in a shortened HF vertical antenna?**

A. Lower Q
B. Greater structural strength
C. Higher losses
D. Improved radiation efficiency

**D** Top loading is a technique that can reduce loading-coil losses. The method requires that a capacitive hat be added above the coil. The added capacitance at the top of the antenna allows a smaller value of loading inductance. This results in lower system losses, thus improving antenna radiation efficiency.

**E9D15 What is the approximate input terminal impedance at the center of a folded dipole antenna?**

A. 300 ohms
B. 72 ohms
C. 50 ohms
D. 450 ohms

**A** The input impedance of a dipole is approximately 73 ohms. In a folded dipole antenna, the current is divided between the two parallel wires. That means that the current at the feed point of a folded dipole is half of what it is in a dipole. From the power formula $P = I^2 \times Z$, you can see that with the same power and half the current, you'll also have four times the impedance. In this case approximately 300 ohms.

**E9D16 Why is a loading coil often used with an HF mobile antenna?**

A. To improve reception
B. To lower the losses
C. To lower the Q
D. To tune out the capacitive reactance

**D** An HF mobile antenna is usually less than a quarter wavelength long, which means the feed point has a capacitive reactance. The loading coil is inductive and is used to tune out the capacitive reactance.

**E9D17 What is an advantage of using a trap antenna?**

A. It has high directivity in the higher-frequency bands
B. It has high gain
C. It minimizes harmonic radiation
D. It may be used for multi-band operation

**D** A trap antenna may be used for multi-band operation.

**E9D18 What happens at the base feed-point of a fixed length HF mobile antenna as the frequency of operation is lowered?**

A. The resistance decreases and the capacitive reactance decreases
B. The resistance decreases and the capacitive reactance increases
C. The resistance increases and the capacitive reactance decreases
D. The resistance increases and the capacitive reactance increases

**B** Lowering the frequency of operation has the same effect as shortening the antenna. (In terms of wavelength it is shorter.) That means that the resistance decreases and the capacitive reactance increases.

**E9D19 What is the beamwidth of a symmetrical pattern antenna with a gain of 30 dB as compared to an isotropic radiator?**

A. 3.2 degrees
B. 6.4 degrees
C. 37 degrees
D. 60 degrees

**B** Do you remember the formula? A gain of 30 dB is a gain of 1000. The beamwidth can be estimated by

$$\theta = \frac{203}{\sqrt{\text{Gain Ratio}}} = \frac{203}{\sqrt{1000}} = \frac{203}{31.6} = 6.4 \text{ degrees}$$

**E9D20 What is the beamwidth of a symmetrical pattern antenna with a gain of 15 dB as compared to an isotropic radiator?**

A. 72 degrees
B. 52 degrees
C. 36 degrees
D. 3.6 degrees

**C** A gain of 15 dB is a gain of 31.6. The beamwidth can be estimated by

$$\theta = \frac{203}{\sqrt{\text{Gain Ratio}}} = \frac{203}{\sqrt{31.6}} = \frac{203}{5.6} = 36.25 \text{ degrees}$$

This is approximately 36 degrees.

**E9D21** **What is the beamwidth of a symmetrical pattern antenna with a gain of 12 dB as compared to an isotropic radiator?**

A. 34 degrees
B. 45 degrees
C. 58 degrees
D. 51 degrees

**D** A gain of 12 dB is a gain of 15.8. The beamwidth can be estimated by

$$\theta = \frac{203}{\sqrt{\text{Gain Ratio}}} = \frac{203}{\sqrt{15.8}} = \frac{203}{3.97} = 51 \text{ degrees}$$

## E9E Matching antennas to feed lines; characteristics of open and shorted feed lines: 1/8 wavelength; 1/4 wavelength; 1/2 wavelength; feed lines: coax versus open-wire; velocity factor; electrical length; transformation characteristics of line terminated in impedance not equal to characteristic impedance; use of antenna analyzers

**E9E01** **What system matches a high-impedance transmission line to a lower impedance antenna by connecting the line to the driven element in two places, spaced a fraction of a wavelength each side of element center?**

A. The gamma matching system
B. The delta matching system
C. The omega matching system
D. The stub matching system

**B** A delta match network matches a high-impedance transmission line to a lower impedance antenna by connecting the line to the driven element in two places spaced a fraction of a wavelength each side of the element center. The principle is illustrated in the drawing.

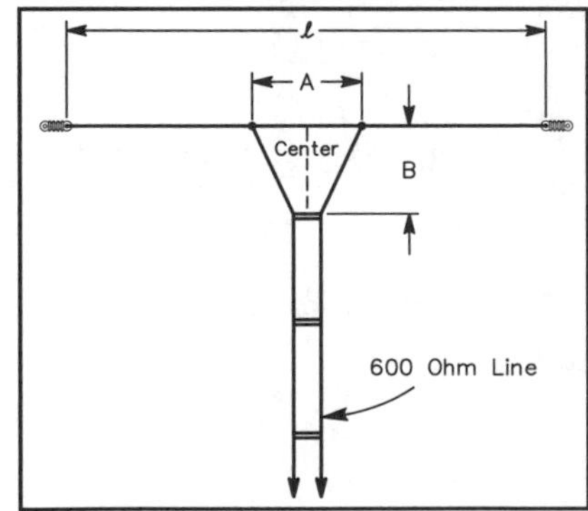


**The delta matching system is used to match a high-impedance transmission line to a lower-impedance antenna. The feed line attaches to the driven element in two places spaced a fraction of a wavelength on each side of the element center.**

**E9E02 What system matches an unbalanced feed line to an antenna by feeding the driven element both at the center of the element and at a fraction of a wavelength to one side of center?**

A. The gamma matching system
B. The delta matching system
C. The omega matching system
D. The stub matching system

**A** A gamma matching system matches an unbalanced feed line to an antenna by feeding the driven element both at the center of the element and at a fraction of a wavelength to one side of center. This is illustrated in the drawing.

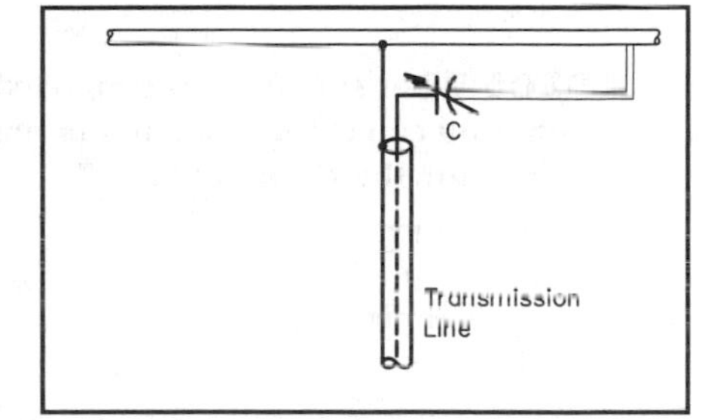


**The gamma matching system is used to match an unbalanced feed line to an antenna. The feed line attaches to the center of the driven element and to a point that is a fraction of a wavelength to one side of center.**

**E9E03 What impedance matching system uses a short perpendicular section of transmission line connected to the feed line near the antenna?**

A. The gamma matching system
B. The delta matching system
C. The omega matching system
D. The stub matching system

**D** The stub matching system uses a short perpendicular section of transmission line connected to the feed line near the antenna. You can see how this works in the drawing.

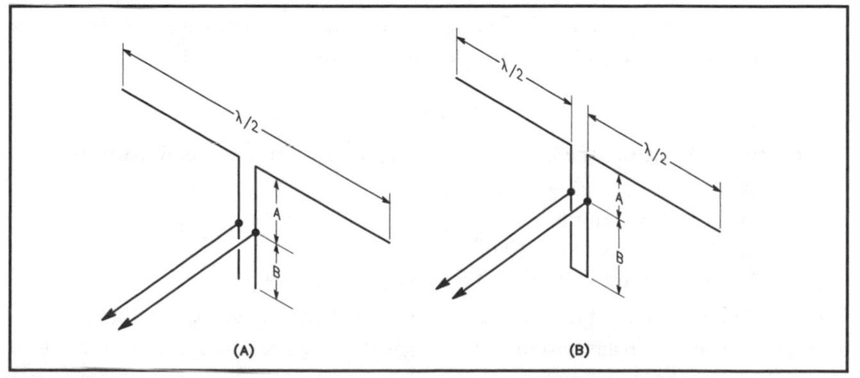


**The stub matching system uses a short perpendicular section of transmission line connected to the feed line near the antenna. Dimensions A + B equal ¼ wavelength.**

**E9E04 What should be the approximate capacitance of the resonating capacitor in a gamma matching circuit on a Yagi beam antenna for the 20-meter band?**

A. 14 pF
B. 140 pF
C. 1400 pF
D. 0.14 pF

**B** The rule of thumb for the capacitor value in a gamma matching circuit is 7 pF per meter of wavelength. A 20-meter gamma match will have a capacitor value of around 140 pF.

**E9E05 What should be the approximate capacitance of the resonating capacitor in a gamma matching circuit on a Yagi beam antenna for the 10-meter band?**

A. 0.2 pF
B. 0.7 pF
C. 700 pF
D. 70 pF

**D** Using the same rule of thumb as the previous question, 7 pF times 10 gives a value of 70 pF.

**E9E06 What is the velocity factor of a transmission line?**

A. The ratio of the characteristic impedance of the line to the terminating impedance
B. The index of shielding for coaxial cable
C. The velocity of the wave on the transmission line multiplied by the velocity of light in a vacuum
D. The velocity of the wave on the transmission line divided by the velocity of light in a vacuum

**D** The velocity factor of a transmission line is the velocity of the wave in the line divided by the velocity of light in a vacuum.

**E9E07 What determines the velocity factor in a transmission line?**

A. The termination impedance
B. The line length
C. Dielectrics in the line
D. The center conductor resistivity

**C** The presence of dielectric materials reduces the velocity of an electromagnetic wave in a transmission line, since those waves travel more slowly in materials other than a vacuum.

**E9E08 Why is the physical length of a coaxial cable transmission line shorter than its electrical length?**

A. Skin effect is less pronounced in the coaxial cable
B. The characteristic impedance is higher in a parallel feed line
C. The surge impedance is higher in a parallel feed line
D. RF energy moves slower along the coaxial cable

**D** The electrical length of a line is measured in wavelengths at a given frequency. To calculate the physical length of line for a given electrical length, you multiply the electrical (free space) length by the velocity factor. Keep reading and you'll soon come to an example of this.

**E9E09 What is the typical velocity factor for a coaxial cable with polyethylene dielectric?**

A. 2.70
B. 0.66
C. 0.30
D. 0.10

**B** The typical velocity factor for a coaxial cable with polyethylene dielectric is 0.66. In other words, the speed of an electromagnetic wave in typical RG-8 coax is about two-thirds the speed of light in a vacuum.

**E9E10 What would be the physical length of a typical coaxial transmission line that is electrically one-quarter wavelength long at 14.1 MHz? (Assume a velocity factor of 0.66.)**

A. 20 meters
B. 2.3 meters
C. 3.5 meters
D. 0.2 meters

**C** The 14.1 MHz frequency corresponds to a free-space wavelength of 21.3 meter (300 divided by the frequency in MHz). Since we wish to have a ¼-wave line, the free-space length would be 5.3 meters. This is multiplied by the velocity factor to give 3.5 meters.

**E9E11 What is the physical length of a parallel conductor feed line that is electrically one-half wavelength long at 14.10 MHz? (Assume a velocity factor of 0.95.)**

A. 15 meters
B. 20 meters
C. 10 meters
D. 71 meters

**C** Here you apply the same technique as in the previous question. The free-space wavelength is 21.3 meters (300/14.1). We desire a ½-wavelength line, which would have a free-space length of 10.6 meters. This is multiplied by the velocity factor to give 10 meters.

**E9E12 What parameter best describes the interactions at the load end of a mismatched transmission line?**

A. Characteristic impedance
B. Reflection coefficient
C. Velocity factor
D. Dielectric Constant

**B** The reflection coefficient is the ratio of reflected voltage (or current) to the incident voltage (or current) at the same point on a line. The reflection coefficient is determined by the relationship between the feed line characteristic impedance and the actual load impedance. That makes the reflection coefficient a good parameter to describe the interactions at the load end of a mismatched transmission line.

**E9E13 Which of the following measurements describes a mismatched transmission line?**

A. An SWR less than 1:1
B. A reflection coefficient greater than 1
C. A dielectric constant greater than 1
D. An SWR greater than 1:1

**D** If there is a mismatch, the SWR will be greater than 1:1. An SWR less than 1:1 is not possible. Neither is it possible to have a dielectric constant or reflection coefficient greater than 1.

**E9E14 What characteristic will 450-ohm ladder line have at 50 MHz, as compared to 0.195-inch-diameter coaxial cable (such as RG-58)?**

A. Lower loss in dB/100 feet
B. Higher SWR
C. Smaller reflection coefficient
D. Lower velocity factor

**A** The ladder line will typically have less than a tenth the loss per 100 feet compared to the RG-58.

**E9E15 What is the term for the ratio of the actual velocity at which a signal travels through a transmission line to the speed of light in a vacuum?**

A. Velocity factor
B. Characteristic impedance
C. Surge impedance
D. Standing wave ratio

**A** The ratio of the actual velocity at which a signal travels through a transmission line to the speed of light in a vacuum is called the velocity factor.

**E9E16 What would be the physical length of a typical coaxial transmission line that is electrically one-quarter wavelength long at 7.2 MHz? (Assume a velocity factor of 0.66.)**

A. 10 meters
B. 6.9 meters
C. 24 meters
D. 50 meters

**B** The free-space wavelength is 41.6 meters (300 divided by 7.2). You want a ¼-wavelength line, which would have a free-space length of 10.4 meters. Multiply this by the velocity factor (0.66) to give you 6.9 meters.

**E9E17 What kind of impedance does a 1/8-wavelength transmission line present to a generator when the line is shorted at the far end?**

A. A capacitive reactance
B. The same as the characteristic impedance of the line
C. An inductive reactance
D. The same as the input impedance to the final generator stage

**C** Now you come to a series of questions about various line lengths and terminations. You'll find the answers in the Table 9-1, which shows input impedance to various length line sections that are terminated in a short or an open circuit. From the table, you see that an 1/8-wavelength transmission line that is shorted at the far end exhibits an inductive reactance at its input.

**Table 9-1**

**Properties of open and shorted Feed-Line Sections**

| *Length* | *Termination* | *Impedance* |
|---|---|---|
| 1/8 wavelength | Shorted | inductive |
| 1/8 wavelength | Open | capacitive |
| ¼ wavelength | Shorted | very high impedance |
| ¼ wavelength | Open | very low impedance |
| ½ wavelength | Shorted | very low impedance |
| ½ wavelength | Open | very high impedance |

**E9E18 What kind of impedance does a 1/8-wavelength transmission line present to a generator when the line is open at the far end?**

A. The same as the characteristic impedance of the line
B. An inductive reactance
C. A capacitive reactance
D. The same as the input impedance of the final generator stage

**C** From the table, you can see that the open ended 1/8-wavelength transmission line looks capacitive to the generator.

**E9E19 What kind of impedance does a 1/4-wavelength transmission line present to a generator when the line is open at the far end?**

A. A very high impedance
B. A very low impedance
C. The same as the characteristic impedance of the line
D. The same as the input impedance to the final generator stage

**B** From the table, you can see that the open ended 1/4-wavelength transmission line has a very low impedance at its input.

**E9E20 What kind of impedance does a 1/4-wavelength transmission line present to a generator when the line is shorted at the far end?**

A. A very high impedance
B. A very low impedance
C. The same as the characteristic impedance of the transmission line
D. The same as the generator output impedance

**A** From the table, you can see that the shorted 1/4-wavelength transmission line presents a very high impedance to the generator.

**E9E21 What kind of impedance does a 1/2-wavelength transmission line present to a generator when the line is shorted at the far end?**

A. A very high impedance
B. A very low impedance
C. The same as the characteristic impedance of the line
D. The same as the output impedance of the generator

**B** In the table, you find that a shorted 1/2-wavelength transmission line presents a very low impedance at its input.

**E9E22 What kind of impedance does a 1/2-wavelength transmission line present to a generator when the line is open at the far end?**

A. A very high impedance
B. A very low impedance
C. The same as the characteristic impedance of the line
D. The same as the output impedance of the generator

**A** Once again in the table, you can see that an open 1/2-wavelength transmission line presents a very high impedance to the generator.

# About the ARRL

The seed for Amateur Radio was planted in the 1890s, when Guglielmo Marconi began his experiments in wireless telegraphy. Soon he was joined by dozens, then hundreds, of others who were enthusiastic about sending and receiving messages through the air—some with a commercial interest, but others solely out of a love for this new communications medium. The United States government began licensing Amateur Radio operators in 1912.

By 1914, there were thousands of Amateur Radio operators—hams—in the United States. Hiram Percy Maxim, a leading Hartford, Connecticut, inventor and industrialist saw the need for an organization to band together this fledgling group of radio experimenters. In May 1914 he founded the American Radio Relay League (ARRL) to meet that need.

Today ARRL, with approximately 170,000 members, is the largest organization of radio amateurs in the United States. The ARRL is a not-for-profit organization that:

- promotes interest in Amateur Radio communications and experimentation
- represents US radio amateurs in legislative matters, and
- maintains fraternalism and a high standard of conduct among Amateur Radio operators.

At ARRL headquarters in the Hartford suburb of Newington, the staff helps serve the needs of members. ARRL is also International Secretariat for the International Amateur Radio Union, which is made up of similar societies in 150 countries around the world.

ARRL publishes the monthly journal *QST*, as well as newsletters and many publications covering all aspects of Amateur Radio. Its headquarters station, W1AW, transmits Morse code practice sessions and bulletins of interest to radio amateurs. The ARRL also coordinates an extensive field organization, which includes volunteers who provide technical information and other support for radio amateurs as well as communications for public-service activities. ARRL also represents US amateurs with the Federal Communications Commission and other government agencies in the US and abroad.

Membership in ARRL means much more than receiving *QST* each month. In addition to the services already described, ARRL offers membership services on a personal level, such as the ARRL Volunteer Examiner Coordinator Program and a QSL bureau.

Full ARRL membership (available only to licensed radio amateurs in the US) gives you a voice in how the affairs of the organization are governed. ARRL policy is set by a Board of Directors (one from each of 15 Divisions). Each year, one-third of the ARRL Board of Directors stands for election by the full members they represent. The day-to-day operation of ARRL HQ is managed by an Executive Vice President and a Chief Financial Officer.

No matter what aspect of Amateur Radio attracts you, ARRL membership is relevant and important. There would be no Amateur Radio as we know it today were it not for the ARRL. We would be happy to welcome you as a member! (An Amateur Radio license is not required for Associate membership.) For more information about ARRL and answers to any questions you may have about Amateur Radio, write or call:

ARRL—The national association for Amateur Radio
225 Main Street
Newington, CT 06111-1494
(860) 594-0200

Prospective new amateurs call:
**800-32-NEW HAM** (800-326-3942)
You can also contact us via e-mail at **newham@arrl.org**
Or check out *ARRLWeb* at **www.arrl.org/**

# Notes

# Notes